Buckeye Memories

FROM THE COUCH, THE STANDS, AND THE PRESS BOX

Book Design & Production:
Columbus Publishing Lab
www.ColumbusPublishingLab.com

Paperback ISBN: 978-1-63337-524-6
E-Book ISBN: 978-1-63337-525-3

Printed in the United States of America
1 3 5 7 9 10 8 6 4 2

Buckeye Memories

FROM THE COUCH, THE STANDS, AND THE PRESS BOX

Steve Basford
and a few Fun Facts

proving
press

TABLE OF CONTENTS

FOREWORD

by Jack Kramer

MY FATHER SHARED WITH ME much of the Ohio State football lore that highlighted games and seasons from the 1930s to the 1950s.

He told me all about the 1942 season when the Buckeyes edged Georgia in the final poll for their first ever national championship. He always kept my interest with unusual statistics from the "Snow Bowl" loss to Michigan in 1950 when the two teams combined for 45 punts. Dad described the 1956 loss at Iowa as a game marked by hot verbal exchanges between Woody Hayes and Hawkeyes Coach Forest Evashevski over the condition of the field. A year later, Ohio State fell in its opener, a third straight setback spanning two seasons. But the Buckeyes ran the table, my father remembered well, and claimed the conference title and a Rose Bowl victory before sharing a national championship with Auburn.

However, since the late 1960s, I have missed my father's recall of OSU on the gridiron. That void in my sports life has now been filled by Steve Basford in his book *Buckeye Memories from the Couch, the Stands, and the Press Box*. As you will discover, the book is a detailed, colorful, and well-written review of the Buckeyes, authored by a talented sports broadcaster and game statistician who had been in the stadium witnessing every

Ohio State football home game since the second game in 1970, until the 2020 pandemic year.

Steve, by the way, was my statistician and right-hand man in the press box from 1981 to 1990 when I announced Ohio State football games for flagship station WOSU-TV. The telecasts were treated as "live" programs with no edits and then shown statewide on Saturday night and Sunday morning on more than twenty PBS stations throughout Ohio. While viewing the game replays, we had the chance to evaluate our own performances, from the producer and director to those of us in the broadcast booth. Steve's stats were always spot on!

You have heard the expression, "The devil is in the details," referring to elements hidden in the details that seem simple at first look. But in the case of a game statistician, the calculation of such details requires much more effort and, above all, speed and precision. As a phenomenal statistician throughout his career, Steve has executed his role to perfection, one contest after another. In addition to the accomplished work he performed for me and WOSU-TV, he has served as a statistician for NBC, ESPN, Big Ten Network, Spectrum Sports, Columbus Sports Network, and several other media outlets.

Steve, in fact, has been both a play-by-play sportscaster and statistician for over 2,000 events spanning football, basketball, baseball, softball, and a few other sports. He is currently the play-by-play announcer for Ohio Wesleyan University and has announced more than 500 college and high school contests for numerous radio, television, and online media.

On the microphone, Steve has always offered a vivid commentary that obviously is not present when he completes his statistician assignments. As if he were on radio or television covering the Buckeyes in their 2002 national championship year, Steve writes in his book that his eyes and ears often picked up very interesting seconds of action on and off the field. He notes that the television camera caught Coach Jim Tressel trailing Maurice Clarett down the sidelines in the opening win over Texas

Tech. He adds that Purdue fans serenaded the Ohio State team chanting "Overrated," to which the Ohio State fans responded, "Undefeated." And in the national title victory, he writes that karma occurred when a questionable call against Miami was preceded by replays showing a grab of Chris Gamble's jersey when he may have caught the ball inbounds anyway.

You, the reader, will also appreciate Steve's love for unique "stats." In 2002, for example, the Buckeyes had only two more first downs than their opponents, and seven of the team's last eleven wins were by seven points or less.

And, Ohio State, which has won 17 of the last 19 games versus Michigan, has beaten the Wolverines every thirteenth year since 1929. Guess what? The year 2020 would have been the next in the sequence since the Buckeyes' triumph in 2007. Leave it to Steve to uncover this and nearly 500 more "fun facts."

I am certain that you will thoroughly enjoy reading Steve's spotlight on several decades of Ohio State football about which he has researched and written beginning with the 1968 season. He has acquired so much specific and insightful information from many sources and locations like the couch, the stands, and the press box.

Go Bucks. Thank you, Steve!

Jack Kramer, who lives near Dayton, Ohio, was the television play-by-play announcer for Ohio State football from 1981 to 1990.

FOREWORD

by Jeff Logan

I FIRST MET THE BASFORD FAMILY some 40 years ago, but Steve could probably tell you the exact date, because that is what Steve is all about. Following my Ohio State football career and a short stint in the NFL, I returned to Columbus and began working in sports broadcast journalism. It seems like the Basford family has been a part of my broadcasting career every step of the way. Mark Basford was a producer when we were on the air with QUBE, the predecessor to cable television and interactive viewing. His sister, Beverly, had a long career with the Ohio State Alumni Association. I also got to meet their parents, who were terrific individuals and very proud of their children.

I always joke with Steve that he is the "cornucopia of worthless information," knowing and recalling facts and figures better than anyone I have ever come across. While at times these may seem mundane, I have come to the realization that sports moments, especially in the history of Ohio State, have a major impact on people's lives.

Steve and I have worked very closely over the past 25 years doing live high school football games for television. Prior to every broadcast, we challenge each other with a trivia question, and rarely have I been able to stump the master! I realize how important these moments are for so many, and I applaud Steve for sharing this with all of you.

I will leave you with this trivia question. Who are the only two father and son combinations to play for the legendary Woody Hayes at Ohio State?

INTRODUCTION

THREE MEMORABLE MOMENTS in attending (or not attending) OSU games stick out in my mind.

- When I was nine, my friend and I belonged to the YMCA, and we would take the bus from Upper Arlington to the downtown branch. After one Saturday morning of swimming, I called home on a pay phone— that gives you an idea of how long ago it was—to tell my mother that I would be staying longer. She said, "Your dad has tickets to the OSU game. Do you want to go?" I said, "No. I'm having too much fun at the Y."

- In 1970, I had a sprained foot and did not try to go to the opening game against Texas A&M.

- For about three months in 2006, I had an illness that left me with no energy. Yet I did not miss a home game, and I flew down to Texas for the Buckeyes' big match with the Longhorns.

People who know me would give me a break on the first one since I was only nine, would say that not missing those 2006 games was consistent with my passion for OSU football, and would have had my head examined for not finding a way to hobble to the 1970 game. On that last matter, I would agree.

For missing the 1970 game, they would invoke the story of Giles Pellerin, the Southern California Trojans Super Fan who attended 797 consecutive USC football games, home and away. This excerpt is from the *Los Angeles Times* (Oliver was his brother):

> *He was hospitalized after an emergency appendectomy in 1949 and had to fool the nurses to get to the USC-Oregon game. "He called me on Friday [before the game] and said, 'Be here Saturday at noon,'" Oliver Pellerin said. Giles told the nurses he was going for a walk, watched the Trojans win, 40-13, then returned, not bothering to explain why his face was sunburned.*

The 1970 Texas A&M game is the last home game that I have missed before the 2020 COVID-affected season. I realize that there may be many of you who have not missed a home or away game in that time. My intention in this book is not to suggest that I am the biggest OSU fan. In fact, whenever OSU is not at home, I continue my quest to have seen each of the 130 Football Bowl Subdivision teams in person. As of this writing, I have seen 123 of the 130. If I had gone to the bowl games against Brigham Young (three chances), Texas A&M (two chances), and Air Force between 1982 and 1998, I would have missed only four of the 130. This idea of seeing all the teams occurred to me about 20 years ago when I saw a list of all the teams in *USA Today*. I counted how many I had seen, and the total of 77 seemed fairly high at the time. You can see my history at https://sites.google.com/site/stevescollegefootballpage.

Another factor in not attending OSU road games is the fact that when there is no conflict with an OSU home game, I am the play-by-play announcer for Ohio Wesleyan home football, men's basketball, and women's basketball games streamed on the OWU website.

These activities have caused me to miss watching the Michigan games live in 2009 (I was at Clemson watching the Tigers beat Virginia); in 2011 (I was at Marshall watching the Thundering Herd beat East Carolina); and in 2015, 2017, and 2019, the last three while broadcasting Ohio Wesleyan basketball games. Trust me, I am a huge OSU football fan, as you will see.

My intention also is not to tell you what you probably already know. It is to share memories, anecdotes, and little-known facts that make the OSU football experience so compelling to us in Buckeye Nation. It is not quite Paul Harvey's, "Now you know the rest of the story," but these are my stories, just as you have your vivid and fond memories. I am a fanatic for trivia, coincidences, and statistics, so you will see a heavy dose of these. I will also sprinkle in some stories from my experiences of broadcasting and keeping stats for high school games on TV and radio.

For one game in 1978, and starting in 1979, and with the exception of the 1991 and 1992 seasons, I have been a statistician in the press box—the 1979 and 1980 home games for Time Warner telecasts, from 1981 through 1990 for the WOSU-TV delayed telecasts, and since 1993 as part of the athletics department's official statistics crew for home games. The team has had good fortune during the first year of each:

- 1978: In my only game, Woody Hayes won his last game.

- 1979: The team was 11-0 in the regular season.

- 1981: The team beat Michigan and won the bowl game in the same season for the first time since 1968.

- 1993: The team was 10-1-1, ending a streak of 13 years with at least three losses.

So, I have enjoyed the OSU football experience from the couch, the stands, and the press box.

By the way, during the 1975 Penn State game, I was in the Time Warner truck outside the stadium, winding and rewinding the broadcast tapes. I do not count that as missing a game!

Inspired by Billy Crystal's monologue in *City Slickers*: "Your twenties... Your thirties... Your forties..." I break down the book's chapters by decade, starting with the Buckeyes' 1968 national championship team.

What connection do the Fibonacci Sequence and George Bush have with the OSU-Michigan rivalry? Read on!

CHAPTER 1

The 1950s

The Early Years

I WAS BORN IN 1951, not coincidentally as part of the baby boom that followed the Snow Bowl of 1950—omen #1. Our house was in Clintonville, about three miles from Ohio Stadium, on Kensington Place East, which along with Kensington Place West formed a U almost like a horseshoe—omen #2.

I know that I went to a few games in the 1950s, but I do not know which ones. My dad worked for the Abel Company that sold auto supplies and had auto repair shops in the Lazarus Department Store branches, and he would occasionally get tickets from the Abel family to sit with them. At a game, he would say, "Be sure to thank Mr. Abel for inviting us to come to the game."

We would park in the polo fields that stretched south of the stadium to King Avenue. When I heard men in the parking area calling, "Who needs tickets?" I thought that they were giving them away!

I do recall telling my mother after one of the games that the best part of the game was when an official fell down.

My friends and I would compete to be OSU's Heisman Trophy recipient Hopalong Cassady when we played for fun, though we were too young to know exactly what he did. For some reason, I wanted 55 to be my jersey number, so my mother sewed scarlet numbers depicting "55" onto a gray sweatshirt for me.

Everybody knows of Woody Hayes's disdain for passing, but the statistics from 1954 (Woody's first national championship) through 1959 are beyond belief compared to today: from a low of 18 yards per game to a high of 80 in 1959 in those six years. His first three teams averaged 144 yards per game, but the Buckeyes would not average 100 passing yards per game from 1954 to 1964.

Watching footage from the 1950s, I find it interesting to see that the Ohio Stadium field had 5-yard numerals (5, 15, 25, etc.) painted on the field, as Louisiana State's field still does.

Before the 1959 season, my family (my siblings are Beverly and Mark) moved from Clintonville to Upper Arlington, so we were still about three miles from Ohio Stadium. One year, it was unusual to see a policeman directing traffic after the games near our house where Zollinger Road dead ends at North Star. The 3-5-1 record in 1959 would be their worst record since then.

CHAPTER 2

The 1960s
Becoming Consumed with College Football

I ACTUALLY BECAME MORE FAMILIAR with OSU basketball before OSU football. The 1960s were the glory years of coach Fred Taylor and players Jerry Lucas, John Havlicek, Mel Nowell, Larry Siegfried, and Gary Bradds, and it seemed as if the basketball games were always televised on Channel 4. When Jimmy Crum opened with, "Live from Saint John Arena..." I would get goosebumps. The word *Saint* made me think that this was a holy shrine.

Our house was near a woody (no pun intended) area called Wakefield Forest, and when the 1959 basketball game against Wake Forest came on TV, I wondered if there was a connection, if these two universities were three miles apart.

Our fourth-grade class went to an OSU basketball practice on a field trip and saw Jerry Lucas and the other stars, but I don't recall seeing any of their games on TV. The Gary Bradds years are fairly vivid. I went to only two games before college, and one was in the middle of his six straight games of at least 40 points. At that game, Bradds went to the free throw line to shoot two free throws with 38 points and his replacement ready to come in, and he made them both.

With a few exceptions, I didn't see any OSU football games on TV until 1967. I do recall watching Cleveland Browns games every Sunday and seeing them win the 1964 NFL Championship game, a game that my dad attended. What I remember was uniquely designed end zones, with Ohio Stadium's having diamond designs. Watching the 1966 UCLA-Michigan State Rose Bowl, I wondered, *Don't the Trojans know that the Spartan quarterback is always going to pitch the ball to the running back?* I had not learned the nature of an option play yet. An assistant coach on that UCLA team was John Cooper.

I was confused that the Buckeyes had a player named Tom Perdue, amused that a player named Jim Nein wore #9, and really amused when a newspaper printed a photo of Paul Fender and Ed Bender side-by-side, showing their names on their jerseys.

I recall OSU Athletic Director Richard Larkins saying that some of his math acumen was the fact that he could multiply 81,000, the approximate capacity of Ohio Stadium, times $6.00.

The Sunday edition of the *Columbus Dispatch* contained photos of key plays, and the editors' style of identifying the players was unique. Placed next to a player was a rectangle containing an arrow pointing to him, and the text inside the rectangle read, for example, "Warfield, O" —always *O* for *Ohio*.

My dad was from Waterloo, Iowa, where Woody's brother Ike had been a veterinarian—omen #3—and spent two years at the University of Iowa before the army transferred him to Ohio State. On one occasion when the Buckeyes and Hawkeyes met, I asked him who he was pulling for. He said, "Ohio State," as if it were obvious.

In the 1960s, boys would get their hair cut on Saturdays, and the barber shop would have the game on the radio. My brother Mark and I would go to Alfred's Barber Shop in the Kingsdale Shopping Center. Alfred would give us a penny for the gumball machine, and if it dispensed a black gumball, he would give us another penny. I can remember listening to the 51-15 win over Illinois in Alfred's Barber Shop. One time at Alfred's, I picked up the morning *Columbus Citizen-Journal* and saw a photo of a friend who had won a prize at the Columbus Jets baseball game. The prize was a pony!

The *Columbus Dispatch* let kids sell newspapers—with a page containing the rosters wrapped around the first section—at the games, and Mark and I did this a few times. The *Dispatch* employee recorded our names when we checked in, and we got our first bundle of about 25 for no charge. When we came back to the truck for our next bundle, we gave the *Dispatch* employee whatever the established rate per bundle was and kept the difference. We had to check out with the *Dispatch* employee to ensure that we didn't keep all of the cash from our last bundle. If we didn't check out, we were not allowed to work the next game, because the staff member had our name on a list. We were supposed to call out "Football lineups!" to the arriving fans, and to us young kids, their tips seemed generous. When we were done, Mother would pick us up on Lane Avenue, and we would spend part of our two-dollar fortune at the University City Shopping Center McDonald's where Mark and I would eventually work.

Mark sold the papers at the 1967 home game against Arizona, but I did not. A fan asked Mark if he wanted his extra ticket for free, and Mark's answer was obvious. Mark was not quite eleven years old! Can you imagine that today—a ten-year-old entering an OSU game on his own?

I recall watching the 1961 Michigan game on TV at age ten. I remember Sam Tidmore, who would play for the Cleveland Browns, catching a touchdown pass at the end of the game to make the final score 50-20. Paul Warfield, who would become the WOSU-TV color announcer when I did the stats from 1981 to 1990, ran for 122 yards on six carries and had 61 yards on two receptions. Bob Ferguson ran for 152 yards and four touchdowns. This was the year that the Buckeyes had a perfect Big Ten record but did not play in the Rose Bowl because the OSU Faculty Council voted to reject the bid.

The 1964 Michigan game is the first game that I can identify as having attended. It was a sunny day, but according to *Sports Illustrated*, "With temperatures as low as six degrees in the morning leading up to the game and a modern-day estimate of wind chills around -30 degrees with winds up to 25 miles-per-hour, the 1964 Big Ten Championship clash is the coldest game Ohio State has ever played in." Still, the attendance was only 27 fans short of the stadium record to that point.

That morning, I went with my dad to his office near Port Columbus to pick up two of his associates from Michigan—Wolverine fans who were also going to the game. I was amused that one of the men was named Jack Gleason. I told them that their quarterback Bob Timberlake must be pretty good. Timberlake, from Franklin, Ohio, who would go on to play for the New York Giants, threw a touchdown pass and kicked a field goal and the PAT. I knew that Illinois's quarterback Fred Custardo also was a kicker, so in my naïveté as a 13-year-old, I thought that quarterbacks doing double duty was common in college football.

Michigan beat another OSU, Oregon State, in the Rose Bowl that season. An assistant coach on that Oregon State team was John Cooper. The year 1964 was the only one between 1951 and 1968 that Michigan won the Big Ten championship. The year 1964 was the only one between 1951 and 1968 that I attended an OSU-Michigan game. It's all my fault.

I did not attend another game until 1967, when I was a guest of a friend at the Purdue debacle, a 41-6 loss. Purdue had quarterback Mike Phipps and halfback/defensive halfback Leroy Keyes, and the Boilers led 35-0 at halftime. In his book *Ohio State Football: The Great Tradition*, Jack Park mentions Woody thanking Purdue Coach Mollenkopf for "holding down the score" by pulling most of his starters in the third quarter. This was Woody's worst loss at OSU. Mark and I had attended the first two losses of 1967— Mark at the Arizona game and me at the Purdue game.

On October 28, 1967, the Buckeyes lost at home to Illinois 17-13. It would be the last OSU loss until the infamous 24-12 loss at Michigan in

1969, which ended a 22-game winning streak and was the last home loss until 1971. I was in Iowa at the time for my grandfather's funeral, taking my first flight ever.

My dad and I went to the home Wisconsin game in 1967, which was played in a rainstorm and is notable for the lowest attendance since the 1950 Snow Bowl: 65,470. Our seats were in bleachers along the track on the visitors' side.

1968 (10-0)

On Sundays following games, there was a one-hour recap show on TV very much like the ESPN *College Football Final* show, though it seemed like every show had a 45-minute segment where they showed the OSU game drive-through style.

This was the year of the Super Sophomores: Rex Kern, Leo Hayden, Jan White, Bruce Jankowski, Larry Zelina, John Brockington, Jim Stillwagon, Jack Tatum, Mark Debevc, Doug Adams, Mike Sensibaugh, and Tim Anderson. Apologies to those whom I omitted.

In their debut, the Buckeyes saw Southern Methodist, coached by future Iowa coach Hayden Fry, throw 76 passes and finish with 437 yards passing, but the defense had five interceptions in the 35-14 win. Mike Sensibaugh punted 11 times, unusual for such a lopsided game, including twice on third down in the first half. Dave Brungard ran for 101 yards and scored three times, twice on receptions. The Mustangs outgained the Buckeyes 487-372 in total yards. The official account shows in one drive the Buckeyes with a third down-and-½ yard play on the SMU 2 ½-yard line. Watching footage from the game, you can see rows of empty seats under the scoreboard in a corner and many male fans wearing dress shirts and ties.

This was the year that the rule was implemented to stop the clock after first downs. *Sports Illustrated* printed a story about how the rule change led to the boom in the number of plays and the scoring. The Buckeyes would average the second highest number of plays per game in the nation, and *The Ohio State University 1969 Football Information* publication the next year would refer to the "hurry up" offense. In that *Sports Illustrated* story, Woody said, "We are moving so fast I frequently can't get a play in from the sidelines. We'll hit 100 plays a game soon." SMU was close, totaling 98 plays in the game.

My dad was able to get tickets for all five of us (the attendance was only 70,191) to the Oregon game, which OSU led only 7-6 at halftime and won 21-6. All three touchdowns by the Buckeyes came on "exceptional plays," as the box score describes: a 35-yard run by Jim Otis (#35); a return of a punt that Mike Polaski blocked and caught in the air; and a 55-yard pass from Ron Maciejowski to Bruce Jankowski, a play that Woody called "from Pole to Pole." In fact, on all three touchdowns, the player scoring was untouched. The Buckeyes threw four interceptions but outgained the Ducks 456-140 in total yards, and Oregon had no first downs in the second half. About 20 years later, I would interview Maciejowski at a high school game where his son was playing. Otis ran for 102 yards, and 10 others had carries.

In the big game that year, #1 Purdue returned to Columbus, and the Buckeyes won 13-0. The first half was scoreless, meaning that the Oregon and Purdue games had a combined first half score of 7-6 and that the last four quarters between OSU and Purdue had a combined score of 6-6. On the first possession of the second half, Ted Provost returned a Mike Phipps interception 35 yards for a touchdown. The ball had been spotted on the right hash mark, and Phipps's pass was nearly to the left sideline. In 1967, Purdue's first score came on a 30-yard interception return. Bill Long, who had thrown two interceptions in as many passes the week before, came in for an injured Rex Kern and converted his only run of the day into his only touchdown of the year, a 14-yard run. The Buckeyes outgained the Boilermakers 411-186, with Jim Otis rushing for 144 yards. The defense held Keyes to 19 yards on seven carries and threw Phipps for 58 yards in losses and minus four net on the ground.

Four times, the box score informed that "Next week's game will start at 2:20 p.m.," providing better customer service than the current practice of TV networks releasing a start time the Sunday before.

The Buckeyes rolled up 565 total yards, with Kern accounting for 291 (121 on the ground) in a 45-21 win over Northwestern.

The first road game of the year saw the Buckeyes lead Illinois 24-0, the Illini tie it at 24-24 on three scores and three two-point conversions, and Maciejowski replace an injured Kern and lead the Buckeyes to a score and a 31-24 win.

In the days following the Buckeyes' 25-20 win over Michigan State where the defense recorded six turnovers, Bruce Jankowski was on the cover of *Sports Illustrated* making an over-the-shoulder catch. The blurb read: "THE BUCKEYES ARE BACK."

In place of Kern, Maciejowski ran for 124 yards and three touchdowns and passed for 153 and another score in a 43-8 win at Wisconsin, with 33 of the points scored in the second half. It was the Buckeyes' first ever game on an artificial surface.

Otis ran for 166 yards in a 33-27 win at Iowa, with the team leading 26-6 at the end of three quarters and the Hawkeyes scoring three touchdowns in the fourth.

The Buckeyes ran for 421 yards—Otis,143 with four touchdowns; Kern, 96; and Zelina, 92—in the 50-14 win over Michigan, leading only 21-14 at the half. Otis launched the ball into the stands after the last of his four touchdowns. Otis's four scores matched Bob Ferguson's four in the 1961 Michigan game, and the 50 points matched the Buckeyes' output in the same game. Jack Tatum had a hard blind side hit on the Wolverine quarterback, which produced an iconic photo. The defense picked off three Wolverine passes. Michigan had given up only 11.7 points per game coming into the contest.

In the 27-16 win over USC in the Rose Bowl, the Buckeyes trailed the Trojans 10-0 after O.J. Simpson's 80-yard run (as Lou Holtz said, 80 was all that he needed) but tied it 10-10 just before halftime and let the defense control the second half. The Buckeyes' short scoring "drives" in the second half would resemble the ones they had against Miami in January 2003, when they won their next national championship on the field. The Buckeyes recovered three fumbles and intercepted two Trojan passes, one by Simpson. Simpson's 27 carries other than the 80-yard burst netted only 91 yards. Otis ran for 101 yards, Hayden for 90, and the Buckeyes won despite being outgained, 366-361.

Kern threw touchdown passes to Leo Hayden and Ray Gillian in the fourth quarter. The two of them entered the game with a combined one touchdown and four receptions and finished the year with 10 combined receptions. After his touchdown, Gillian threw the ball into the crowd as Jim Otis had done after his last score against Michigan—no penalty for unsportsmanlike conduct at the time!

USC scored a touchdown with 45 seconds on a controversial catch in the back of the end zone by Sam Dickerson where it appeared that Mike Polaski intercepted the pass. Woody went nuts (surprising?), but the replay (or as Curt Gowdy called it, "the rerun") shows that it was a good call, a simultaneous catch that goes to the offensive player. Curt Gowdy also informed us that the band was playing "Hurry Up, Sloopy."

I enjoyed Gowdy's mellow voice calling various sports over the years. In 1970, he autographed my program at St. John Arena when he called the basketball tournament games.

I get a chuckle looking at the stats document online (partly hand-written), the players' averages (rushing, receiving, punting) with two decimal places, and the individual tackles broken out into groups: linemen, linebackers, and defensive backs.

After the season, Woody wrote his spiral-bound *Hotline to Victory* book, which I still possess.

FUN FACTS:

- With one more game than in 1967, the 34 rushing touchdowns were more than double the previous total of 16, and the 323 points were more than double the total of 145 in 1967.

- Seniors (Bill Long was the only one) accounted for only 65 of the 4,402 total offense yards.

- Seniors accounted for only 42 of the 1,384 receiving yards.

- Dave Brungard and Ed Bender combined for three receptions, all for touchdowns.

- The only two teams to outgain the Buckeyes were in the first and last games of the year. The defense recorded five turnovers in each of those games.

- The 77 points scored in the last two games of the season, the two most important games, were the most in consecutive games.

1969 (8-1)

Before the Michigan game, many fans, including me, say that this may have been OSU's finest team ever. The closest margin before the Michigan upset was 27 points; the scoring average was 42.5. These were team records to this point:

- total offense

- points

- plays in a game

- rushing yards in a nine-game season
- first downs rushing in a nine-game season
- first downs passing
- season rushing yards—Jim Otis
- points in a season—Jim Otis
- extra points—Stan White
- total offense in a season—Rex Kern

In the spring, my Upper Arlington High School arranged for Rex Kern and Brian Donovan to come to our senior party as part of the entertainment. I asked Rex how his physical condition was since he had been injured in 1968. Fortunately, this was way before the HIPAA Privacy Rule!

As basketball Coach Fred Taylor was preparing for the upcoming season, Texas Christian football coach Fred Taylor brought his Horned Frogs to Columbus. This was my first game as an OSU student. My friend Wayne and I would get season tickets in each of our four years. Rex Kern's first pass was for 50 yards to Bruce Jankowski but was called back on a penalty. After the walkoff, on what looked like an instant replay, Kern threw a 58-yard touchdown pass to Jankowski. And Woody hated passing? The Buckeyes' last three touchdowns, including the last two in the Rose Bowl, were through the air. This year, the freshmen students sat in the temporary stands in the south end zone, and my seats were along the left side as you face the field. The Buckeyes scored at least two touchdowns in each quarter, and Kevin Rusnak at quarterback got in the action with a 62-yard (must have been the magic number in the 62-0 win) bomb to Tom Campana in the last minute of play. Otis ran for 121 yards.

My first game as an OSU student would have the biggest margin of victory in any of Woody's 276 games and the most plays ever in a game

(101), to be tied a few weeks later against Illinois. My dad and Mark were at this game too, and at halftime, with the rain coming down and the score 33-0 on the way to a 62-0 final, Dad yelled up to us that it was time to go home.

For obvious reasons, the play-by-play showed shorthand for "Maciejowski"—"Macey" and "Macy." It also used a convention that we do not use today: the total playing time excludes the time of intermission.

The Buckeyes traveled to Seattle and beat Washington 41-14. The scoring plays in the official stats show OSU touchdowns by "kern" and "korn"—apparently, the Shift key was on the fritz—and rushing and passing by "Korn." Kern ran for 139 yards and Otis for 111.

In their 54-21 win over Michigan State, the Buckeyes scored half their points in the first quarter, including an interception return by Mark Debevc and a 73-yard punt return by Zelina for scores. For lovers of round numbers, the Buckeyes had a 400-300 edge in total yards.

In the 34-7 win at Minnesota, the Gophers had a 443-429 edge in total yards but lost five fumbles. Otis ran for 138 yards.

In the 41-0 win over Illinois, the Buckeyes had a 101-59 edge in plays (tying the record of 101 plays in the TCU game) and a 564-156 edge in total yards. The box score shows Illini quarterback Steve Livas with 57 yards lost in rushes and a net of minus 27 yards rushing. Otis ran for 167, and Kern passed for 193. The play-by-play includes, "Otis banged over left guard"; "Jackson was spilled by Stillwagon"; "Hayden dodged through left tackle"; and "Brockington bulled through left guard." I wonder now if Gus Johnson had done the descriptions. In the postgame notes, Illini coach Jim Valek described the Buckeyes as "pretty good."

The Buckeyes held Northwestern to minus 29 yards rushing—the box score shows Wildcat quarterback Maurie Daigneau with minus 100 yards—in the 35-6 win. In 1967, Wildcat quarterbacks had minus 40 against the Buckeyes. Otis ran for 127 yards. Future sports columnist and author Rick Telander had seven punts for the Wildcats.

The Buckeyes had 595 total yards and posted 62 points for the second time this year, 62-7 over Wisconsin, and like the 62-0 TCU game, the first touchdown was a pass to Jankowski, 31 yards from Maciejowski. It was the second straight year that Maciejowski ran and passed for more than 100 yards each against the Badgers while filling in for Kern. Maciejowski and Kevin Rusnak had two touchdown passes each, and Dick Kuhn's two receptions were for touchdowns, his only two of the year.

The Buckeyes gave up only a 98-yard kickoff return by Stan Brown and a touchdown pass by Mike Phipps with 1:12 remaining in the 42-14 win over Purdue in the snow, the Boilermakers playing in Columbus for the third straight year. Hayden ran for 130 yards, Kern ran for two touchdowns, and Zelina had a 57-yard punt return for the last score. Both of Zelina's touchdowns in 1969 came on punt returns. The defense held the Boilers to 29 yards on the ground, and Sensibaugh and Provost each had two of the five Mike Phipps interceptions, making it seven picks of Phipps over the last two years. The Buckeyes threw three interceptions, a bad omen heading into the following week's game at Michigan. Phipps finished second and Kern third in the Heisman Trophy voting in 1969.

The Michigan game was played on the Wolverines' artificial turf, where first year Coach Bo Schembechler had been photographed sweeping with a broom earlier in the year. He wore a mock turtleneck shirt at games his first year, but not often enough to set a fashion statement as Jim Tressel would with his sweater vest.

The Buckeyes followed the three interceptions from the previous week with six against the Wolverines in the 24-12 upset that broke the 22-game winning streak. Barry Pierson had three of the interceptions, and his 60-yard punt return was the biggest play of the game.

The Buckeyes' first drive saw an option pitch to fullback Jim Otis and a scramble pass to Otis! The Buckeyes had a 12-7 lead after Jan White's 22-yard catch and run, and all the scoring was in the first half. Otis carried his weight in the game, rushing for 144 yards and becoming the Buckeyes' first back with at least 1,000 yards with his 1,027.

If there had been video replays in those days, I would have liked to have seen if Garvie Craw really did break the plane of the end zone in the second quarter. Why is there a guy wearing a scarlet jacket celebrating with the Michigan players as they left the field?

It looks odd to see tailback Leo Hayden lined up practically piggy-back behind fullback Jim Otis in the I formation. Woody was incredibly calm on the sidelines, far from his demeanor in the 1971 and 1977 games in Ann Arbor. Michigan ran for 266 yards, losing only one the entire game. The total offense difference was only one yard, 374-373 in favor of Michigan.

This came in front of the largest crowd to see an OSU game, breaking the previous high in the Rose Bowl the previous year. After this game and through November 13, 1976, the Buckeyes would have seven regular season losses, all by seven points or less, and two ties.

FUN FACTS:
- Players with 99 of the 113 receptions would return for 1970.

- Jim Otis (96 points) outscored the opponents (93).

- Otis had 1,027 rushing yards, and the opponents had 883.

- Bruce Jankowksi and Jan White each had 23 receptions and five touchdowns.

- The defense gave up a total of 14 points in the first quarter, for the second straight year, and seven points in the third quarter.

- The Buckeyes scored more points in the first (121) and second (103) quarter than the opponents scored in the year (93).

- With a coach who did not like to pass, the Buckeyes had 78 more passing yards than the opponents on 30 fewer attempts.

- Kern averaged 7.4 yards per pass attempt for the second straight year.

- Only two other Big Ten teams, Purdue and Michigan, had an overall winning record, and the Buckeyes played them in the last two games of the year.

- In addition to Kern finishing third in the Heisman Trophy voting, Otis was seventh and Tatum was tenth.

- Kern finished ahead of Archie Manning in the Heisman Trophy voting. Each had nine touchdown passes, though Manning had 130 more passes.

CHAPTER 3

The 1970s
Oh, So Close, Part 1

THE BUCKEYES WERE A NEAR DYNASTY in the 1970s seasons. They had the lead in the fourth quarter in the Rose Bowl of the 1970 season, the 1974 Michigan State game, and the Rose Bowls of the 1974 and 1979 seasons, and lost all four. They also had the lead in the fourth quarter of the 1973 Michigan game that ended in a tie. These cost them a perfect season in each case.

1970 (9-1)

With the 1968 Super Sophomores now in their senior year, the biggest hole to replace was Jim Otis. Brockington did the job, rushing for 1,142 and 17 touchdowns. The Buckeyes were the only Big Ten team to have only nine regular season games.

Buckeyes fans survived a blasphemous prospect—the notion to replace "Hang On, Sloopy" with Blood, Sweat & Tears's "Hi-De-Ho." The sight of the cheerleaders performing slowly to "Hi-De-Ho" was quite a contrast to the high-energy "Hang On, Sloopy."

The first seven opponents had a losing record in 1969. For the third straight year, the Buckeyes opened against a team from Texas with a 56-13 win over Texas A&M. The Buckeyes had 513 total yards with 415 on the ground. As I stated in the Introduction, this was the last home game that I missed until the 2020 pandemic season. This was the Aggies' third game, coming off a win at LSU, and they would lose at Michigan 14-10 the next week.

In the 34-10 win over Duke, the Blue Devils led 3-0 at the end of the first quarter, and the Buckeyes led only 6-3 at halftime. The Buckeyes' first half score came with 13 seconds remaining, with Ken Luttner returning a blocked punt 45 yards for a touchdown. Hayden ran for 165 yards, Brockington for 117, and Kern for 113.

In the 29-0 win over Michigan State in East Lansing, the play-by-play shows a fourth quarter drive when Brockington carried nine straight times from the Spartan 26 to the one, with Maciejowski scoring on a keeper on fourth down. Brockington finished with 126 yards on 30 carries.

Brockington added 187 yards on 28 carries in a 28-8 win over Minnesota, with the Buckeyes scoring all their points in the first half.

As in 1968, the Buckeyes had a struggle with Illinois in Champaign, trailing 20-14 at halftime and leading 27-23 at the end of the third quarter before finishing strong in a 48-29 win. Kern had a 76-yard touchdown run, the longest run in OSU history at the time. In the fourth quarter with the score 34-23, on fourth and six from the Illini 31, the Buckeyes surprised Illinois as Hayden took an inside reverse to the end zone.

Here are some comments from the play-by-play:

"Robinson repeated at the right side."
"Navarro picked his way through left tackle."
"Maciejowski slanted outside."
"Hayden smashed left tackle."
"Robinson slanted outside."
"Brockington vaulted the center."

"Coburn cracked the left side."

"Coburn drilled left tackle."

"Coburn smacked over the left side." (Earlier, he had cracked the left side.)

"Coburn dove over left tackle."

For the second straight week, the Buckeyes trailed at halftime, this time 10-3 against Northwestern before winning 24-10. Brockington carried 42 times for 161 yards. Rick Telander had an interception for the Wildcats. Wildcat quarterback Maurie Daigneau, who had minus 100 yards rushing in the previous year's game, improved to minus 37 in this game.

The Wisconsin game at Madison had the Buckeyes with only a 10-7 lead at halftime before winning 24-7. The Badgers picked off five Buckeye passes, yet the Buckeyes had more passing yards than on the ground. Brockington ran for 83 yards and all three touchdowns.

For the fourth straight week, the Buckeyes struggled in the first half, tied 7-7 with Purdue in West Lafayette, and won 10-7 on a 30-yard Fred Schram field goal with 2:04 remaining. Maciejowski ("Mac-ski" in the play-by-play) had 30 of the 53 yards of the winning drive on two carries. The Boilers' only score came on a 96-yard kickoff return by Stan Brown, the second straight year that he had taken a kick back the distance against the Buckeyes. The defense was solid, with the team holding a 255-71 advantage in total yards and holding the Boilers to three first downs. Brockington had 136 yards on the ground. Each team punted 12 times and completed only two passes, with future TV analyst Gary Danielson only two-for-twelve for 17 yards for the Boilers. He completed two more passes, but they were intercepted by the Buckeyes' defense.

In the 20-9 win over Michigan, the Buckeyes converted a Wolverine fumble on the opening kickoff into a 28-yard field goal by Schram. A 26-yard touchdown pass from Kern to Jankowski was one of only three scoring passes on the year for the senior quarterback and the only score of the year for Jankowski. Stan White's interception and return to the Michigan 9-yard line in the fourth quarter set up Hayden's 4-yard run for the final score.

Woody had predicted the Buckeyes would run for 250 yards, and they came within eight as the Buckeyes totaled 242 (117 from Hayden) and held the Wolverines to 37.

I went to my first of three Rose Bowls (also after the 1972 and 1973 seasons) with three friends. Wearing a turtleneck, I thought that I would be the most over-dressed of the four of us on the flight, but it turned out that they and practically every other guy on the plane wore a dress shirt and tie! The package deal cost $259 for the flight, motel, parade ticket, bus to the game, and eight-dollar game ticket. Other companies had a package as low as $209.

I saw on a sign at a hotel that the singer Freda Payne, whose hit was "Band of Gold," was performing. I also had a chat with the comedian Leonard Barr.

This was my first trip to Southern California, and it was spectacular, of course. The Rose Bowl game was not. Just as in the 1969 Rose Bowl win over USC, the Buckeyes trailed 10-0; they scored twice to take a 14-10 lead at halftime.

OSU led 17-13 at the end of the third quarter and was deep in Stanford's territory, but John Brockington was stopped on fourth and one on the first play of the fourth quarter, and Stanford's Heisman Trophy quarterback Jim Plunkett rallied his team to a 27-17 win. With under three minutes to play and the score 27-17, Plunkett fumbled on the OSU 17-yard line. Stan White recovered and lateralled to Harry Howard, who took it all the way to the end zone—except that it was a forward lateral. A touchdown would have made things interesting. Twenty-six years later, Arizona State had a similar illegal forward lateral play toward the same end zone off of a blocked Buckeyes field goal attempt in the Rose Bowl.

The Buckeyes outgained Stanford 439-408 in total yards, using a wishbone formation and running for 364 yards, with Kern running for 129 and Brockington for 101. They even had two rushes by Jankowski for 41 yards, his only two carries of the year. Woody was quoted in *The New York Times* as saying Kern "developed a charley horse and wasn't too effective."

For those of you who insist on precision, the box score, which you can see online, again shows the players' rushing average with two decimal places! The punt return teams took the day off; none of the combined five punts had a return.

I had figured out before the game that after we got back from the game we would have time to go to the Kings hockey game. On the bus leaving the game, I worked up the nerve to ask my buddies, "So, still want to go to the hockey game?" The silence and crushed looks gave me my answer. I recall that Jim Murray, columnist for the *Los Angeles Times*, referring to Stanford's student base, had as his headline, "Yes, Pater, We Won."

The next day, we had time to see two movies. One was *Five Easy Pieces* at Grauman's Chinese Theatre, and the other was *Madron*, starring Richard Boone and Leslie Caron. We may have been the only four people ever to have seen *Madron*. Our Ford Pinto rental car died on the last day, but somehow we were able to return it to the rental office.

Rex Kern battled injuries, and his completion rate fell to 46%, with the team at 44% and only four touchdown passes.

FUN FACTS:

- The two games against the Teams From the State Up North each had a combined score of 29 points.

- For the second straight year, the defense gave up 93 points in the regular season.

- In 1968 through 1970, the three years of the Super Sophomores, the rushing yards in nine regular season games were 2,758 in 1968, 2,774 in 1969, and 2,761 in 1970.

- The two games with the lowest combined score in the three years of the Super Sophomores both came against Purdue—13 in 1968 and 17 in 1970.

- The 3,125 rushing yards in the 10 games were a team record to this point.

- Brockington had 1,142 rushing yards, and the opponents had 1,108.

- Brockington (17) and Kern (7) had more rushing touchdowns than the opponents (6).

- Brockington led the team in rushing yards and kickoff return yards.

- Larry Zelina averaged 7.3 yards per carry for his career.

- The three games with the fewest points allowed came on the road.

1971 (6-4)

The 1970 freshman team had a 2-1 record, scoring a total of 28 points, giving up 15, and completing only 28% of their passes. I went to a few games, which they played on Fridays, in the stadium with a few hundred fans in attendance. The players on this team had much better stats as varsity players in 1971.

The 1971 season was all about replacing the Super Sophomores, playing on the first artificial turf, playing the first ever 10 game regular season, coping with injuries, and close losses—all four by seven points or less. WOSU-TV televised some of the games.

The 10th games for 1971 and beyond were added in the past year. *The Ohio State University 1970 Football Information* publication had listed only nine games for 1971 through 1976.

Replacing the Super Sophomores seemed to be a non-issue when the Buckeyes beat Iowa in the opener, 52-21. John Bledsoe ran for 151 yards and two touchdowns, both of his touchdowns on the year, and quarterback Don Lamka ran for 100 yards and four scores, half of his touchdowns on the year, as the team ran for 402 yards.

The Buckeyes lost to Colorado the next week, 20-14, trailing 13-0 at halftime. Playing from behind, Don Lamka had 255 yards passing and 60 rushing, with 11 completions to Dick Wakefield for 172 yards. Lamka accounted for both touchdowns in the fourth quarter, with a 1-yard run and a 14-yard pass to Rick Middleton, the first of only two touchdown passes on the year. In the postgame notes, Woody said that Lamka separated his non-throwing left shoulder on the third play of the game.

Cliff Branch's 68-yard punt return for a score was the difference in the game. The Buffaloes' 10-2 record that year was the best in the 11 seasons for Coach Eddie Crowder, who left the field with the game ball. Tom Campana, who would play both offense and defense in his OSU career, had an interception.

The punting duty for the Buffaloes belonged to defensive back John "Bad Dude" Stearns, who would go on to an extended baseball career as a catcher for the New York Mets and would return to Columbus in 2007 as the manager of the minor league Columbus Clippers. His last punt pinned the Buckeyes at their own 5-yard line with a minute remaining. The box score shows that he was credited with saving a touchdown by committing a pass interference penalty. I would attend a meeting when he became the manager of the Clippers.

The California game, a 35-3 win, was on an incredibly hot day in Columbus. The Buckeyes had a 430-135 edge in total yards. Lamka played, but sophomore Greg Hare had the most passes with 12. In the middle of the second quarter, Woody ordered a punt—on second (no typo) down and 28 from the OSU 21.

In the 24-10 win over Illinois in Champaign, Rick Galbos ran for

112 yards and Morris Bradshaw for 95. In the postgame notes, Woody said that three starters were lost due to injuries during the game, and Illinois Coach Bob Blackman said that he had never been so disappointed in his life. Illinois had a 414-292 edge in total offense but four turnovers. The Buckeyes completed two passes for eight yards.

The play-by-play states, "White kicks off north dribbler picked up by B. Wright."

In the 27-7 over Indiana in Bloomington, the Buckeyes had 263 yards passing, with 204 by Greg Hare. The Hoosier quarterback was Ted McNulty from my high school class at Upper Arlington. After the game, I recall Woody saying that the Buckeyes had won the Three-I League, after beating Iowa, Illinois, and Indiana.

The 31-6 win over Wisconsin was the Morris Bradshaw show, with the future Oakland Raider running for a touchdown—the longest in OSU history—and returning a kickoff for a score, each one 88 yards long. He finished with 123 yards rushing, and Galbos added 100. I recall that Bradshaw was not named the Player of the Game by the television staff, losing out to the Badgers' Rufus Ferguson, who rushed for 136 yards. In the postgame notes, both Woody and Badger Coach John Jardine described the Buckeye defense, which recorded seven turnovers, as "bend-but-don't-break." The Buckeyes' edge in total offense was only 399-383.

In Minneapolis, the Buckeyes stopped Minnesota's attempt for a two-point conversion ("inches short," according to the play-by-play) after an 80-yard drive with 39 seconds remaining, recovered the onside kick, and escaped with a 14-12 win. Wakefield had the Buckeyes' second and last touchdown catch of the year. The Buckeyes scored 14 points in each of the two games when they had a touchdown pass. At 6-1, it would be the last win of the year.

The game against Michigan State was a 10-10 tie at halftime, with the Spartans scoring on an 11-yard drive in the fourth quarter after recovering a Buckeye fumble to win 17-10. The play-by-play lists the first play of the drive as, "Matthews stormed over right guard for 4." Each team had less than 200 yards total offense, combining for three completions out of 22 passes for 29 yards. Galbos's 91 yards rushing was almost half of the team's 185 total yards. At the end of 1971, this was the only game of the top 10 attended games in Ohio Stadium that the Buckeyes lost.

The next game, against Northwestern, was similar. The Buckeyes led 10-7 at halftime, but they gave up a Wildcat score in the fourth quarter to lose 14-10. The Buckeyes reached the Wildcat 21-yard line after the Wildcat go-ahead touchdown but threw an interception. Northwestern's score in the first half was on a 93-yard kickoff return. Maurie Daigneau improved his rushing stats against the Buckeyes to minus four in this game. The play-by-play states, "Robinson managed to get one hard yard," "Galbos tapped the middle for FD," "Lamka was spilled ..." and "Lamka was smeared trying to pass."

The only way to watch the Michigan game, a 10-7 loss, without being in Ann Arbor was on a closed-circuit feed to Mershon Auditorium on the OSU campus, and I was there. It was weird watching a game without any TV commentary or sound but in an auditorium full of screaming fans. It was a game played in snow early and in sunshine later.

Tom Campana's 85-yard punt return—he would have 166 yards on returns in the game—in the third quarter gave the Buckeyes a 7-3 lead. It was the second longest punt return in OSU history at the time and the longest in the Big Ten that year. The TV camera did not pick up Campana catching the punt; instead, you saw a white-jerseyed player streaking into view on the left side of the screen and running to paydirt, spiking the football as he scored. The Michigan punter tried to coax a penalty by falling to the turf on the punt after being brushed by a Buckeye defender. Thirty eight years later, I would interview Tom's brother Tim, a former Ohio Wesleyan player, during an OWU broadcast and had him give his take on the crazy game.

Campana's score came with 2:07 remaining in the third quarter, and Michigan's Billy Taylor ran 21 yards for the final score with 2:07 remaining in the game. On the next possession, Lamka's high pass for Wakefield was intercepted by Thom Darden over Wakefield's back, triggering Woody's explosion. The Buckeyes were outgained 335-138. Two Wolverine quarterbacks completed one pass each. Campana passed Larry Zelina for most career punt return yards, by six yards.

It was a year of what-ifs. What if the Buckeyes had avoided the Colorado punt return and the Northwestern kickoff return? What if the Buckeyes had not fumbled against Michigan State? What if Darden's interception had been ruled pass interference? What if the Buckeyes had avoided the injuries?

The last four games saw 17 as the most points scored by either the Buckeyes or the opponents.

FUN FACTS:

- Campana had 447 of the team's 481 punt return yards. The other 34 yards were by an offensive lineman and a defensive lineman.

- Campana had 447 punt return yards, and the opponents had a total of 182.

- The defense gave up only 13 points in the first quarter and 14 in the third. It had given up 12 points in the third quarter in 1970.

- The defense gave up 120 points, the same as in 1970.

- For the second straight year, the Buckeyes had a 24-10 win over one of the Illinois teams in October and a 10-7 road game in November.

- The Buckeyes and the opponents were separated by one first down.

- The Buckeyes and the opponents each had two touchdown passes, even though the opponents had 56 more passes and 24 more completions.

- The edge in rushing touchdowns was 26-12.

- The 1971 team accomplished something that the Super Sophomores did not do in either 1969 or 1970—avoid a double digit loss. The last non-national championship Buckeye team to avoid a double digit loss was the 1955 team.

1972 (9-2)

The 1971 freshman team had a 3-0 record, beating Indiana, Kentucky, and Ohio University by a combined 120-43 score. *The Ohio State University 1972 Football Information* publication has the stats for the team, with Champ Henson averaging 7.6 yards per carry.

In 1972, OSU had a Varsity Reserve team that went 2-0, with 562 yards rushing and 82 passing. Cornelius Greene tied Bruce Elia for the team lead with three rushing touchdowns, the number three matching his completions.

This was the first year of freshman eligibility, and Archie Griffin would make an impact, but not in the opening 21-0 win over Iowa. Sophomore Champ Henson did, with 79 rushing yards and two touchdowns. Randy Keith added 81 yards and the other score. The Buckeyes had a bye week after this game.

The North Carolina game, a 29-14 win, was Archie's breakout game, with his 239 yards setting a single game record. It seemed as if Archie broke more tackles in that game than most running backs break in their career. Here is a trivia question that I like to spring on friends: Who had the longest run for the Buckeyes in the 1972 North Carolina game? You can see their brains churning, and when they figure out that it's Archie's breakout game, that's their answer. Ah, but Elmer Lippert had a 68-yard run, to Archie's long of 55. Elmer had 116 yards on the day—his high for the year—and averaged 5.1 yards per carry in his OSU career. The 68-yard run represented 10% of his 688 career total. Cornelius Greene, wearing #25, made his freshman debut late, throwing his only pass of the year for an incompletion and rushing three times for minus 14. Spoiler alert: 1973 would be different for him.

This was the only game in my four years as a student that my friend Wayne missed. I walked the three miles back home, thinking all the way, "Wayne is going to be so upset that he missed this game."

The Buckeyes intercepted four Golden Bear passes in a 35-18 win over California in Berkeley. Rick Middleton, who would broadcast three high school games with me for WINF-FM in his home Delaware County in 2010, had two of the picks. The *Columbus Dispatch* reporter Paul Hornung wrote that the Buckeyes scored five touchdowns in a 21-minute span.

Archie found his hometown of Columbus a welcome site, as he ran for 192 yards in the 26-7 win over Illinois. He had 431 of his 867 yards on the year in the North Carolina and Illinois games. Henson ran for three touchdowns.

The Buckeyes had 386 of their 396 yards on the ground in the 44-7 win over Indiana, with Henson gaining 116. Archie had the only two receptions, for 10 yards. This game commemorated the 50th year of Ohio Stadium, and I still have my slightly water-logged program.

Greg Hare passed for 120 yards and showed his running ability (hint: see the Michigan game) with 118 yards, and Henson had 122 yards rushing in the 28-20 win at Wisconsin.

Henson ran for 131 yards in the 27-19 win over Minnesota, his third straight week with a new career high. Paul Hornung wrote in *The Columbus Dispatch* that the Buckeyes defense was missing five starters, including Randy Gradishar.

The Buckeyes lost three fumbles and two interceptions in the 19-12 loss to Michigan State in East Lansing. For the second straight year against the Spartans, the game was tied at halftime, and Michigan State scored the winning touchdown in the second half after a Buckeye fumble. This one was on a 6-yard "drive," while last year's took only 11 yards. Ted Powell had a touchdown catch for the second straight game, and his two would lead the Buckeyes for the year. MSU's Dirk Krijt kicked four field goals in his first varsity game.

The Spartans had a 334-107 edge in rushing yardage. The last two trips to The State Up North, including in Ann Arbor in 1971, produced a total of 185 yards rushing. It was a going-away present for retiring Spartan Coach Duffy Daugherty.

Champ Henson had an OSU record 44 carries for 153 yards and all four touchdowns in the 27-14 win at Northwestern, setting another record with 19 touchdowns in a season. John Brockington had the previous high of 42 carries, also against Northwestern. The Buckeyes defense continued to show no mercy for Wildcat quarterbacks, and Mitch Anderson netted minus 43 yards on the ground. Ted Powell continued to be an effective target for Hare with three catches for 75 yards.

Woody said that when you pass, three things are possible and two of them are bad. In the 14-11 win over Michigan, he proved it. Greg Hare passed three times, completed one, and had one incompletion and an interception. The one reception went to Archie, and I basically missed it. My seat was behind a pillar, and the pass hit a blind spot. All three passes were in the second half. In the last two matchups between these teams, the winning team combined for three completions.

In the first drive of the second half, Hare had a 35-yard run and Archie the remaining 30 on the next play for a 14-3 lead. The defense had two huge goal line stands which were disputed by Bo Schembechler.

Including this game, the two teams had scored 21 points each in the last two games. Michigan had a 344-192 edge in total offense and had almost twice as many plays, 83 to 44. In the past two years, the Michigan advantage in yards was 679-330. The Wolverines had broken a 21 game regular season (22 overall) win streak by the Buckeyes in 1969, and this win broke a Michigan 21 game regular season win streak. If Michigan had won, it would have been their 22nd straight in Woody's 22nd year at OSU.

Famous postgame photos of tough guys Woody, Archie, and John Hicks in tears in the locker room appeared in the newspapers.

My friend Marvin and I went to the Rose Bowl, my second trip in three years. I was a big NFL fan in those days, so on a Sunday, the thirty-first, I watched the Cowboys-Redskins playoff game in the hotel room, something that I would never do today, while Marvin went to Long Beach to see the RMS Queen Mary. For the second time in three years, I had a great time in Southern California—but not when seeing Southern California trounce the Buckeyes 42-17 in the Rose Bowl. Half of the game was enjoyable, as the halftime score was 7-7. The Buckeyes outrushed USC 285-207 and had one more play, but the Trojans' Sam Cunningham scored four touchdowns, all in the second half.

The 42 points were the most given up in any of Woody's games, which meant that I had been to the top two, including the 1967 Purdue game. The attendance set an all-time record for a "modern collegiate" game, according to the notes.

FUN FACTS:
- Archie and Champ Henson each had 772 yards rushing in the regular season.
- Cornelius Greene had more kickoff returns (three) than passes (one).
- The top three kickoff returners were freshmen—Brian Baschnagel, Griffin, and Greene. They had 471 of the 518 yards.

- Baschnagel was the leading kick returner and punt returner.

- Four Buckeyes had games with at least 100 yards rushing—Griffin, Henson, Hare, and Lippert—a freshman, a sophomore, and two juniors.

- The edge in rushing touchdowns was 34-10.

- Henson had twice as many rushing touchdowns (20) as the opponents.

1973 (10-0-1)

In the opening 56-7 win over Minnesota, Archie had a 93-yard kickoff return for a touchdown to go along with his 129 yards on the ground, starting his 31 regular season game streak of 100 plus, and Neal Colzie had a 78-yard punt return for a score. Greene had 84 yards rushing in his first start, and Henson had 81, with the team rushing for 383. Future NFL Coach Tony Dungy completed his first college pass as a backup for the Gophers.

After a bye week, the Buckeyes beat Texas Christian 37-3, to make the combined score of the last two games against the Horned Frogs 99-3. Archie had 119 yards on the ground with a 68-yard score, and Greene had 113 with a 72-yard score, but Henson was injured. The team ran for 396. The Buckeyes' six pass completions came to six different receivers from three different quarterbacks.

Bruce Elia switched from linebacker to fullback against Washington State and recorded the first two of his 14 touchdowns of the year in the 27-3 win. Archie ran for 128 yards, with 92 in the second half. In the postgame notes, Cougar Coach Jim Sweeney called Greene the quickest quarterback that he had ever seen.

The scoring declined for the third straight game, but the defense blanked Wisconsin 24-0. Archie ran for 169 yards, and the Buckeyes rushed for 423.

Archie had 130 yards, Elia had his best output of 123, and the Buckeyes ran for 365 in the 37-7 win over Indiana in Bloomington. Colzie had a 55-yard interception return for a score. The radio broadcaster struggled to pronounce the last name of freshman Nick Buonamici.

Archie had "only" 105 of the team's rushing 425 yards in the 60-0 trouncing of Northwestern, a game that was scoreless in the first quarter. The 425 yards were distributed to 14 ball carriers. For the seventh straight year, the defense held the Wildcat quarterback to negative yardage on the ground—minus 32 by two quarterbacks this time. Wildcat coach John Pont, who played for Woody at Miami, had been the coach at Indiana the previous year, so this made it 104-7 in the two games for him.

The Buckeyes had an all-time team record of 84 rushes for 341 yards—108 by Archie—and 95 plays, almost twice as many as Illinois, in the 30-0 win in Champaign in front of the only non-sellout crowd of the year. Pete Johnson had the first score of his career. The Illini completed five passes thrown by five different players to four different receivers.

The defense recorded its third straight shutout and held the Spartans to four first downs, all on the ground, in a 35-0 win over Michigan State. The teams combined for 37 yards passing, six by the Spartans. Archie ran for 131 yards, and Colzie had a 43-yard punt return for a score among his 170 return yards in the game. The Spartan quarterback with both of their two passes was former walk-on and future college coach Ty Willingham, who also had their most carries.

Archie broke his own record with 246 yards rushing, and 13 ball carriers combined to run for 447 yards in the 55-13 win over Iowa. In the postgame notes, Woody said, "Corny threw the ball very well today," apparently referring to his only completion, a 41-yard touchdown pass to Dave Hazel.

Greene's one completion was one more than the Buckeyes had the next week in the 10-10 tie at Michigan. Greg Hare had all four passes, as the Buckeyes suffered from a Greene Thumb—Corny had injured his.

Counting this game, the Buckeyes had a total of one completion in the last two Michigan games.

The Buckeyes had a 10-0 lead, survived two missed field goals by the Wolverines, and went to the Rose Bowl after the vote of the conference athletic directors. In the last three years, the teams now had scored 31 points each.

Archie was running so well in the first half—99 of his 163 yards—that I said to myself *Perhaps he is worthy of the Heisman Trophy*, unheard of for a sophomore. Tom Skladany had a leg injury on a kickoff in the second quarter and was done for the season. Mike and Mike took his place for the punting duty—Bartoszek in the Michigan game and Keeton in the Rose Bowl.

The two starting quarterbacks were Cornelius Greene and Dennis Franklin. What do Greene and Franklin have in common? They are both counties in Ohio.

Mark and I went to the Rose Bowl, a 42-21 win over USC, the Buckeyes matching the 42 points that the Trojans scored on the Buckeyes the previous year. We used the Richard Lewis (no relation to the comedian, an OSU alumnus) Travel Agency. The package cost us a whopping $414 each and included the flight, lodging, a ticket to the Tournament of Roses parade, a bus to the game, and a box lunch. We gave up on waiting for the chicken in the lunch to thaw. I opened my first checking account to pay for this trip.

During our stay, we took the #5 bus to Inglewood to see the Lakers play in the Fabulous Forum. We bought tickets from a scalper, paying the face value of $2.00. When we got to the seats, they were already occupied. Looking at our tickets, we saw that they were for a previous game. Thank goodness that ticket scanners were years in the future.

The OSU float in the parade produced an ironic chuckle from Buckeye fans. It showed a gigantic quarterback cocking his arm for a pass, this for a team that had about seven times as many rushing yards as passing yards and had Cornelius Greene, who would finish at 43%, coming off his injury. The float proved to be prophetic, as Greene passed early, finishing 6-for-8 for 129 yards, with each of the six completions gaining a first down. The 129 yards were more than what the team had in the previous four games combined. Future assistant coach Fred Pagac caught four for 89 yards; the four catches nearly matched his season total of five coming into the game, and the 89 yards were more than the 70 that he had entering the game. The Trojans had a 27-20 edge in first downs.

Our seats were in the north end zone, so Archie's 47-yard touchdown run as he followed his blockers (the box score called it a 47-yard "blast") to seal it came right at us. Freshman Pete Johnson had 94 of his 205 season's yards and three of his six touchdowns in the game.

It didn't seem like a 27-year time warp, but the handwritten stats now found online show the date on one page as January 1, 1947!

Notre Dame beat Alabama 24-23 in the Sugar Bowl, with a key play a late Crimson Tide missed PAT kick. A different outcome may have given the Buckeyes instead of the Irish a national championship.

FUN FACTS:

- The last two games, away from home, had attendances of 105,223 and 105,267.

- The 42 points in the Rose Bowl remain the most scored by a winning Big Ten team since the 1948 game. Only Penn State's 49 in the loss in the 2017 game is higher.

- Archie's 2,444 rushing yards after two years matched Rex Kern's career passing yards.

- Archie also led the team in kickoff returns.

- Archie ran for 1,577 yards, and the opponents ran for 1,458.

- Bruce Elia and Cornelius Greene each had more points than the opponents did for the year.

- Five Buckeyes—Elia, Greene, Griffin, Johnson, Henson—had as many or more rushing touchdowns than the opponents did for the year.

- Elia, Greene, and Griffin had more total touchdowns than the opponents did for the year.

- The edge in rushing touchdowns was 47-4.

- Four of Pete Johnson's six touchdowns came in the last two games.

- The Buckeyes had 22 first downs passing the entire season. In 2018, they would have at least 22 first downs passing in three games.

- The Buckeyes scored more points in each quarter than the opponents scored the entire season.

- The Buckeyes gave up a total of three points in the first quarter and seven points in the third quarter the entire season.

- The defense gave up 20 points in the first seven games and 44 in the last three.

- Greene had the longest run of the year, 72 yards, but Greg Hare had the longest pass of the year, 55 yards.

- Bill Ezzo's only reception of the year was the team's longest, 55 yards.

- The opponents threw 123 more passes and completed 60 more passes than the Buckeyes, but the Buckeyes had a five to three advantage in touchdown passes.

- The Buckeyes had an 805-42 advantage in punt return yards.

- Eleven Buckeyes had a longer run than the opponents' longest run of 19 yards.

- Neal Colzie had the longest punt return and interception return.

- Five opponents had one PAT kick in a game, and no opponent had more than one.

- The Buckeyes lost one fumble per 108 carries, and the opponents lost one per 35 carries.

- Both OSU and USC had a tie game in which each team had one touchdown and gave up the lead. USC and Oklahoma played to a 7-7 tie.

- *The Ohio State University 1973 Football Information* publication informed that single game tickets ranged from $5.00 up to $8.00.

1974 (10-2)

The season started with a rare opener on the road, a 34-19 win at Minnesota. Archie had 133 of the team's 350 yards on the ground. The Buckeyes' worst ball carrier was "Center Pass," who carried once for a 12-yard loss. These days, it's recorded as a team rush. Dungy was now the starting quarterback for the Gophers, and he completed only five of 19 passes.

Back in Columbus, the home OSU beat the visiting OSU, 51-10 over Oregon State. Lenny Willis returned the second half kickoff 97 yards for a score. Archie had 134 of the 386 rushing yards, but he was outscored by his brother Ray, who had two touchdowns to his one. The box score lists Archie's touchdown as by "Griffin" and Ray's two by "R. Griffin."

The Buckeyes scored a touchdown in each quarter in the 28-9 win over SMU. Archie had 156 yards, and Brian Baschnagel had 140 on only seven carries along with three catches for 38 yards. The team ran for 357 yards.

The Buckeyes traveled to Pullman, Washington, and beat Washington State 42-7. Archie had 196 yards as 11 Buckeyes had a carry for their 351 yards. For lovers of round numbers, the attendance is listed as 50,000.

The Badgers scored first, but the Buckeyes had the last 52 in the 52-7 win over Wisconsin. Archie ran for 112, but he was topped by Greene's 146 as the team ran for 359. Amazingly, first downs were even at 23 each. The defense picked off five passes, four in the second half, with Bruce Ruhl tying a team record with three. Skladany had his kicking duties cut in half with kickoffs but no punts. In the postgame notes, Badgers Coach John Jardine called the Buckeyes the best team he had ever faced.

Sixteen players carried the ball for 333 yards, 146 by Archie, in the 49-9 win over Indiana. A bigger surprise was having 235 passing yards by Corny, with two receivers topping 100 yards—111 by Baschnagel and 108 by Dave Hazel.

Archie averaged almost 10 yards per carry for his 173 yards in the 55-7 win at Northwestern. The defense picked off three Wildcat passes and held quarterback Mitch Anderson to 20 yards in rushing losses.

The 49-7 win over Illinois was Woody's 200th career win, and the Victory Bell rang 200 times. The Griffins combined for 230 yards rushing, 144 by Archie to give him a record 18 straight regular season games with more than 100. Corny ran and passed for 127 yards each, and the Buckeyes recorded a then-team record 644 total yards.

The Buckeyes had a 13-3 lead at Michigan State in the fourth quarter, but the Spartans rallied for their 16-13 win. Buckeye fans were irate over the finish, as Henson was ruled stopped short of the goal line, and the Spartan defenders would not unpile in time for the Buckeyes to line up for another play. The defense gave up touchdowns on a 44-yard pass and an 88-yard run in the fourth quarter. On Levi Jackson's 88-yard run, MSU fans swarmed into the end zone. Woody's comments in the postgame notes are surprisingly composed compared to his reported anger in the locker room. Archie ran for 140 yards.

Corny rested his arm in the 35-10 win at Iowa, passing only twice, both in the first half. Archie ran for 175, giving him 421 in the last two years against the Hawkeyes, and the team ran for 384. For the second straight year against Iowa, the Buckeyes completed only one pass, and it was to Dave Hazel each time. Amazingly, the Hawkeyes had a 24-22 edge in first downs.

The Buckeyes and Wolverines had tied the previous year, and they were dead even in rushing yards at 195 each this year in the Buckeyes' 12-10 win. At halftime, they were separated by two rushing yards and one passing yard. Three of Tom Klaban's four field goals were at least 43 yards, and the Wolverines missed a late field goal for the second straight year. Skladany got his kicks, too, averaging 45.2 on five punts. For the second straight year, the visiting team lost a 10-0 lead. Archie ran for 111 yards.

Freshman Jeff Logan muffed a punt, but, fortunately, he recovered it. I have worked stats for Jeff on broadcasts since 1979, and occasionally I will chide him about it.

The holidays came early, as Santa Claus was spotted on the stadium track. I did not have season tickets in 1974, so I had to buy from scalpers at each game. For the Michigan game, I had to pay a king's ransom of $25.00. The news that night broadcast footage of a student who could not find a buyer for his ticket. He said, "I'll take fifty cents for it!" I recall that Woody was quoted as wondering if the Man Upstairs was testing his team after the Michigan State loss. The Buckeyes' three completions ran their combined total to four in the last three Michigan games.

In the third straight Rose Bowl against USC, the Trojans scored a late touchdown and a two-point conversion to win 18-17. Twenty-five of the 35 points were scored in the fourth quarter. On the last play, Skladany tried a 62-yard field goal that was well short.

A key play occurred when Colzie intercepted a pass but drew a penalty when he spiked the ball out of bounds. I recall a few years later on a similar play, Marv Homan, broadcasting a game, said that the Buckeyes once lost a Rose Bowl on a play like that.

Archie had only 75 yards, but his streak of 100-yard games was still intact, as the record keeping does not include bowl games. Both he and Anthony Davis suffered a rib injury in the game.

The Buckeyes' two losses in 1974 came by a total of four points.

FUN FACTS:

- Corny and Archie had the two highest single-season total offense totals in team history.

- The Buckeyes gave up a total of three points in the third quarter the entire season, which meant that in the last two seasons, they had given up a total of 10 points in the third quarter.

- The Buckeyes scored more points in the second quarter than their opponents scored the entire season.

- For the second straight year, the longest pass was 55 yards.

- For the second straight year, Neal Colzie had the longest interception return and punt return.

- The six players who had interceptions each had at least three.

- The opponents threw 141 more passes and completed 49 more, but the Buckeyes had the same number of touchdown passes—nine.

- Opponents had one more offensive play on the year.

- Four Buckeyes—Griffin, Henson, Greene, Johnson—had as many or more rushing touchdowns as the opponents.

- The edge in rushing touchdowns was 48-6.

1975 (11-1)

The backfield of Archie, Pete, Baschnagel, and Corny was considered the best in the country. They represented three different states and the District of Columbia—Ohio, New York, and Pennsylvania, with Corny from DC. *The Ohio State University 1975 Football Information* publication mentioned that "Ohio State expects to have a good football team in 1975."

During 1975, I saw the movie *Return to Campus*, directed by former OSU player Harold Cornsweet, at the theater in the Graceland Shopping Center. The IMDB.com website (which gives it 3.0 stars out of 10) summary describes it this way: "A 55-year old former high school football player finally gets to fulfill his life-long dream and play in the big game in this autobiographical fantasy." Supposedly it took place at Ohio State, with game footage cut, spliced, and mashed up. In one sequence, a quarterback launches a pass, and the film cuts to a player catching a punt. In another, the team prepares for the upcoming game against "Motor Dame."

Mark and I went to the opening Michigan State game in East Lansing, a 21-0 revenge win over the Spartans. Archie ran for 108 yards, and Corny hit Lenny Willis with a 64-yard touchdown pass. Craig Cassady tied a team record with three interceptions.

We left for the game before sunrise. On the way back, we had dinner at a Ponderosa Steakhouse in Ann Arbor and made it home before midnight in time to see Bud Kaatz's half-hour recap on Channel 6.

The 17-9 game against Penn State was the game when I worked in the Time Warner broadcast truck instead of being in the stadium. Before sunrise, we went to Worthington to board the truck. I had a part-time job for Time Warner. One of my tasks was to go to a transmitter building on Morse Road in the middle of nowhere, now across the street from the Easton Town Center, and press two switches to bring the Pittsburgh Pirates broadcast to our subscribers. I quickly became a fan of Bob Prince, their play-by-play announcer.

It was only a 10-9 score before Pete Johnson scored with 4:47 left in the game. Archie ran for 128 yards and had the team's longest reception of 23 yards, which, in the postgame notes, Woody called an impossible catch and Joe Paterno called a great catch. Johnson added 112 yards, and Baschnagel had the longest run of the game, 49 yards, playing against his home state.

In the 32-7 win over North Carolina, Archie ran for 157, giving him a total of 396 in his two games against the Tar Heels. Pete Johnson added 148 yards and scored all five touchdowns. On the last one, he had a slow start getting the snap, but he still scored. Duncan Griffin had his only interception of the year.

In the Los Angeles Coliseum, the Buckeyes dominated UCLA 28-7 at halftime and cruised to a 41-20 win. Interestingly, the Buckeyes wore their home uniforms. Interviewed at halftime, Woody said that he always treats a game as if it were nothing to nothing. If so, the game would have ended in a tie, since each team scored 13 in the second half.

The Bruins scored first on a pass from John Sciarra to James Sarpy, and Keith Jackson said on the air, "…and it grows quiet along the banks of the Olentangy." Miffed at the time, I thought to myself *How does he know what the mood is thousands of miles away?*

With UCLA deep in OSU territory in the second half, Sciarra threw a fourth down pass that was ruled pass interference, and the story was that OSU linebacker Ken Kuhn asked an official something like, "Excuse me, sir, but if the pass is tipped before the contact, pass interference cannot be called, can it?" After some deliberation, the official signaled a deflection and Buckeyes' ball. Kuhn would have an interception later.

For the second straight game, two Buckeyes ran for 100 plus—Archie for 160 and Corny for 120. Corny actually had 122 in the first half and minus two in the second. I kept my own stats while watching the game on TV, and they were amazingly close to the official stats.

When he later became a commentator on ABC, Bruins Coach Dick Vermeil would be very pro-OSU, it seemed, especially in the 1997 Rose Bowl. The attendance of 55,248 was the lowest at an OSU game all year. The Bruins had two extra-point kicks, breaking a 26-game streak where no opponent had more than one.

In the 49-0 win over Iowa, five Buckeyes ran for at least 49 yards each, and 12 players had a carry, with Archie gaining 120. Johnson ran for three touchdowns, and freshman quarterback Rod Gerald carried only twice, scoring both times on runs of 45 and 14 yards in the fourth quarter. Corny was a perfect eight-for-eight passing for 117 yards. Skladany took the day off on his punting duties.

Forcing six turnovers, the Buckeyes recorded their second straight shutout at home, 56-0 over Wisconsin. The Badgers fumbled 10 times, losing five. Counting the opener against Michigan State, no Big Ten team had scored on the Buckeyes in three contests. Archie ran for 107 yards, getting only two carries in the second half, and Tim Fox had a 75-yard punt return for a touchdown. Six ball carriers ran for a touchdown.

My entire family went to the Purdue game, a 35-6 win in West Lafayette. Archie ran for 130 yards and set the record for the all-time rushing yards, topping the previous mark of Ed Marinaro of Cornell. Johnson added 131 yards. With the Boilers kicking two field goals, no Big Ten team had scored a touchdown in four matchups, and the defense had not been scored on in the second half.

A few weeks later, Woody appeared at the downtown Lazarus Department Store to sign autographs, and he signed the back of my photos from the Purdue game. Lazarus would host sports figures often, and I met Pete Rose, Oscar Robertson, and the tennis Amritraj brothers at the Lazarus events.

The score was only 17-14 after three quarters against Indiana before Johnson scored with 6:22 left for a 24-14 win. Earlier in the fourth quarter, the Buckeyes had a 16-play drive end at the Indiana 1-yard line on a fumble. Archie and Johnson ran for 150 yards each, the second straight game of over 100 for each. Only four of the Buckeyes' 76 plays were passes. Other than one play in the last 21 seconds of the first half, the Buckeyes had only three possessions in the first 30 minutes.

Illinois scored the first three points and the Buckeyes the last 40 in the 40-3 win in Champaign. Tom Skladany may have upstaged Archie's 127 yards by kicking a Big Ten record (at the time) 59-yard field goal. In his career, it was the only successful field goal out of nine attempts of at least 50 yards. He also averaged 56.5 yards on four punts, with a long of 68. The field goal broke the previous record of 57 yards set by the Illini's Dan Beaver three weeks prior to this game in the same stadium.

Tim Fox scored his second touchdown of the year on a 20-yard interception return, demonstrating his athletic ability by doing a head over heels front flip after each one. One of them was a perfect 10, but the other perhaps a 9.1, based on a slightly awkward finish. Fox had the Buckeyes' only punt return and interception return for a score in 1975.

In the 38-6 win over Minnesota, each of the four backfield players—Archie, Corny, Pete, and Brian—ran for touchdowns. Archie ran for 124 yards and was the leading receiver with 48 yards. Pete Johnson, whom Gopher coach Cal Stoll in the postgame notes called a "buffalo," ran for 90 yards and a touchdown. Also in the notes, Woody described the running, 360 yards, as only fair.

Griffin—Ray, not Archie—set up the winning touchdown the next week in the 21-14 comeback over Michigan. After the tying drive in the fourth quarter, he intercepted Rick Leach's pass and returned it 29 yards to the three, setting up Pete's winning touchdown on the next play. Ray picked the perfect time for his only interception of the year, and it was the team's longest of the year.

To everyone's shock, each team threw unexpected passes. Pete Johnson caught a 7-yard touchdown pass for the first score and would score all three touchdowns. Michigan running back Gordon Bell threw a touchdown pass. The *Sports Illustrated* story on the game described it this way (not verbatim): "A fan yelled 'They're passing!' in the same way that you would say, 'He stole my wallet!'"

Down 14-7 in the fourth quarter, Baschnagel caught a Greene pass for 17 yards on the right sideline on third down and was knocked out of the game on a hard hit. It was the first of five straight plays to gain at least 11 yards. Archie would be bottled up until this drive, finishing with 46 yards, but he had the 11-yard run. Pete scored from the one on fourth down.

Archie's streak of 100-yard games was snapped at 31, but no one was complaining. Ironically, Michigan had two players over 100, Gordon Bell and Rob Lytle, and had twice as many rush yards as the Buckeyes. ABC's Bill Flemming interviewed Cornelius Greene and Aaron Brown after the game. His line was something like, "OSU's colors are scarlet and gray, but today, they're Greene and Brown."

The Buckeyes were 3-0-1 against Michigan from 1972 through 1975 despite being outgained in each game.

The Rose Bowl 23-10 loss to UCLA in a re-match was painful to watch. The Buckeyes dominated the first half, giving up only nine yards rushing and 48 total, but they led only 3-0. UCLA finished with 202 yards on the ground and 212 passing. Counting the 13-3 run that they had to finish the first meeting, the Bruins had outscored the Buckeyes 36-13 in the two games. The Buckeyes lost despite having a 20-19 edge in first downs.

For the second straight Rose Bowl, Archie suffered an injury, a broken left hand on the third play of the game. He still managed to run for 93 yards.

Archie won his second Heisman. Michigan's Charles Woodson would match Archie's four touchdowns when he won the Heisman in 1997, but he was a defensive player and a punt returner. These two Heisman winners who scored only four touchdowns were both born in Ohio—Woodson was born in Fremont.

FUN FACTS:

- Archie and Corny left as the top two career total offense leaders in team history.

- For the second time in three years, the Buckeyes had a player, Johnson this year, who outscored the opponents.

- Pete Johnson had half of the team's 52 touchdowns. His 25 rushing touchdowns were 19 more than the opponents' total.

- Corny's eight rushing touchdowns were two more than the opponents' total.

- The edge in rushing touchdowns was 44-6.

- Johnson had 1,059 yards rushing to join Archie in surpassing the 1,000 yard mark.

- The defense gave up only 16 points in the first quarter and 13 in the second.

- The Buckeyes scored more points in the second quarter than the opponents scored the entire season and more points in the fourth quarter than the opponents scored the entire season.

- Cornelius Greene had all but four of the team's pass attempts.

- Corny's 21 completions in three Rose Bowls resulted in 17 first downs.

- For the second straight year, the Buckeyes and the opponents had the same number of touchdown passes—six in this year. The opponents had 103 more passes and 37 more completions.

- Four players had a longer run than Archie—Johnson (60 yards, the longest), Greene, Rod Gerald, and Baschnagel—but Archie had the longest kickoff return of 53 yards.

1976 (9-2-1)

For a few years, a high school all-star game was held in Ohio Stadium in the summer. I went to the 1976 game, which was played in a downpour, and saw future Buckeye stars Ken Fritz and Mike Guess.

Similar to replacing the Super-Sophomores-Turned-Seniors in 1971, the 1976 team was replacing the Freshmen-Eligible-Turned-Seniors—Archie, Brian Baschnagel, Corny, Fox, Kuhn, and others—of the previous year. Similar to 1971, touchdown passes were at a premium—two in 1971 and one in 1976. Jim Pacenta and Rod Gerald had combined to complete only one of four passes in 1975.

Jeff Logan would fill in capably for Archie and run for 1,248 yards. He had the longest run (75 yards), punt return (68), and kickoff return (49). He also completed his only pass, for 36 yards. Woody pointed out that he had a 60-yard run called back.

The Buckeyes passed twice—Logan's was the only completed—and ran for 463 yards in the opening 49-21 win over Michigan State. Logan did it all; he had his 75-yard run and his 68-yard punt return. He ran for 112 yards, and Gerald added 104. Johnson was a yard short of being the third Buckeye with more than 100 yards. For the Spartans, as Jack Buck would say in the 1988 World Series, "I can't believe what I just saw," Kirk Gibson caught an 82-yard bomb for a touchdown.

The Buckeyes beat Penn State for the second straight year, 12-7 in Happy Valley. The pre-game show on ABC had an interview with Jeff Logan, who shared that Penn State had been interested in him as a recruit. He would run for 160 yards in the game, getting his jersey shredded on one play. Rod Gerald and Bob Hyatt each had eight yard touchdown runs. For Hyatt, it was a fourth and one play and his only carry of the season, and he would finish his career with a total of five carries. For the second straight game, the Buckeyes completed only one pass.

The yard markers that the chain gang used in that game were unique. The official planted a stick to measure, then another piece of the apparatus rotated to achieve the full 10 yards. On one measurement, the first stick appeared to give the Nittany Lions the first down, only to reveal that the gain was short after the second piece was rotated. The attendance was 62,503, a Beaver Stadium record, which looks odd compared to the current 100,000-plus capacity in the expanded stadium.

The Buckeyes had a 21-7 lead at halftime against Missouri before losing 22-21. The Tigers were using backup quarterback Pete Woods, and he completed a touchdown pass with 12 seconds left and scored the winning two-point conversion, with the Tigers getting a second chance after a holding call against the Buckeyes. The account of the touchdown and two, two-point plays in the official recap requires seven lines to describe.

Make that three straight games of completing one pass for the Buckeyes. The number of plays was as close as the score—each team with 73—and the 22-21 edge in first downs by the Tigers matched the score. Logan and Johnson each ran for over 100 yards.

For the third time in 12 months, the Buckeyes played UCLA, resulting in a 10-10 tie in Columbus in a nationally televised game (!) that left each team with a 1-1-1 record in the three games. Skladany's 25-yard field goal in the fourth quarter produced the final score. The pass completions doubled to two, and the Buckeyes managed only 222 yards on offense.

The pass completions escalated to four—to four different receivers—in the 34-14 win over Iowa. The Buckeyes' four completions went for 73 yards, while the Hawkeyes' six covered only 39 yards. Johnson ran for three touchdowns on runs of one, one, and three yards. The score was 34-0 after three quarters.

Logan ran for 113 yards in the 30-20 win at Wisconsin, with the Buckeyes scoring 20 in the second quarter in front of a record crowd at Camp Randall Stadium. I was in Athens, Ohio, at the time, seeing the Bobcats beat Miami.

Logan followed that with a season high 175 yards and two scores in the 24-3 win over Purdue, a game that was only 3-0 at halftime. Jim Pacenta completed five of nine passes in place of Gerald, who injured his lower back and was out until the Orange Bowl.

My entire family went to the Indiana game in Bloomington, a 47-7 OSU win. Buckeyes defensive lineman Nick Buonamici intercepted a pass at the Ohio State 5-yard line and rumbled upfield, handing the ball to Ray Griffin on what appeared to be an illegal forward lateral to complete the 95-yard scoring play, causing Hoosiers coach Lee Corso to have a fit. It was the longest interception return in OSU history at the time.

The Hoosiers took a 7-6 lead, prompting Corso to have his picture taken with the team and with the scoreboard in the background. As the rain came down in the fourth quarter, the others in my family took shelter, but I toughed it out and saw sophomore Ron Springs score two more touchdowns, his only two of the season. He finished with 107 yards. Pacenta's 59-yard pass to Jim Harrell produced the only passing touchdown of the year.

For the second straight game, the Buckeyes scored on a monstrous interception return in the first quarter, an 81-yard return by Ed Thompson in the 42-10 win over Illinois. Johnson scored four touchdowns, the longest being four yards. Dave Adkins put bookends on the scoring with a 19-yard interception return in the fourth quarter. The defense had five interceptions, and eleven Buckeyes had carries for the team's 271 rushing yards. In the postgame notes, Woody assured that the team would not look past Minnesota.

All the scoring was in the first half when the Buckeyes beat the Gophers 9-3 in Minneapolis. Logan ran for 116 yards, and Pacenta ran four yards for the only touchdown and the only touchdown of his OSU career. Tony Dungy passed for 201 yards for Minnesota.

The first half was scoreless, but Michigan beat the Buckeyes 22-0 in Columbus, the number 22 matching the OSU win streak that the Wolverines snapped in 1969, and matching the 22 that Missouri scored in the only other loss this year. In front of a record crowd at Ohio Stadium, the Wolverines took a page from the Buckeyes' book and did not complete a pass in six attempts. The Buckeyes had three of the four longest plays in the game, but they were outgained 366-173. In the pre-game, a broadcaster informed that the OSU band had performed *Ohio Script!*

I was fortunate to get a ticket for this game by seeing an OSU employee whom I did business with, outside St. John Arena. This was one of only three OSU home games that I left before the game was over, when the game was out of hand in the fourth quarter. The loss to Michigan was the Buckeyes' first shutout loss since 1964. Yes, I was there for that loss, also to Michigan.

The Buckeyes beat Colorado 27-10 in the Orange Bowl. With the Buckeyes down 10-0, Woody shuffled the backfield, Gerald replacing Pacenta at quarterback; Logan switching from tailback to fullback, replacing Pete Johnson; and Springs coming in at tailback. On Logan's first carry as a fullback, he ran 36 yards for a touchdown to get the Buckeyes on the scoreboard. Springs ran for 98 yards, Gerald for 81 yards, and Logan for 79. The four quarterbacks, two for each team, combined for 10 of 30 passes. Harrell had a 44-yard catch, giving him the two longest receptions of the year.

At various times, the Buckeyes were down 3-0, down 10-0, down 10-7, tied at 10-10, up 20-10, and up 27-10—and those same scores occurred in the 1969 Rose Bowl win over USC. In that Rose Bowl, if the Trojans had not been credited with the controversial touchdown catch by Sam Dickerson, the final score would have been 27-10, the same as this Orange Bowl. Pete Johnson scored with 24 seconds left in the first half in this game; the Buckeyes had scored with three seconds left before halftime in the 1969 Rose Bowl.

FUN FACTS:
- Pete Johnson's 19 rushing touchdowns were nine more than the opponents' total.
- Johnson's 19 total touchdowns matched the opponents' total.
- The edge in rushing touchdowns was 36-10.
- Ray Griffin and Dave Adkins each had one interception on the year, but both resulted in touchdowns.
- Nick Buonamici, a defensive lineman, had three interceptions, leading the team with 103 yards on returns. Bob Brudzinski, a defensive end, tied for the team lead with four interceptions.
- The Buckeyes completed only 45% of their passes, but the opponents completed only 41%.

1977 (9-3)

The BBC network spent time in Columbus to film a documentary on Woody. I recall it vividly, and you can see snippets on a web search, but the only reference that I can find online is for this VHS tape on eBay:

> *Woody Hayes: The Football Coach* is an uncensored, behind the scenes look at one of America's most famous sports figures. Filmed by the BBC in the weeks leading up to Ohio State's season opener in 1977... contains exclusive interviews with the coach, and follows Woody into practices (even into the huddle), team meetings, film review sessions, the halftime locker room, and more. The result is a complete picture of Woody

Hayes, one that reveals him to be much more than just a foot-ball coach. Learn what the Buckeyes legend thought about his critics, witness his trademark intensity firsthand, and marvel at his motivational techniques. This program is uncensored and contains some coarse language.

The show contained a segment on the Buckeyes attending the *Star Wars* movie at a theater across from campus on High Street that no longer exists, the same theater where I saw it. Jeff Logan was featured promi-nently on the BBC show, and he and Ray Griffin appear on the cover of the *Ohio State Football 1977 Official Press Guide*.

In 1977, my seats were on bleachers along the track near the visiting team's locker room. In other words, the view was as if you were an OSU player on the sideline, except at the extreme right end and with the players blocking your view.

At one game, Miss America happened to be there, and she and her entourage walked by our location. As you can imagine, this caused quite a reaction from those around me—but perhaps not the reaction that you imagined: "Get out of the way! We can't see the game!"

The kicking duties in 1977 belonged to two players from Franklin County. David McKee of Upper Arlington was the punter, and Vlade Janakievski of Whitehall was the placekicker.

Springs ran for 114 yards and the only touchdown in the opening 10-0 win over the Miami Hurricanes. Rushing yards were 287 to minus 13 in favor of the Buckeyes, as the Hurricane quarterback had minus 63.

The defense pitched its second straight shutout in the 38-7 win over Minnesota, with the kicking team giving up a 100-yard return for the only score. Springs ran for 147 yards, and ten other Buckeyes chipped in for the team's 385. A banged up Jeff Logan was not one of them. Greg Castignola's only pass went 38 yards to Doug Donley for a score. Donley, a running back in high school, had only two receptions on the year and would be a rare Buckeye to catch a touchdown pass in all four of his years. Keith Jackson would share that Donley's nickname was "White Lightning." The Gopher passing was very 1976-OSU-like: one for eight for 15 yards.

The biggest non-conference game of the 1970s was the 29-28 loss to Oklahoma on a 41-yard field goal with three seconds left, following an onside kick recovery. The Buckeyes trailed 20-0 before running off 28 straight points. The Sooners had a huge break when a running back fumbled and a teammate accidentally kicked the ball forward into the hands of another Sooner.

Both quarterbacks, Rod Gerald and Thomas Lott, left the game with an injury, as did Jeff Logan and Tom Cousineau for the Buckeyes and the Sooners' future Heisman Trophy winner, Billy Sims. Pressed into duty, Ray Griffin switched from defensive back to running back.

Greg Castignola threw a 16-yard touchdown pass to Jimmy Moore, his only touchdown catch of the year, deflected by a Sooner defender. After two weeks of action, Castignola was three-for-three with two touchdowns. Fifty-four of the 57 points were scored on the north side of the field with my seats, of course, being on the south side. The Buckeyes made the most of their 202 total yards. The teams combined to lose six of ten fumbles.

As Barry Switzer ran in front of me into the locker room celebrating the win, I yelled at him, "You were lucky, Barry!" Recounting the game in his book *Bootlegger's Boy*, Switzer wrote, "I've got to be the luckiest guy alive," and said in his postgame comments, "We were still lucky." You can draw your own conclusions. Just sayin'.

In reality, his book contains a mistake when it states that Oklahoma led 20-0 in the third quarter. The Buckeyes scored 14 in the second quarter after trailing 20-0.

In some small fashion, an OSU coach would beat Oklahoma that season, as the Arkansas Razorbacks, under former Buckeyes assistant coach Lou Holtz, beat the Sooners 31-6 in the Orange Bowl.

This marked the second straight season that the Buckeyes lost a one-point game to a Big Eight Conference team in Columbus in the third game of the season. The 22-21 loss to Missouri in 1976 came with 12 seconds left. In those two games, the Buckeyes had 38 yards passing combined.

Bad news was the theme of the day. After the game, Mark and I saw *The Bad News Bears* at the Drake Union.

As in 1968, the Buckeyes scored 35 points in the SMU game, winning 35-7 in a night game at the Cotton Bowl. The Buckeyes had seven interceptions, with Mike Guess tying a team record of three. Eleven Buckeyes carried the ball for the 360 yards. Joel Payton scored twice and had the longest run of the game and his longest of the year, 44 yards.

Guess followed up that performance with a 65-yard interception return for a touchdown on the first possession of the game in the 46-0 win over Purdue. The halftime score was 39-0, and Springs ran for 151 of the team's 391 yards. The five completions went to five receivers.

Gerald ran for 101 yards (corrected from 100 in a letter from D.C. Koehl of OSU's Sports Information Department to Iowa's Director George Wine) and passed for 91 in the 27-6 win at Iowa.

Springs ran for 130 yards, with a long of 72; Logan had 88, with a long of 63; and the team totaled 300 yards on the ground in the 35-15 win at Northwestern. The two teams combined to lose seven of 13 fumbles.

On the second play of the 42-0 win over Wisconsin, Gerald threw a 79-yard touchdown pass to Harrell, the longest completion in OSU history at the time. The team's six receptions to six different receivers averaged almost 27 yards per catch. Springs ran for 104 of the team's 287 yards.

The defense posted its second straight shutout in the 35-0 win at Illinois, the score being only 7-0 at halftime. Springs led 11 ball carriers with 132 of the team's 402 rushing yards.

The Buckeyes were tied 7-7 at halftime, but they pulled away to a 35-7 win over Indiana. It was the second straight week where the team scored seven in the first half and 28 in the second. It was Logan's turn to lead the rushers with 148 of the team's 368 yards, 115 of them in the second half.

In the 14-6 loss at Michigan, the Buckeyes had a 23-10 edge in first downs and almost twice as many yards, but they lost two costly fumbles, one triggering Woody's wrath. Each team had only one penalty for five yards.

Rod Gerald improved his passing percentage from 35% in 1976 to 59%, helped by 13-of-16 against the Wolverines.

After a scoreless first quarter against Alabama in the Sugar Bowl, the Buckeyes lost 35-6 in a game matching Woody against Bear Bryant, the two active coaches with the most career wins. Jim Harrell had the only touchdown on a 38-yard pass from Gerald to make the score 21-6.

The Buckeyes defense recorded four shutouts, but the offense could score only six points in each of their last two games. Ron Springs made it five years in a row that a running back had at least 1,000 yards, finishing with 1,166. Harrell had averaged 20.5 yards per catch in 1976 and upped it to 24.8 in 1977, again with the longest catch of the year, 79 yards.

FUN FACTS:

- Mike Guess had the longest interception and punt return, and Ray Griffin had the longest kickoff return. Both attended Columbus Eastmoor High School.

- The Buckeyes had a 39-11 edge in rushing touchdowns.

- Joel Payton (13) had more rushing touchdowns than the opponents.

- The Buckeyes had a 6-4 edge in passing touchdowns, even though the opponents had 88 more passes and 24 more completions.

- Jim Harrell averaged 22.7 yards for his 28 career receptions.

- In the two non-sellout games, the Buckeyes scored 35 points, at Southern Methodist and Northwestern.

- Opposing coaches with Ohio connections included
- Lou Saban (Miami Hurricanes), who played for the Cleveland Browns
- Ron Meyer (SMU) from Westerville
- Jim Young (Purdue), who was an assistant coach at Miami in Oxford
- Bob Commings (Iowa), a Youngstown native and Massillon High School coach
- John Pont (Northwestern), a Canton native and head coach at Miami in Oxford
- Dave McClain (Wisconsin), an Upper Sandusky native and former OSU assistant
- Gary Moeller (Illinois), a Lima native and OSU player
- Bo Schembechler (Michigan), a Barberton native, Miami player and coach, and OSU assistant

1978 (7-4-1)

I got it in my head that perhaps visiting radio stations would want someone to keep statistics for their broadcasts and feed them information, so I wrote (snail mail, of course) to OSU Sports Information Director Marv Homan to ask if he had contact information for each station. He graciously sent me a typed response that I still have, though I didn't follow through on it.

Two questions led up to the Penn State opener. Would Rod Gerald be on the field for the Buckeyes' first possession? Would freshman Art Schlichter be on the field for the Buckeyes' first possession? The answers were yes and yes, as Schlichter came out as quarterback and Gerald as a wide receiver. The defense gave up only one touchdown, and the Buckeyes had the edge in total offense, 336-287, but Schlichter threw five interceptions in the 19-0 loss to the Nittany Lions, who were playing their third game and would go undefeated in the regular season. The offense also lost three fumbles. Gerald led all receivers with 91 yards.

Schlichter went from 26 passes to seven in the 27-10 win at Minnesota, but he ran for two touchdowns. Schlichter had run only three times against Penn State, but he had 15 carries in this game. The Buckeyes had a 300-99 edge in rushing yards.

The rushing jumped to 373 yards in the 34-28 win over Baylor, with Paul Campbell gaining 109, Calvin Murray 93, Schlichter 71, and Springs 62.

As in 1968 and 1977, the Buckeyes scored 35 points against SMU but gave up the same in this game in a 35-35 tie. The Mustangs missed a 47-yard field goal with two seconds remaining. SMU had 107 plays (98 in 1968), 341 yards on 57 passes (76 passes in 1978), a 31-16 edge in first downs, and 501 total yards. The Buckeyes led 35-21 at the end of three quarters. Murray ran for 105 yards.

The Purdue game was tied 10-10 in the third quarter in West Lafayette, but the Boilermakers pulled away for a 27-16 win. Ricardo Volley scored the Buckeyes' first touchdown on a 49-yard wrap-around draw play, and Gerald had a 60-yard touchdown catch, his only one of the year. Schlichter passed for 289 yards, the total offense edge was 507-328, and the first downs were 27-20 in favor of the Buckeyes, but they lost four fumbles.

The Buckeyes had no turnovers in the 31-7 win over Iowa. The total offense edge was 423-216, and 78 of Schlichter's 102 passing yards came on a scoring strike to Donley. There was Hope for the Buckeyes, as Bob Hope dotted the I in *Script Ohio*. Years later, one of my cohorts on the OSU official stats crew said with a Freudian slip, "Who are some of the celebrities to dot the I, other than Bing Crosby?"

The Buckeyes ran for 511 yards in the 63-20 win over Northwestern. Murray had 103, Springs 98, Ricky Johnson 83, and Schlichter 68. The

Wildcats' quarterback Kevin Strasser had minus 33 net yards on the ground. The offense tied their record of 33 first downs and set a record with 30 first downs rushing.

I watched the 49-14 win over Wisconsin on Time Warner's pay-per-view package. Three scores came on defense or special teams—a blocked punt, a 96-yard kickoff return by Tyrone Hicks, and a 61-yard interception return by Vince Skillings. The Badgers lost by 35 despite having more total yards, 327-316. All of this prompted Woody on his show that night to praise his defense but say that the offense was not that good.

The Illinois game was only 14-7 at halftime before the Buckeyes pulled away, 45-7. The Buckeyes dominated the total offense stats, 429-191. Eleven ball carriers combined for 293 yards. It would be Woody's last win at Ohio Stadium.

Ricky Johnson ran for 109 yards, including a 46-yard touchdown run, in the 21-18 win over Indiana in Bloomington, Woody's last win. Mike Guess intercepted at the Hoosier 27-yard line with 1:37 left to seal the win.

This was my first game doing stats in a broadcast, working the game for Time Warner. Cleveland Browns' broadcaster Gib Shanley did the play-by-play, and former New York Giants Coach Allie Sherman was the analyst. During the game, I handed Gib a note stating that in the last three times that the Buckeyes played in Bloomington, the scores were 27-7, 37-7, and 47-7. Allie added, "and all 7s." After the game, Mark and I had the task of returning Allie's rental car to the Indianapolis airport.

The Buckeyes scored first on a Bob Atha field goal in the first quarter, but they were done scoring in the 14-3 loss to Michigan, the only time that Woody's teams would lose three straight to the Wolverines. The turf was so worn that Schlichter slipped when making his cuts.

After the game, I had enough time to go to the Upper Arlington-Watterson high school basketball game before going to the only *Woody*

Hayes Show that I would attend, which turned out to be his last ever show. At one point, the floor director tried in vain to get Woody's attention to break for a commercial and finally threw up his arms in defeat. At the end of the show, defensive lineman Byron Cato walked by, and my mother wished him good luck.

Other moments from the *Woody Hayes Show* over the years included these two memorable ones:

- The host informing Woody that the show was the longest running on TV, longer than *The Lucy Show*.

- Woody's wife, Anne, filled in for Woody once when the team was on the West Coast. I recall the host saying that the next game was a big one, to which Anne, in full Woody mode, replied, "Ted, they're all big."

I would occasionally see Mrs. Hayes at the Super Duper grocery store in the Lane Avenue shopping center, which was not far from their house.

In the span of 15 days, I was at Woody's last home win, his last road win, his last home loss, and his last TV show.

The 17-15 loss to Clemson in the Gator Bowl seemed like a long game, and not just because it started on a Friday and ended on a Saturday. The Buckeyes outgained the Tigers 355-330 and had no turnovers until … Schlichter's interception that led to Woody's punch. Woody's last game was also Clemson Coach Danny Ford's first game.

For stat geeks: Schlichter's season passing completion percentage was exactly .500 before that interception. I recall that Tom Cousineau, commenting on the officiating crew from the Southeastern Conference, said that on one occasion an official said to him something like, "Son, that's intimidation."

That same night, the men's basketball team upset top-ranked Duke 90-84 in overtime in a semifinal game of the Eastern College

Athletic Conference Holiday Classic at New York's Madison Square Garden.

FUN FACTS:

- Campbell, Schlichter, and Springs had 591, 590, and 585 yards rushing, respectively.

- The edge in rushing touchdowns was 37-16.

- Seven Buckeyes had a longer run than the opponents' long of 28 yards.

- The opponents' passing stats are superior in all categories, but the Buckeyes had touchdown passes of 78 and 60 yards, compared to the opponents' longest completion of 45 yards.

1979 (11-1)

New coach Earle Bruce made an appearance at an Arthur Treacher's Fish & Chips on Hamilton Road on the east side of Columbus, and I went there and may have obtained an autograph.

This year would start my streak of working games in the press box (except for 1991 and 1992) as I did the stats for Time Warner's telecasts in 1979 and 1980. Before the first game against Syracuse, the producer instructed our broadcasters John Gordon (who broadcast for the Orioles, Yankees, and Twins) and Jeff Logan to emphasize what was new this year—the new coach, a new offense, and a new turf that replaced the one that was so slippery the year before.

The offense ran for 383 yards—Schlichter for 91 and Murray for 86—in the 31-8 win over Syracuse. Four different Buckeyes scored a touchdown. What else was new? Freshman linebacker Marcus Marek called the defensive signals. Art Monk, who would gain 12,721 receiving yards in the NFL, had 114 for Syracuse.

Coach Bruce was prophetic after the Syracuse game when he stated in the postgame notes, "I expect to see a tough Minnesota team next week." The Buckeyes trailed the Gophers 14-0 and 17-7 at halftime before blanking them in the second half and rallying to win 21-17, with Schlichter scoring on a 32-yard run in the fourth quarter. Schlichter ran for 86 and passed for 152. Minnesota had a 505-295 edge in total offense and 80-49 in plays. Bad omen: the Gophers' Garry White (see the Rose Bowl) ran for 221 yards, with 147 in the first half. He added 67 more on receptions.

The defense gave up 408 yards in the 45-29 win over Washington State. The biggest play was an 86-yard catch-and-run (mostly run, the longest completion in OSU history at the time) by Murray, who added two scores on the ground. Schlichter passed for 233 yards, with 138 going to Donley. Six of Schlichter's completions gained 224 yards; the other two gained nine. Tyrone Hicks recovered a blocked punt for a touchdown. (Good omen: a similar play would happen again this year.)

Again the prophet, Earle said, in the postgame notes, "I don't know much about UCLA, but that's sure going to be a challenge for us."

In the first of two trips to southern California, the Buckeyes rallied with an 80-yard drive in eight plays—Schlichter was six-for-six—to beat UCLA 17-13 before "a national television audience." Schlichter's shortest pass of the game was the two yard touchdown to Paul Campbell, who had switched from running back to tight end, with 46 seconds left. Murray kept it up against Pacific-8 teams, running for 117 yards and a 34-yard touchdown.

After two games on the road, the Buckeyes had two comeback wins in the fourth quarter.

The Buckeyes had almost twice as many yards as Northwestern, but they won only 16-7, leading 13-7 in the fourth quarter before a 50-yard Bob Atha field goal. Campbell returned to running back and had 113 yards on the ground. The Wildcats' quarterback Chris Capstran had minus 64 net yards on the ground.

After scoring a combined 33 points in the last two games, the Buckeyes' average score in the next five was 45-4. The defense pitched back-to-back shutouts of Wisconsin and Michigan State.

The Buckeyes outgained Indiana 503-289 in total yards in the 47-6 win. Volley ran for 97 yards and Campbell for 93, and they combined for 169 in the first half. Donley was the recipient of 103 of the 156 passing yards.

Eleven Buckeyes carried the ball, and eight had a reception as the total offense tally was 572-206 in the 59-0 win over Wisconsin. Murray ran for 135, all in the first half, and Ray Ellis returned an interception 27 yards (matching his jersey number) for a touchdown. Schlichter and Greg Castignola combined for 12 carries for only 13 yards, but they scored three touchdowns.

The total offense was even more lopsided, 533-113, in the 42-0 win over Michigan State. Volley ran for 132 yards, and Donley had two touchdown catches and 122 of Schlichter's 154 passing yards.

Murray ran for 98 yards in the 44-7 win over Illinois in Champaign. Todd Bell was the leading tackler and returned a blocked punt for a touchdown. (Good omen: he would do it again this year.)

The Buckeyes were outgained 229-185 by Iowa, but they won easily 34-7, recovering five Hawkeye fumbles. Iowa had a 13-11 edge in first downs, but they had only one in the first half. Eleven Buckeyes carried the ball for a total of only 110 yards.

My dad got us five tickets to the Michigan game in Ann Arbor, an 18-15 win. The weather was perfect, and, somehow, we were able to park on a street instead of in a massive parking lot.

Bo started a freshman quarterback, but their offense jump started when he switched to John Wangler, who found freshman Anthony Carter with a 59-yard touchdown catch and another catch for 66 yards, for 125 of their 147 passing yards. The Buckeyes had one offensive touchdown—their first against Michigan since 1975—on an 18-yard reception by

Chuck Hunter which was tipped by defensive back Mike Jolly. Hunter had come to OSU as a fullback, and his catch raised the Buckeyes' total to three receptions for scores against Michigan in the 1970s.

Todd Bell's return of a blocked punt for the winning score came right at us in the south end zone. Michigan had three more possessions, but they had to punt twice. My last concern was that Michigan would kick a field goal to spoil our perfect season, but Marek intercepted a pass with three seconds remaining. He also had 15 tackles.

It was the Buckeyes' third comeback win in the fourth quarter of the year, all on the road.

The other four in my family went to the Rose Bowl, which USC won 17-16 on a late drive. I dropped them off at the airport, then drove to the movie theater at the Continent to see *Going in Style*, which I hoped would be a good omen. I watched most of the game on New Year's Day back at the airport after taking a friend for his flight.

The Buckeyes had a familiar Rose Bowl deficit of 10-0, but they ran off 16 straight for a 16-10 lead. Schlichter passed for 297 yards, including a 67-yard pass to Gary Williams with 21 seconds remaining in the first half. Both Williams and Donley had over 100 yards receiving in the game, and each had his longest gain of the season.

Both teams missed scoring chances near the end zone. An odd play that you may see once in a lifetime was in the fourth quarter, when USC's Vic Rakhshani was called for offensive pass interference in the end zone, which by rule is a touchback with possession going to the Buckeyes.

Charles White ran for 247 yards—almost exactly half of them in each half—the second time this season that an opponent named White would top the 200 yard mark. His touchdown with 1:32 was the winner. Vlade had three field goals to tie the Rose Bowl record, the last one giving the Buckeyes the 16-10 lead before the winning drive.

The last two games—Michigan and USC—each had a combined

score of 33 points, with Vlade kicking five field goals and the team scoring a total of two offensive touchdowns, both on passes.

The last two bowl games were losses by scores of 17-15 and 17-16.

The defense gave up only 17 points in the second quarter on the year. Unfortunately, seven of those came in the Rose Bowl.

FUN FACTS:

- Calvin Murray had the longest run and reception of the year.

- Paul Campbell and Ron Barwig combined for three receptions, two for touchdowns. Barwig's was the first score of the Earle Bruce era, and Campbell's was the winning touchdown in the UCLA game. Campbell, Barwig, and freshman Brad Dwelle combined for seven receptions, four for touchdowns, all as a tight end.

- The two longest touchdown passes—86 yards to Calvin Murray and 67 yards to Gary Williams—came against Washington State and USC of the current Pacific-12. The shortest touchdown pass—two yards to Campbell— came against UCLA of the current Pacific-12.

- The opponents threw 57 more passes and had 25 more completions, but the Buckeyes had a 16-9 advantage in touchdown passes.

- The Buckeyes had a 28-6 advantage in rushing touchdowns.

- Schlichter and Murray had as many or more rushing touchdowns as the opponents.

Not-So-Fun Fact: The Buckeyes were in six Rose Bowls in the seasons of the 1970s, not trailing at halftime in any of them, but winning only one. The halftime scores were:

- 1970: 14-10
- 1972: 7-7
- 1973: 14-14
- 1974: 7-3
- 1975: 3-0
- 1979: 10-10

CHAPTER 4

The 1980s
The WOSU-TV Years

1980 (9-3)

LOOKING AT THE MEDIA GUIDES in the 1980s, it's interesting to see the planned matchups in the future schedules that eventually fell through:

- 1985: UCLA at home, replaced by the Pitt Panthers
- 1986: at UCLA
- 1987: Texas A&M at home—this would have been back-to-back games against the Aggies following the Cotton Bowl in the previous year
- 1989: at Texas A&M

A new addition to the coaching staff was one future national championship head coach replacing another with Nick Saban taking over from Pete Carroll, who became the defensive coordinator at North Carolina State.

This was my second year doing the stats for Time Warner, though I was able to work the stats for the opener on ESPN, with John Sanders (not Saunders) and Paul Maguire as the broadcasters. Somehow, I knew that Maguire—the AFL's all-time leader in punts and punt yards—had the most punts in a season, so I ribbed him about that (in hindsight, probably not a wise move). They used a stat that I had prepared when Mark Sullivan made a tackle. My stat was that he had had two tackles for loss in the 1980 Rose Bowl, on Charles White and Paul McDonald. After the game, my ESPN contact was so happy with my work that he doubled my pay from $25 to $50.

The opener was against Syracuse for the second straight year. The Buckeyes trailed 21-3 and 21-9 at halftime before winning 31-21, scoring 31 again in this opener. Doug Donley (wearing #47) had a 47-yard touchdown catch to start the second half, making it his fourth year with a touchdown reception. It was the team's longest pass play of the year. Vlade had three field goals, giving him six in the last two games, and earned the game ball from Coach Bruce. Murray rushed for 117 yards, and Joe Morris, older brother of future Michigan star Jamie, led all rushers with 150 for Syracuse.

It was odd to see some Buckeyes jerseys with the player's name on the back and some without. In the postgame notes, both coaches referred to the heat, 85 degrees at kickoff, and Bruce predicted for the next game, "We're going to have our hands full this week."

They didn't, blanking Minnesota 47-0 and making their scoring run 75-0 going back to the previous week. It was another 85-degree day at kickoff. Vlade had four field goals, giving him ten in the last three games. All five touchdowns were on the ground, with quarterbacks Schlichter and Atha combining for three.

The Buckeyes and Arizona State combined for 991 yards of total offense, 591 by the Buckeyes, in the 38-21 win. Murray ran for 98 yards, Schlichter passed for 271, and Donley had 133 receiving. Mike Pagel passed for 288 yards—208 in the second half—and two touchdowns for the Sun Devils; I would work a few high school playoff game broadcasts with him in Cleveland in the mid-1990s. The Arizona State coach was Darryl Rogers, who coached Michigan State from 1976 to 1979, and in the postgame notes he said that Donley reminded him of Kirk Gibson.

The UCLA game was only 3-0 at halftime in favor of the Bruins, but UCLA won 17-0 in Columbus. It was the second straight year that the winning team in this matchup scored 17 points. In the postgame notes, Bruce said that the reason Schlichter exited the game in the fourth quarter was that he had a slight concussion.

In the 63-0 win over Northwestern, Murray ran for three touchdowns and 120 of the team's 418 yards, and the Buckeyes had an edge of 575-222 in total yards. The halftime score was 42-0. Todd Bell found the end zone again with a 50-yard interception return. The other eight touchdowns were on the ground. In the postgame notes, Bruce said that they ran four different running plays and two or three different passing plays.

Murray almost doubled his output the next week, celebrating his birthday by rushing for 224 yards and two touchdowns in the 27-17 win over Indiana. It was the fourth highest performance by a Buckeye at the time. The Buckeyes had 382 yards as a team on the ground.

The defense held the Badgers to 157 yards in the 21-0 win over Wisconsin. Sophomore Tim Spencer had his best game to this point with 81 yards. It was the fourth straight game without a passing touchdown. It was the defense's third shutout in six games and the second straight shutout of the Badgers. Spoiler alert: Things would change in this series.

The offense rolled up 603 total yards in the 48-16 win at Michigan State. Murray ran for 115 yards, and Atha had the team's longest run of the year, 63 yards for a touchdown in the fourth quarter. Gary Williams had 113 yards in receptions and two touchdowns, including one with seven seconds left in the first half where no one on defense covered him. Schlichter passed for 212, with 173 in the first half.

My parents and I drove to that game, and I worked the stats for Time Warner. This was Halloween weekend, and at dinner the night before the game, we ate at a restaurant where the staff wore costumes. Our server was in character as Harpo Marx, and he took our orders without saying a word.

For the second straight game, we had a team with over 600 yards— this time the visiting Illini— as the Buckeyes won a wild game, 49-42. Illinois had their last score with 11 seconds remaining and had a 659-398 edge in total offense. The Illini's Dave Wilson passed for 621 yards, with 344 in the second half, and six touchdowns to close to within seven points after trailing 35-7 in the third quarter. Schlichter passed for 284 and four scores. Five players in the game had over 100 yards receiving: 137 for Donley and 120 for Williams. Mike White was the first-year Illini coach. He had coached against the Buckeyes in 1972 as the head coach of California and had been Stanford's quarterback coach when the Buckeyes lost in the Rose Bowl on New Year's Day of 1971.

Late in the game, Jeff said, "Our statistician, Steve Basford, is on his sixth pencil."

The Buckeyes had a 494-147 edge in total yards in the 41-7 win at Iowa, as Murray ran for 183 yards.

The Michigan game in 1980 is the only one since 1966 where I had little recollection of the details and had to do some major research. The 9-3 score probably had something to do with that. It was not an all-field goals game; Michigan's PAT attempt after their touchdown in the third quarter was no good. This marked the fourth straight Michigan game in Columbus where the Buckeyes could not score a touchdown. The two teams combined to complete 19 of 49 passes. The Buckeyes had the longest run and the three longest completions.

Bo must have had a short memory when he called it in the postgame notes the "biggest win I've ever had." The 9-3 score would match the Buckeyes' record each year from 1980 through 1985.

In the Fiesta Bowl against Penn State, the Buckeyes scored 19 straight for a 19-7 lead, but they gave up 24 straight to lose 31-19. Schlichter passed for 302 yards, giving him 599 in his last two bowl games, and three touchdowns, with 244 yards in the first half. Donley had 122 yards receiving and Williams 112, the second straight year that both topped 100 in the bowl game.

As the Nittany Lions pulled away, before every commercial break, NBC played the song *Celebration*, with its first line, "Celebrate good times, come on!" Sorry, Kool and the Gang. That song makes me ill each time I hear it.

After a two year hiatus, the Buckeyes had a back with at least 1,000 yards rushing (Calvin Murray with 1,267), a streak that would continue through 1984.

FUN FACTS:

- The team scored only three fewer points than in the previous year.

- The defense gave up 23 points in four road games, with two shutouts.

- The edge in interceptions was 25-10.

- The edge in rushing touchdowns was 33-7.

- Spencer, Murray, and Schlichter had as many or more rushing touchdowns as the opponents did.

- Schlichter had 11 of his 15 passing touchdowns in the last five games.

- Schlichter had 2,255 yards of total offense, nine more than last year, and one less touchdown than last year.

- Spencer was third on the team in carries, but he led with eight rushing touchdowns.

- The opponents had one more yard in penalties than the Buckeyes.

1981 (9-3)

Time Warner decided to stop televising the games, so I wrote a letter to WOSU-TV, which showed the games on a delay, asking if they could use me for the stats. Through a stroke of luck, they were making major changes that year, with Marv Homan and Kaye Kessler no longer the broadcasters. I got the job and held it for the last ten years that they produced the OSU games, ending in 1990.

I learned in the phone call that the broadcasters would be Jack Kramer (I assumed that it was spelled Cramer) and Cornelius Greene. Jack is a graduate of Indiana University, as was John Gordon. Jeff Logan would replace Cornelius midway in the 1981 season and return in 1982, and Paul Warfield would be Jack's broadcast partner from 1983 to 1990.

The broadcasts were also on the USA Network in 1981, so when Jack and his broadcast partner recorded the pre-game stand-up, they would do it a second time, this time with the USA logo on their stick microphones.

In the beginning, I would pass my notes to Jack on an index card. Broadcasters are getting information from several sources, such as their broadcast partner and the director. Over the years, I noticed that my index cards often were lost among other cards that the broadcasters had, so I switched to yellow Post-It notes. The color made them noticeable, and the broadcasters could mount them on an eye-level surface. After a few games, the producers supplied me with a headset so that I could communicate with a staff member located in the studio in the Fawcett Center for stats on graphics.

Jack had a huge cork board about an inch thick for his spotting charts. He had the OSU offensive alignment and opponent defensive alignment on one side, and the reverse on the opposite, two deep at each position. He had pushpins to be placed next to the name of each player in the game at the time, and our spotter Jim Henderson's job, among others, would be to watch for each substitution to adjust the pushpin to the new player's name. For a tackle, he would point to the player/pushpin on the chart, and for a block, he would point to the player with one hand and put his other arm at a 90-degree angle to signify the block. *Columbus Citizen-Journal* columnist Tom Keys and OSU tennis coach John Daly also served as spotters. Since these games were on commercial-free TV, the broadcasters often would not get a break and would need to keep on talking throughout the timeouts.

One of the perks in the press box in my early years was enjoying the sumptuous pre-game meals, a different one every game and ranging from omelets to full Thanksgiving dinners for the Michigan game. Before the stadium was renovated in 2000, after a game, I could leave the press box through a door that opened onto B Deck and walk down the steps in the stands to the track. With each step, the view of the field became more amazing

Thirty years after meeting Jack, he asked me to take over the maintenance of his website for his broadcasts of high school sports in western Ohio.

1981 was an odd year. The pass defense struggled in many games, yet the Buckeyes beat Michigan and won the bowl game in the same season for the first time since 1968, and would repeat the feat in 1982, but not again until 1998.

Villanova had discontinued their football program, so the Buckeyes were able to pick up four of their players, including Anthony Griggs, who led the Buckeyes with four interceptions and was third in tackles.

The season started with a bang in the 34-13 win over Duke, with Tim Spencer running 82 yards for a touchdown on the Buckeyes' first play. Spencer finished with 172 yards and three touchdowns, and the 82-yard run was the second longest in OSU history, coming ten years after Morris

Bradshaw's 88-yard run against Wisconsin in 1971. It was only 14-13 at halftime, as Duke scored with one second left. The 34 points against the Blue Devils were the same output as in the 1970 matchup in Columbus.

Near the end of the game, Jack asked me to jot down my name so that he could give me credit on the air. I must have been destined to be a doctor—he read it as *Steve Barford*.

In the 27-13 win over Michigan State, the Spartans' Morten Andersen kicked a 63-yard field goal. Without anything to refer to, I was 99% sure that this was a Big Ten record, so I scribbled "Big Ten record" on a note to Jack, who read it on the air. I was recalling Tom Skladany's 59-yard record kick in 1975, and luckily, it was true!

Schlichter was injured during the game, so Bob Atha took his place. He scored on a 27-yard quarterback draw—the play-by-play shows "untouched"—with one minute left, his only rushing touchdown of the year. It was the Buckeyes' longest run of the game. On TV, Coach Bruce could be heard shouting, "Tom! Tom!" to Atha, the code for the quarterback draw play. In a video on the 1968 team, Coach Bruce said that the "Tom" play had been around at least since the 1960s, when he was an assistant under Woody. Atha added the extra point, his third of the game, and followed that by kicking off to the Spartans ... all this to go along with two field goals and five punts, with a long of 52 yards. It was the second straight year Atha ran for a touchdown in the fourth quarter against the Spartans, having two the previous year.

Jack and Jeff went to Palo Alto to record their broadcast of the Stanford game, a 24-19 win, and didn't even bring me back a T-shirt. In the pre-game stand-up, Jeff described Schlichter as "a winner." The ESPN broadcasters said that Schlichter and John Elway were potential Heisman winners. The Buckeyes led 24-6 at the end of three quarters, but Stanford could not score again in the last nine minutes after scoring twice in the fourth quarter. The last Stanford drive was stopped on a fumble caused by Jeff Cisco and recovered by Marcus Marek, the only turnover for either team. Cisco is the son of former Buckeye football player and MLB pitcher Galen Cisco, and Associate Director of Sports Information Steve Snapp called him the Cisco Kid!

Schlichter passed for 240 yards and John Elway for 248 (193 in the second half), but Elway had 12 more completions. Schlichter was named the Vitalis Most Valuable Player of the game. Tight end Brad Dwelle caught two short touchdown passes, his only two scores of the year. Elway was shaken up in the fourth quarter and left the game for several plays.

Each team had 496 total yards, a team record 458 passing yards (260 in the second half) by Schlichter, but Florida State won 36-27 in Columbus. Gary Williams set another record with 13 catches for 220 yards, and Cedric Anderson had a breakout game with 158 receiving yards. FSU scored 17 points on a touchdown off a blocked punt, a touchdown on a fake field goal play, and a 52-yard field goal. Neither team had a turnover.

The Seminole quarterback was Rick Stockstill, born in Sidney, Ohio. I would see him twice as the coach of Middle Tennessee State when I traveled to Murfreesboro to see their games. Before the game, I passed one of the booths in the press box and saw the late Tom Mees of ESPN taping his pre-game comments for a Tallahassee TV station.

The young Buckeye secondary would be under fire much of the year, but they gave up only two completions in Madison. Of course, both were for touchdowns in the Badgers' 24-21 win. The Buckeyes had an edge in total yards of 314-197.

This would be the first of several losses to the Badgers under Coach Bruce, as the Buckeyes won only two of seven between 1981 and 1987. The next day, I ran in the Columbus Marathon, with a time of 3:37:51. I competed against Bill Rodgers ... well, let's just say that I was on the same course.

Illinois passed for 368 yards (251 in the first half) to 11 receivers, giving them 989 passing yards in the last two years in Columbus, and led 27-24 before the Buckeyes scored the last ten in a 34-27 win. Spencer ran for 131 yards and Jimmy Gayle for 119 as the Buckeyes had a 273-18 edge on the ground.

The *Columbus Citizen-Journal* mentioned that the junior varsity team would play Michigan at 1:30 on Monday in Ohio Stadium.

Jimmy Gayle exploded for 186 yards in the 29-10 win over Indiana, a year after Calvin Murray racked up 224 against the Hoosiers. Atha kicked a team-record five field goals.

Purdue's Scott Campbell passed for 516 yards (340 in the second half), but the Buckeyes won 45-33 in West Lafayette. Campbell's 516 yards were the second-most in Big Ten history, behind Dave Wilson's 621 in 1980. I thought that Schlichter had a Heisman-like performance with his 336 yards and three touchdowns, the last on a great catch by John Frank. Williams had 126 receiving yards and Anderson 117 to go along with a blocked punt.

Minnesota's Mike Hohensee passed for 444 yards, making it 960 by the opponents in the last two weeks in a 35-31 win for the Gophers in Minneapolis. He passed for the last two scores of the game in the last seven minutes, the winning touchdown pass tipped by a Buckeye defender. The 444 yards were the third highest in Big Ten history, all coming in the last two years against the Buckeyes. The Gophers' Jay Carroll was efficient, with three receptions for three touchdowns, all in the second half. Spencer ran for 135 yards and two touchdowns.

The Buckeyes racked up 639 yards in a 70-6 thrashing of Northwestern. Schlichter passed for 281 yards (186 in the first half), Spencer ran for 108 and two touchdowns, and Anderson had 102 receiving yards. Mark Eberts had a 52-yard interception for a touchdown, his only interception of the year, and Mike Tomczak had his only touchdown pass of his freshman year, to Trent Penn, Penn's only reception of the year. Two Wildcat quarterbacks had a combined minus 22 yards on the ground.

The *Columbus Dispatch* ran a headline: "Liberty (Bowl) Aims to Match Bucks with Notre Dame."

The Buckeyes were outgained 367-257 in Ann Arbor, but they beat Michigan 14-9. It was the second straight year that they held the Wolverines to nine points. Schlichter had minus 42 yards rushing on the year, compared to 590 as a freshman, and had only nine yards in this game, but he ran for both scores, including the winner on a 6-yard run with 2:50 left behind Vaughn Broadnax's block ... or more accurately, his blocks? The play-by-play shows that Schlichter "danced down the sidelines and into the M end zone." His record against Michigan was 0-2 in Columbus and 2-0 in Ann Arbor.

The 14 points were the lowest output of the year, but no one was complaining. The Wolverines punted once, for 20 yards. Spencer ran for 110 yards, and the defense had three interceptions, two off deflections. The Buckeyes had followed their biggest scoring output with their lowest.

I was working the stats for a Time Warner televised high school playoff game in Dayton that weekend. The dozen of us on the staff checked out of our rooms in the morning and crammed into one room to watch the game. At one point when the ABC production switched their shot to another camera, wreaking havoc with the clarity on the screen, our technical crew shouted, "Iris!"

The Buckeyes did go to the Liberty Bowl, against Navy. As the sideline reporter for the broadcast produced by Metrosports, based in Rockville, Maryland, Jeff Logan was able to get me the job of statistician and Mark the job as spotter.

To prepare for the game, I wanted to get Navy's stats on my own, so I went to the Ohio History Center near the Ohio State Fairgrounds to get their box scores from the *Columbus Dispatch*'s Sunday sports sections. The security clearance for this was impressive—I had to answer several questions explaining why I wanted to look at the newspapers!

We drove to Memphis two days before the game, eating at a KFC in Jackson, Tennessee, where half of the eight customers were OSU fans. We went to the team's hotel that night and shared an elevator ride with President Edward Jennings. The day before the game, we went to Graceland and then that evening to the Liberty Bowl stadium to check it out. We asked a worker there, "What gives with the 30-degree weather? I thought that the South was supposed to be mild in the winter." He replied succinctly, "This is not the South."

Harry Kalas, the Philadelphia Phillies' broadcaster, did the play-by-play, and Hall of Famer Joe Theismann called his first ever game as a color announcer. My gig as the statistician was contingent on the availability of another guy. In our pre-game chat, he said he was suffering from a cold. He had to bail on doing the stats, and I was in. He worked stats for Notre Dame telecasts and shared some of the stats that he kept for their game. The producers let us see some taped action that they had ready to use during the game, including Tomczak's touchdown pass in the Northwestern game.

The 31-28 win over Navy saw each team score at least six points in each quarter and the Buckeyes recover an onside kick to seal it. Navy had a 20-17 lead midway through the third quarter before Jimmy Gayle ran for his second score and Schlichter had his second touchdown pass of the game. The clock was down to one second in the game and Navy was down by 11 points, but, as the play-by-play shows, "Clock operator is resetting 12 seconds on the clock for an unknown reason." The Middies scored a touchdown and a two-point conversion on a "one-handed stab." A few plays before, the play-by-play shows, "Staggers forward to the 1" and "At the last minute, he tries to pass."

The highlight for us was Mark seeing Woody Hayes in the press box and asking the producer if it would be OK to ask Woody to come on to the broadcast for a while. Woody did oblige.

The crew had a get-together at a hotel after the game, and I asked Joe Theismann to confirm the story that his name was actually pronounced *thees-man*, changed by Notre Dame staff to rhyme with "Heisman," and he did.

I still have my handwritten individual rushing stats on yellow legal paper. Compared to the official stats, I match the Navy total and am off by seven for the Buckeyes. I have one more carry for Spencer and one less for Gayle, who scored two touchdowns and was the Buckeyes' outstanding (the official stats have the typo *outstnading*) player on offense. This was Nick Saban's last game as an OSU assistant coach.

In Schlichter's four bowl games, this game had his fewest yards passing (159), fewest completions (11, tied), and the only sub-50% completion rate (11 of 26), but his only win. It was his only bowl where he did not run or pass for all of the touchdowns.

Mark asked me how much I thought we would be paid, and I said, well, last year, I was paid $50.00 for a regular season game by ESPN, and this was a bowl game, so probably $100.00, which would cover the expenses of our trip. When the check came, it was for $25.00, but hey, we are not in it for the money.

Later in the 1980s, the WOSU producers asked me to create some trivia questions that Jack could read on the air, along with a graphic, to challenge our viewers. One of them was: "Who was the last Buckeye to run for a touchdown, pass for a touchdown, kick a PAT, and kick a field goal in the same season?" The answer was Bob Atha, and, interestingly, Earle started him at wide receiver at the Liberty Bowl. If Bob had caught a touchdown pass in that game, his accomplishments would have been off the charts.

FUN FACTS:

- The team scored 387 points for the second straight year. In 1979, they scored 390 points.

- In the two games with the smallest attendance, Minnesota and Navy, the Buckeyes scored 31 points each.

- The last two games, Michigan and Navy, had the highest and second lowest attendances.

- The edge in rushing touchdowns was 30-5.

- Spencer, Gayle, and Schlichter had more rushing touchdowns than the opponents.

- Spencer ran for 1,217 yards, and the opponents ran for 1,135.

- Williams, Frank, and Anderson each had a season that ranked in the top eight in OSU history for number of receptions to this point.

1982 (9-3)

One of my favorite movies in 1982 was the comedy *My Favorite Year*. I am not saying that 1982 season was my favorite year, but based on the following, it was *a* favorite year: the Buckeyes ending on a seven game winning streak after a 2-3 start, Tim Spencer with his second straight year with 1,000-plus yards rushing, the emergence of Mike Tomczak at quarterback, Gary Williams closing out his career with a catch in all 48 games, a second straight win over Michigan, a 47-17 rout of Brigham Young in the Holiday Bowl, etc., etc. The Buckeyes were 5-0 away from home, including the Holiday Bowl win, and 4-3 at home.

One of the stars of *My Favorite Year* was Mark-Linn Baker; coincidentally, I would see him in the Broadway musical *Doonesbury* in New York in 1983. I was in New York then to do the stats for the OSU-Maryland basketball game in the Meadowlands for Chuck Underwood and Vince Chickerella on WTVN radio. But, I digress.

Spencer had another monster first game performance—147 yards in the 21-14 win over Baylor, giving him 319 yards in his two opening games as a starter. Broadnax added 101 yards and the first two touchdowns, and Tomczak, in his debut as a starter, scored the winning touchdown on a 1-yard run.

Three running backs—Spencer, Broadnax, and Kelvin Lindsey—scored a touchdown in the fourth quarter to break a 10-10 tie and beat Michigan State 31-10 in East Lansing. It was Lindsey's only touchdown of the year. The two opposing quarterbacks combined for only 15 completions in 41 attempts. The post-game notes mistakenly reported that Tomczak threw his first touchdown pass as a collegian. It was the second straight game that was tied at the end of the third quarter.

The largest crowd in stadium history witnessed the lowest point of the 1982 season, the 23-20 loss to Stanford. John Elway threw for 407 yards, 284 in the second half, and led the team to the winning score with 34 seconds left following a Tomczak interception in the end zone, not the last time that Elway would break hearts in Ohio. Gary Williams, a quarterback in high school, "took a long lateral left from Tomczak," as the play-by-play shows, and threw a 63-yard pass to Cedric Anderson to set up the Buckeyes' last touchdown for a 20-13 lead. The two teams combined for seven interceptions. It was the third straight game that was tied at the end of the third quarter.

This was the year that Stanford would lose to California on the multi-lateral kickoff return. Cal play-by-play announcer Joe Starkey described it with, "Oh my God! The most amazing, sensational, dramatic, heart-rending, exciting, thrilling finish in the history of college football!"

Florida State scored 13 in the fourth quarter to win going away in Ohio Stadium, 34-17. The Seminoles had 476 total yards, 20 fewer than in last year's win. Brent Offenbecher, from Massillon, where Coach Bruce had gone 20-0 as the head coach, replaced Tomczak during the game and threw his only touchdown pass of the year to Spencer—Spencer's only touchdown catch of the year. Gary Williams had 104 yards in receptions, giving him 324 in the two games against the Seminoles.

After this game, the Buckeyes' next nine losses would be by seven points or less until the 27-17 loss to Michigan in 1985.

The game against the Badgers was played in a "steady to hard rain," according to the play-by-play, and the Buckeyes lost their third straight at home, 6-0. Offenbecher played the entire game at quarterback and had the two longest plays of the game, passes of 34 and 27 yards. Jimmy Gayle ran for 108 yards.

This meant that the Buckeyes were shut out at home for the fourth time in seven seasons, adding to 1976 (Michigan), 1978 (Penn State), and 1980 (UCLA), without being shut out on the road in that time. The streak goes back to 1959, being shut out at home eight times without being shut out on the road.

It had to be the Columbus Marathon jinx at work; this was the second straight year that the Buckeyes lost to Wisconsin the day before the marathon. In 90-degree heat, as a spectator, I watched several runners resort to walking at the halfway point.

Tomczak returned as the starter at Illinois, a 26-21 win. He was only 14 for 34, but for 247 yards, including a 74-yard first quarter strike to Anderson, who finished with 108 yards and would average 27.6 yards per catch this year. The Buckeyes had 490 total yards, with Spencer running for 151. Rich Spangler kicked a 27-yard field goal with three seconds left to break a 21-21 tie, and the defense added a safety.

Anderson had another huge first quarter play, a 72-yard touchdown catch in the 49-25 win at Indiana. The next longest play was a 68-yard punt return for a score by Garcia Lane. Spencer ran for 187 and two touchdowns. On the telecast, former Utah quarterback Lee Grosscup kept informing us that Indiana's shovel passes were the "Utah pass" from his playing days.

In the *Columbus Citizen-Journal,* Jack Torry reported that the JV team edged West Virginia 47-46 in Morgantown, with Kelvin Lindsey running for 189 yards and four touchdowns.

Anderson made it three straight games with a touchdown catch as the offense rolled up 575 yards in the 38-6 win over Purdue. Spencer ran for 168, and Purdue's Scott Campbell had "only" 333 yards passing this year. He had 107 passes in the two games against the Buckeyes.

The defense held Minnesota quarterback Mike Hohensee to 345 yards below his output the previous year, only 99, in a 35-10 win. The Buckeye offense made it two straight games with 500-plus yards of total offense. Spencer ran for 133, joining Archie Griffin as the only Buckeyes with consecutive 1,000-plus seasons.

It would not be the last time that Hohensee would be involved in a game in Columbus, as he would coach the Chicago Rush of the Arena Football League against the Columbus Destroyers in the 2000s at Nationwide Arena.

The offense clicked for 605 yards in the 40-28 win at Northwestern, as five Buckeyes had a rushing touchdown. Tomczak passed for 222, and Gary Williams set an all-time record by recording a catch in his 43rd straight regular season game—not bad for a high school quarterback. Spencer ran for 190 yards.

Jeff Logan was the analyst for this game for WOSU-TV and flew back to Columbus in time to be the analyst for our high school playoff telecast at Gahanna Lincoln High School.

The Buckeyes broke a 14-14 tie at the end of the third quarter and beat Michigan 24-14 in a game that was played, as the play-by-play shows, in a "blowing rain." Spencer ran for 124, in front of an Ohio Stadium record crowd. Even with the win, only six of the top 15 attended games in Ohio Stadium had produced a Buckeye win.

Bo said, in the postgame notes, that "we did not lose, we gave it away." The Buckeyes had three interceptions, one by Marcus Marek, who finished his career four-for-four on interceptions against the Wolverines. Rowland Tatum added an interception, on his birthday. This was in a period of time where the visiting quarterback could ask the referee to stop the game if he thought that the crowd noise was disrupting his signals.

After the game, Jeff and I took off for Dayton to work a televised high school playoff game at Welcome Stadium. Michigan played one more conference game than the Buckeyes and were the Rose Bowl representatives.

The Buckeyes did play in a bowl game in California, a 47-17 thrashing of Brigham Young in the Holiday Bowl, leading only 17-10 at halftime. Spencer ran for 167, with a 61-yard touchdown run. Broadnax had a touchdown run for the fourth straight game, and Jimmy Gayle had two for the second straight bowl game. All six touchdowns were on the ground. The defense held the Cougars to 19 rushing yards.

Brigham Young had future NFL star Steve Young at quarterback, and he passed for 341 yards, with 231 in the first half. One of the negatives was Gary Williams spraining his knee in the third quarter after extending his record to 48 straight games with a catch.

I mentioned earlier the trivia questions that WOSU-TV producers asked me to create. Another one in a few years was this: "Which of these was the quarterback in a winning bowl game as a sophomore: Rex Kern, Cornelius Greene, Rod Gerald, Mike Tomczak?" Jack thought that it was a trick question, since the answer was all of them.

Here is another trivia question, which someone else devised: How many All-Americans has OSU produced?" After giving the answer, the witty Jack said, "This is actually a two part question. The second part is, 'Name them!'"

FUN FACTS:
• The three highest scoring games for the offense came in front of the three lowest attendances—Indiana, Northwestern, and the Holiday Bowl.

- Tim Spencer had 1,538 rushing yards, the highest output of the top four seasons by a player not named Archie Griffin, ranking third.

- Spencer's 1,538 rushing yards were 10 more than the opponents'. He outgained the opponents for the second straight year.

- Tomczak had 1,602 passing yards, the highest output of the top four seasons by a player not named Art Schlichter, ranking fourth.

- Tomczak had 1,784 yards of total offense, the highest output of the top four seasons by a player not named Art Schlichter, ranking fifth.

- The Buckeye quarterbacks completed exactly half of their 240 passes.

- Garcia Lane had 411 of the team's 416 punt return yards.

- The edge in rushing touchdowns was 36-9.

- Spencer (14) and Broadnax (nine) had as many or more rushing touchdowns as the opponents' nine.

- Four Buckeyes had a longer run than the opponents' long of 23 yards.

1983 (9-3)

In the spring of 1983, my buddy Stu Mason asked me to fill in for him on his Saturday morning half-hour *Sports Showcase* radio show on WCVO-FM. I was a play-by-play and color broadcaster for WCVO-FM from 1981 through 1990, and we carried Gahanna, New Albany, and Grandview high school football and basketball games. I could pick any topic for my half-hour segment, and so I asked Archie Griffin to come to the studio near New Albany for an interview. This was way before I mastered the art of recording interviews on a cassette recorder, later graduating to digital recording. Anybody who knows Archie's reputation—and who doesn't?—knows that he would never say no.

Anyway, it was getting closer to broadcast time and no Archie. I was panicking and thinking of a backup plan: I would rely on my memory, talk about potential high school basketball recruits, and have listeners call in to give their opinion … totally assuming that the engineering staff could accommodate that. But, I finally knocked some sense into my head, saying to myself, hey, this is Archie Griffin, you idiot. Of course he'll be here. And, of course, he was, allowing me to ask my hard-hitting questions such as this one: "So, would you say that the NFL is more a business than a sport?"

The 1983 through 1985 seasons had two assistant coaches who would be candidates for the OSU head coach job in 2001—Glen Mason and Jim Tressel.

The Buckeyes led Oregon in the opener only 10-6 at halftime, but they cruised 31-6, with the temperature 94 degrees at kickoff. Tomczak passed for 273 yards—182 in the second half—and Jim Karsatos completed his first career pass. Keith Byars ran five times for only four yards, but he had the first score on a 9-yard catch, his only touchdown catch of the year. Thad Jemison had the first reception of the year and (spoiler alert!) would have the last one of the year. Rowland Tatum had an interception for the second straight game in Ohio Stadium. The last time that Oregon had come to Columbus, in 1968, they also scored six points on a touchdown (and a missed extra point) in the second quarter.

The big game of the year was the road trip to Oklahoma, which the Buckeyes won 24-14, returning the favor from the 1977 game. The WOSU-TV producers first told me that I could go on the flight and work the game, but unfortunately a few days later they said I could not. Was I disappointed? Not on game day, when I found myself recovering from a kidney stone attack that began Friday night. If I had gotten on the plane, that attack would have hit me somewhere over America's heartland. I could just imagine the pilot radioing: "Hello, Peoria? We need an emergency landing. Please have an ambulance ready." I never told the producers about this. In fact, any cohorts reading this book will know this is the first mention of it. I didn't want them to think that I was high-risk for future flights.

John Frank had 108 receiving yards and two touchdown receptions. Two years prior, another tight end, Brad Dwelle, had two in the win at Stanford. Byars started to take off, with 57 yards on the ground and 75 receiving, including a 51-yard reception. After two games, Tomczak was 36-for-50 for 507 yards. The temperature was 93 degrees at kickoff.

The following week, the game at Iowa provided my first flight for a WOSU-TV road game. I was able to fly with the crew to a few games over the years. We would fly out of Don Scott Field, the university's airport on Case Road. This flight was on an eight-seat propeller plane, and each of my flights in the following years would be on six-seat planes. Even though the Buckeyes lost 20-14, this was my favorite flight trip, since it was my first one and the only where we stayed overnight, in the Amana Colonies. At dinner on Friday night, several kids recognized Paul Warfield and asked him for autographs.

Paul, Director of Player Relations for the Cleveland Browns, had to catch a flight to be at their game in San Diego the next day. The producers arranged for him to broadcast the first half and Herb Howenstine the second. Both Paul and Herb joined Jack to tape the pre-game stand-up, and Herb mentioned Iowa Coach Hayden Fry's saying, "We'll take what the other teams give us. We'll scratch where it itches."

Tomczak cooled off to 13 of 34 passes, while Chuck Long passed for 276 yards. Iowa had future college coach Mike Stoops at defensive back. This game and the rematch the following year would feature a player from each team who would be runner-up in a Heisman Trophy competition—Byars finished second to Doug Flutie in 1984, and Long finished second to Bo Jackson in 1985.

Tomczak averaged 30 yards per completion, and the Buckeyes rolled up 487 yards in the 69-18 rout of Minnesota. Byars was yet to have his first 100-yard game, but he scored three times on runs. Twelve Buckeyes had a carry, and four defenders had an interception, with Rowland Tatum's 52-yard return the team's longest of the year. Amazingly, the Gophers had a 20-16 edge in first downs.

Garcia Lane had two nearly identical punt returns—63 and 71 yards—for touchdowns in the third quarter as the Buckeyes beat Purdue 33-22. Byars had his first 100-yard game, with 135 and two touchdowns, and added 120 yards on four receptions. The post-game notes incorrectly have Byars as the player with the two punt returns.

The first time that I saw Byars was when he was running around St. John Arena celebrating Dayton Roth's state championship basketball title in 1981.

Purdue's Scott Campbell slacked off to only 228 yards passing and only 36 attempts. For the second time this year, the Buckeyes faced a defensive back who would become a college coach, Kevin Sumlin, who had his only interception of the year in this game.

The Buckeyes lost a physical game to Illinois 17-13 when the Illini had an 83-yard drive in 37 seconds with 1:06 remaining. The Illini scored on a 47-yard interception return in the first quarter. Byars ran for 168 yards, but Tomczak had to leave in the first quarter with a concussion. Brent Offenbecher took his place, and Jim Karsatos took Offenbecher's place and would get the start the next week. Karl Edwards's 87-yard punt in the game is an all-time Buckeye record.

Karsatos connected with John Frank for 115 yards and a 39-yard score, and Byars ran for two more in the 21-11 win over Michigan State in the rain. In 1991, I would do the stats for the radio broadcasts of the Columbus Thunderbolts arena football games at the Ohio State

Fairgrounds with Randy Rhinehart as the play-by-play announcer and Karsatos as the color announcer.

The Buckeyes had given up 28 points in the last two games, but 15 of those came from the opponent defense—an interception by Illinois and a blocked punt by the Spartans.

Tomczak returned against Wisconsin in the 45-27 win, was 12-for-14 for 162 yards passing, and ran for 62. The Badgers had 12 and a half more minutes of possession, but the Buckeyes had a 525-398 edge in total yards. Byars ran for 174, and Kelvin Bell had two of the team's four interceptions, his third straight game with a pick.

I flew with the WOSU-TV crew to the Indiana game, a 56-17 win. The Buckeyes gave equal time to the four quarters, scoring 14 points in each. This was Sam Wyche's only year coaching the Hoosiers, and his team threw 52 passes, scoring on the final play of the game and adding a two-point conversion. Byars had 169 yards and four touchdowns, and the Buckeyes scored three times on fourth down plays, as the offense had over 500 total yards for the second straight game.

The Buckeyes topped 50 points for the second straight game and the third time this year in a 55-7 rout of Northwestern. The offense was balanced, as only Tomczak had more than 82 yards in any category and five Buckeyes had rushing touchdowns. The Buckeyes had 41 points on 31 plays in the first half. Byars broke the 1,000 yard mark for the season. This came exactly ten years after the last Big Ten sophomore, Archie Griffin, accomplished the feat.

I worked the stats for the game in Ann Arbor, a 24-21 loss, with some adventure. Mark and I got there fairly late, so I jumped out of the car and sprinted the last mile to the stadium. I was to pick up my pass at the production truck, only to see that it was inside the fenced-in perimeter, beyond the ticket and pass kiosk. I told the portal guy that my pass was in that yonder truck, and he believed me!

Tomczak (the official stats show *Tom Czak* in one place) passed 40 times for 298 yards—the most ever by a Buckeye against Michigan to this point—with Frank catching ten passes for 123 yards and Byars running for 115 yards. A key play was a fumble on "Lachey Right," where the left guard Jim Lachey was to pick up the ball placed on the turf by Tomczak. Ten years later, this play, the guard-around "fumblerooski" play, would be ruled illegal.

Michigan Stadium's sunken field structure created the unique experience of a short walk from the press box to street level compared to Ohio Stadium's longer than 100-foot walk.

In the 28-23 Fiesta Bowl win over the Pitt Panthers, the magic number was 39, with Thad Jemison catching a 39-yard touchdown pass from Tomczak with 39 seconds left. The Buckeyes survived a dropped interception by a Panther defender before the winning pass and had to sweat out the Panthers reaching the 24-yard line on their final drive. Jemison finished with 131 yards.

Byars's 99-yard kickoff return was the game-breaker, though he came dangerously close to stepping out of bounds near the end of the return. It was only his second kickoff return of the season, and it gave him the lead in kickoff return yards on the season. He also had the second longest return on the season, 37 yards; the next longest return by any Buckeye was only 33 yards. The *Ohio State Football 1984 Official Media Guide* has a photo of Byars's kickoff return on the cover. The game featured the place-kicker for each team whose style was straight-on instead of soccer-style.

Thirty of the 51 points came in the fourth quarter. Watching the replay, I get a chuckle out of hearing play-by-play broadcaster Charlie Jones rattling off statistics at warp speed in the final seconds of the game.

FUN FACTS:
- The Buckeyes had a 35-7 advantage in rushing touchdowns.
- Byars's 20 touchdowns on the ground were 13 more

than the opponents' total.

- Byars had the longest run and kickoff return.

- Vaughn Broadnax, Doug Smith, Jay Holland, and Roman Bates combined for nine receptions, with four of them resulting in touchdowns.

- Nine of the 11 players who had a reception had a touchdown. The two who did not were tailback John Wooldridge and fullback Barry Walker, who had a combined six receptions.

- Eleven players had a reception, and eleven players had an interception.

- Jim Karsatos had 207 fewer passes than Tomczak, but he had the longest pass play of 63 yards.

- Garcia Lane became the all-time Buckeye leader in punt return yards.

- Lane's three career punt returns for a touchdown were 68, 63, and 71 yards, and came against the two Big Ten Teams from the state of Indiana.

1984 (9-3)

At some point in the 1980s during my career in the Office of Human Resources at OSU, a Channel 4 news team came to my office to film a feature...not on me but on Archie Griffin. He and I shared an office in his short time in the HR department.

The visiting Oregon State Beavers led 14-3 at halftime in the opener before the Buckeyes won 22-14. Oregon State finished with a 387-370 edge in total offense. Byars ran for 182 yards on a career high 34 carries, with 113 in the second half. Tomczak had suffered a broken leg on a running play in the spring game, so Karsatos went the distance. For the Beavers, running back Donald Beavers had a catch and threw a pass.

This was Chris Spielman's debut. I first saw him as a linebacker/fullback for Massillon when working the stats for television in the 1982 championship at Ohio Stadium. Our play-by-play broadcaster at one point said, "So help me, folks, the Tigers do have other players on defense. It's just that Spielman is making all the tackles!"

Five Buckeyes scored rushing touchdowns in the 44-0 shutout of Washington State. Karsatos started, and Tomczak chipped in with five of seven passes and the only touchdown pass, to Byars, who ran for 145 yards. Pepper Johnson recovered a fumble in the end zone to preserve the shutout and had one of the team's three interceptions. On the Cougars' coaching staff was Jim Burrow, father of Joe Burrow.

Byars did it all in the 45-26 win over Iowa: he ran for 120 yards and two touchdowns, caught a 14-yard touchdown pass, and threw a 35-yard left-handed touchdown pass to Mike Lanese, whose only carry netted another touchdown. Larry Kolic returned a Chuck Long pass 25 yards for another score, knocking over Long at the goal line. The score was 31-26 in the third quarter after the Hawkeyes ran off 16 straight points. Iowa had a 458-335 edge in total yards, but turned it over four times, two on fumbles and two on interceptions. In the *Columbus Citizen-Journal,* Tomczak, referring to Byars's multiple touchdowns, mentioned that Walter Payton might have done that, somehow knowing that Payton would be a Chicago Bears teammate in 1985?

The 35-22 win over Minnesota in the Metrodome was a rare night game against Lou Holtz's Golden Gophers. Byars—the box score has *Byers* in a few places—ran for 164 yards, and two of Cris Carter's three catches went for touchdowns.

I flew to the Purdue game with the WOSU-TV crew, a game that the Buckeyes lost 28-23. With five seconds left, Tomczak threw the ball out of bounds to stop the clock, not knowing that it was fourth down. The

Buckeyes had a 570-376 edge in total yards and eight more minutes of possession, but Purdue scored on a 65-yard pass and a 55-yard interception return. Byars ran for 191, becoming the nation's leading rusher, and added 102 reception yards. Tomczak passed for 280 yards.

The Boilers' coach Leon Burtnett waved a white towel during the game to rev up the fans. His quarterback Jim Everett passed for 257 yards.

The 45-38 win over Illinois was the game where the Buckeyes trailed 24-0 and the game where Byars lost his shoe on a 67-yard draw play in the third quarter, the team's longest run of the year. Speaking of Byars's speed, Coach Bruce said, in a quote that appears in a *Sports Illustrated* story, "When Keith's even with ya', he's leavin' ya'." With the score 24-0, the Illini had a 205-22 edge in total yards.

After he scored to make it 24-7, Byars looked into a camera and said, "We're coming back!" The Illini had committed a penalty as Byars scored, so with the extra 15 yards on the kickoff, the Buckeyes were successful on an onside kick—recovered by Joe Jenkins, an Illinois native—and took advantage with a 30-yard scoring strike to Carter. Byars scored five times to tie Pete Johnson's record, the winner with 36 seconds left, and broke Archie's record with 274 on the ground, 195 in the second half. This gave Byars 442 yards in the last two years against Illinois. When he went airborne on one of his touchdowns, Paul Warfield described it as "a la Superman style." He padded his lead as the nation's leading rusher and also became the leading scorer. Five hours after the game was over, he celebrated his birthday. The two teams combined for 549 yards passing and 1,073 total yards. Cris Carter had 134 receiving yards.

At East Lansing, the Buckeyes had nearly twice as many yards as Michigan State, but they survived a missed 43-yard field goal attempt for the tie with three seconds left to win 23-20. Byars needed 40 carries for his 121 yards, and Tomczak passed for 256, with Lanese having 116 receiving yards. Byars scored once after having 12 straight games scoring at least twice. The Spartans scored on a 75-yard pass and a

93-yard kickoff return in the fourth quarter, the longest such plays against the Buckeyes this year.

I worked the stats for WOSU-TV, and after the game, I rode the elevator down with the two governors, Dick Celeste of Ohio and James Blanchard of Michigan.

The Buckeyes lost to Wisconsin for the third time in four years, 16-14 in Madison. Byars ran for 142 and had 91 receiving yards, but Marck Harrison from Columbus Eastmoor High School ran for 203 for the Badgers.

The Buckeyes had a 490-186 edge in total yards in beating Indiana 50-7. John Wooldridge led ten ball carriers with 94 yards, and nine Buckeyes had a catch. Six Buckeyes each had one touchdown.

I flew to the Northwestern game with the WOSU-TV crew, a game that the Buckeyes won 52-3, outgaining the Wildcats 562-149 and scoring all 52 after the first quarter. We flew into Palwaukee Municipal Airport—it is now known as the Chicago Executive Airport and has PWK as its airport code—north of O'Hare and about 16 miles from Evanston. The stadium is near Lake Michigan and like Wrigley Field is known for its wind effect. Rich Spangler's kick for a field goal was headed right for the uprights until the wind caused it to fall like a brick.

Again, 10 Buckeyes carried the ball, with Byars gaining 151, and Tomczak and Karsatos each passed for over 100 yards and two touchdowns. Using alliteration, Cris Carter and Dino Dawson each had two scoring catches. For the second straight year, the Buckeyes scored more than 50 points on Indiana and Northwestern in consecutive games.

The lead was only 7-6 at the end of the third quarter, but Byars had two 2-yard touchdown runs in the fourth quarter in the 21-6 win over Michigan. A key play was a great catch by Mike Lanese on a third-and-12 play.

The stadium had a new scoreboard and some renovations that year which displaced our broadcast location to the roof, in the open but under an awning. This meant that I had no contact with the official stats. At the end of the game, I gave Jack the stat that Keith Byars had 102 yards rushing. To my horror the next day, the official stats in the newspaper had him for 93 yards. I knew that the play in question was a 9-yard loss on a handoff that was mishandled. To my relief, on Monday, the athletics department stated that the 9-yard loss should be credited to Tomczak and that Byars in fact had 102 yards.

This was the only time that a team with two conference losses won the Big Ten championship outright.

In the 20-17 Rose Bowl loss to USC, the Buckeyes had a 403-261 edge in total yards, but like the Rose Bowl game against the Trojans five years previously, they had to settle for three field goals—this time by Rich Spangler, one a Rose Bowl record 52-yarder. The three field goals tied the Rose Bowl record set by Vlade Janakievski, and the two place kickers combined for four field goals of at least 46 yards.

Tomczak threw for 290 yards—giving the Buckeyes 587 passing yards in the last two Rose Bowls—but had three interceptions. Carter's Rose Bowl record of 172 receiving yards was 44 more than the Trojans had as a team.

Byars ran for 109 yards, with 50 on his first carry. He would finish second in the Heisman Trophy voting, and Bernie Kosar was fourth, meaning that two of the top four were from Ohio, with Kosar being a Boardman native. Doug Flutie won the Heisman with a big boost from his Hail Mary pass to win the Miami game.

FUN FACTS:

- Byars, Carter, and Lanese had 42, 41, and 41 receptions, respectively. In his first two years, Lanese, who had come to OSU as a tailback, had a total of one reception for five yards.

- As a freshman, Carter broke the team season record for

touchdown catches with eight.

- The Buckeyes had 35 rushing touchdowns for the second straight year.

- The edge in rushing touchdowns was 35-5.

- Byars's 22 touchdowns on the ground were 17 more than the opponents' total.

- Byars's 24 total touchdowns were one more than the opponents' total.

- Byars's 1,764 yards on the ground were 50 more than the opponents' total.

- For the second straight year, Byars had the team's longest kickoff return, 61 yards.

- Jim Karsatos had 206 fewer passes than Tomczak (last year, it was 207) but again had the longest pass play, this time 57 yards.

- Two of Dino Dawson's four receptions went for touchdowns, including the team's longest pass play of 57 yards.

- The Iowa game had future head coaches from the two teams on their staffs: Jim Tressel, Glen Mason, Gary Blackney, and Mark Dantonio for the Buckeyes, and Bob Stoops, Bill Snyder, Kirk Ferentz, Barry Alvarez, and Dan McCarney for the Hawkeyes.

1985 (9-3)

The big question in the spring game was who would replace Tomczak at quarterback—Jim Karsatos, who would claim it, or Tom Tupa. The *Ohio State Football 1985 Official Media Guide* had the obvious choice of having

Byars's photo on the cover. Labor Day is supposed to be a holiday and a day to relax, but the Buckeyes were neither celebrating nor relaxing when Byars broke a bone in his right foot in practice. With Byars missing the first five games and playing minimally, the Buckeyes would have more yards passing than rushing this year.

The veteran defensive backfield—William White, Terry White, Greg Rogan, and Sonny Gordon—gave themselves a nickname, Men of Brutality, MOB for short.

The Buckeyes had bookend 10-7 wins in 1985, over Pittsburgh in the opener and over Brigham Young in the Citrus Bowl. In each game, the Buckeyes had three points in the first half and scored the last touchdown.

The opening game against Pittsburgh was the first ever night game at Ohio Stadium. Ironically, Pittsburgh was Byars's second choice among colleges to attend. The night before, I broadcast the Gahanna at Eastmoor high school game for WCVO-FM, a game that Gahanna won. The next morning, I realized that I had left our WCVO banner hanging outside the Eastmoor press box. In a panic, I found the phone number of the Eastmoor athletics department in the phone book, called it, and reached Coach Brian Cross, who would coach several high school teams in central Ohio. I was expecting him to be in a foul mood after the close loss, but he could not have been nicer and arranged a time for me to meet him at the stadium and pick up the banner. Coach Cross was noted for wearing shorts at his games no matter what the temperature, and 25 years later, I interviewed him at the halftime of a basketball game that I was broadcasting at Olentangy Orange High School.

Without Byars, the Buckeyes ran for only 48 yards, but Karsatos passed for 246. As in the 1983 Fiesta Bowl, the Buckeyes beat the Panthers by scoring the last touchdown in the fourth quarter. On fourth and goal at the 2-yard line, Jim Karsatos rolled to his right and passed to Cris Carter for the winning score. Several fans spilled onto the track to celebrate with Carter, including a man jumping up and down with a young child in one arm!

The rushing improved in the 36-13 win at Colorado, as John Wooldridge ran for 119 yards and was the leading receiver with eight receptions. The Buffaloes were only three-for-12 in passing.

The two teams combined for 978 yards as the Buckeyes beat Washington State 48-32. Rueben Mayes had rushed for 1,637 yards, and Mark Rypien had passed for 1,927 in 1984, but they managed only 84 and 139 against the Buckeye defense. Wooldridge ran for 103 yards, and both of Lanese's catches went for touchdowns, one of them a 26-yard pass from Carter. Four Cougars had carries and also had a pass attempt.

I flew with the WOSU-TV crew to the Illinois game, a 31-28 loss where Chris White, the coach's son, kicked a 38-yard field goal on the last play, rallying from a 28-14 deficit. If the field goal had been off the mark, it would have been Coach Bruce's only tie in a Big Ten game and the Buckeyes' first Big Ten tie since the 1973 Michigan game. The Buckeyes themselves had rallied from 14-0 down with two Carter touchdown catches in the third quarter. Carter caught seven passes for 147 yards—no other Buckeye had a catch—and freshman Vince Workman ran for 100 yards. The Farm Aid concert had been in the stadium 13 days earlier.

Wooldridge ran for 104 yards and three touchdowns and caught a pass for another in the 48-7 win over Indiana. The offense had 507 yards, with eleven players having at least one carry and ten with at least one catch. Counting this one, the last four games against the Hoosiers had produced 49, 56, 50, and 48 points.

Byars made his first appearance of the year and had 106 yards and the last two touchdowns in the 41-27 win over Purdue. The Boilers' Jim Everett passed for 497 yards.

The Buckeyes trailed Minnesota 19-10 in the Metrodome (temperature: 72 degrees), but they scored 13 in the fourth quarter to win 23-19. Karsatos hit Ed Taggart with a 1-yard pass on fourth-and-goal for the first touchdown in the fourth quarter—not quite as dramatic as the pass to Carter in the Pitt game—to cap a 90-yard, 16-play drive. Karsatos had sneaked on fourth-and-one at the Gopher 11 moments before. Workman had the winning touchdown, set up by a William White interception. The defense had a stop on a fourth-and-one at their own 12 with 48 seconds left, on a 79-yard Gopher drive. The Gophers had a 360-281 advantage in total yards.

The #1 Iowa Hawkeyes came to Columbus in a game that the Buckeyes won 22-13 in a monsoon, with the lights reflecting off of the puddled field. Sonny Gordon blocked a punt for a safety, and the defense picked off four of Chuck Long's passes, two by Spielman. Iowa also lost a fumble, making it a total of nine turnovers in Columbus in the last two years. For the second straight game, the defense had a huge stop on fourth-and-one, this time at their own 10-yard line. George Cooper had a breakout game with 104 yards, and Wooldridge had a 57-yard scoring run on his first carry of the game in the second quarter. The 57-yard run would be the team's longest of the season. Workman scored on a 4-yard run, but looking at the replay, we saw his knee go down at the 2-yard line. Jack gave me a wide-open look of surprise at the Buckeyes' good fortune, but he said nothing on the air. The World Wide Web would come a few years later, but on this day, *WWW* stood for *Wooldridge, Workman, and White*—William White had the longest interception return of 10 yards.

Karsatos had touchdown passes to Carter, Lanese, and Ed Taggart in the first half and beat Northwestern in Evanston, 35-17. Carter and Lanese had a little dance routine that they did together after touchdowns, and they had two performances today. Lanese had 108 receiving yards, and his 75-yard score was the team's longest pass play of the year. Karsatos finished with 275 yards passing. Only 26,477 fans showed up in threatening weather.

The Buckeyes had a 365-222 edge in total yards on one less play, but they lost to Wisconsin for the fourth time in five years, 12-7 in Columbus. Carter had 131 of Karsatos's 263 passing yards and the team's only touchdown. Karsatos completed 12 consecutive passes, tying the team record. Wisconsin was the last team to win in Columbus, in 1982, and it was the largest crowd to see OSU lose at Ohio Stadium.

Carter caught a 36-yard touchdown pass on fourth down and 15 to cut the lead to 20-17 in the fourth quarter, but Jim Harbaugh connected on a 77-yard strike to John Kolesar 51 seconds later as Michigan won 27-17. Harbaugh's pass came on second-and-seven at his own 23 over a blitzing Sonny Gordon, and it was the longest pass play against the Buckeye defense all year. Both OSU and Michigan had lost a road game in 1985 on a field goal in the final play, Michigan having lost at Iowa.

The 10-7 Citrus Bowl win over Brigham Young, the defending national champions, saw Larry Kolic intercept a pass for the Buckeyes' only touchdown. It was his second interception of the game and of the season. Cris Carter had a one-handed catch along a sideline that is highlight-reel worthy.

With three seconds left in the game, Terry White intercepted a pass in the end zone, the defense's fourth pick and sixth forced turnover of the game. The offense set up in the victory formation ... and the NBC broadcast left to cover another game. Thankfully for Buckeye fans, we did not have a similar fiasco as in the 1968 Oakland Raiders-New York Jets "Heidi Game," when NBC left the game with the Jets seemingly comfortably ahead, only to see—or not see—the Raiders score two touchdowns to win.

For the second straight bowl game, the Buckeyes had no rushing touchdowns. Four of the six forced turnovers ended up in one end zone or the other, as William White added an interception and Greg Rogan recovered a fumble for touchbacks.

FUN FACTS:

- The Washington State Cougars and the BYU Cougars each had one touchdown pass against the Buckeyes' defense.

- Mike Lanese had the longest reception of the year, 75

yards, and a higher average gain per catch than Cris Carter.

- Lanese also had the longest punt return.

- The opponents had 56 more passes but only 20 more passing yards. The Buckeyes had a 20-10 edge in passing touchdowns.

- The edge in interceptions was 21-8.

- The defense gave up 17.7 points per game, following 17.3 in 1982, 17.2 in 1983, and 16.7 in 1984.

- Four of the top nine performances in all of major college football for season passing touchdowns were by Big Ten quarterbacks. Chuck Long was #2, Jim Everett was #3, Karsatos was tied for #7, and Jim Harbaugh was tied for #9.

1986 (10-3)

The Buckeyes went 10-3, breaking their streak of going 9-3 in six straight years by playing an extra game, the opening Kickoff Classic in the New Jersey Meadowlands. After losses to Alabama in the Kickoff Classic and at Washington, the Buckeyes won nine straight before losing to Michigan, and the nine straight would be the longest between 1980 and 1994.

The Buckeyes led Alabama 10-6 after three quarters, but they gave up ten points in the fourth quarter in the 16-10 loss. Jamie Holland's 26-yard run was the only touchdown, set up by a Sonny Gordon interception and Cris Carter's 100th career reception. Two passes from Karsatos to Carter produced interference calls on the Tide with no time on the clock at the end of the game, giving the Buckeyes one more—unsuccessful—shot to Carter from the 18. The play-by-play describes an early play as, "Karsatos overthrows lunging Taggert on squareout left."

The offense had only one touchdown again and only 186 yards in the 40-7 loss to Washington in Seattle. After a scoreless first quarter, the Huskies scored 24 in the second and extended it to 27-0 before a Carter 9-yard touchdown catch.

The Buckeyes recorded their first win by finally playing in Columbus and beating Colorado 13-10, on a 19-yard Pat O'Morrow field goal with 25 seconds left. The 78-yard drive was helped by a controversial pass interference penalty. With only 233 yards of offense, it was the third straight game with only one touchdown that year and the fourth straight dating back to the previous year. Twenty-five seconds must have been a lucky charm, as Carter had the touchdown again with 25 seconds left in the first half following a William White interception. Colorado's coaching staff included future head coaches Gerry DiNardo, Les Miles, Gary Barnett, and Lou Tepper.

The offense had 715 yards, a Big Ten record and nearly as many as the first three games combined, in the 64-6 demolition of Utah, with Vince Workman running for 168 yards and Jaymes Bryant, wearing #41, giving a Byars-like performance with 145. Half of George Cooper's eight carries went for touchdowns; he would score six on the year. The running game accounted for 394 yards, and the passing game added 321. The 64 points matched the total of the previous six games. It was the 600th win for the program.

The last three opponents—Washington, Colorado, and Utah—are current Pacific-12 teams, though Colorado and Utah were not at the time.

After six straight years of matches decided by seven points or less in this rivalry, the Buckeyes beat Illinois 14-0. Both scores were unconventional, as Karsatos rumbled for a 10-yard touchdown run, and Workman threw a 10-yard pass to Nate Harris. The defense recorded five turnovers.

I flew with the WOSU-TV crew to the Indiana game, a 24-22 win, as Bryant ran for 131 yards, and the defense recorded five more turnovers. Spielman was called for a late hit on IU quarterback Brian Dewitz, his high school teammate, and celebrated his birthday with one of the team's three interceptions. Sonny Gordon had the other two. Down 24-14, the Hurryin' Hoosiers had a 15-play, 85-yard drive in 6:16 for their last score with 2:12 left.

I flew with the crew again the next week to the Purdue game, a 39-11 win. The offense had 263 yards on the ground—129 by Bryant—and 281 passing. Carter, Harris, and Holland had touchdown catches, with Carter totaling 118 yards. Freshman David Brown had a 100-yard interception return, a Big Ten record. Matt Frantz had practically instant-replay field goals of 21, 22, 22, and 21-yards. Indiana's lone field goal was 23 yards long. On the way back, Jack said that the first night game in Ross-Ade Stadium had the feel of a high school playoff game.

Bryant and Carter, who had 127 yards receiving, each scored twice in the 33-0 shutout of Minnesota in a steady rainstorm, with the defense holding the Gophers to 189 yards. A squirrel that ran on the field may have had more yardage than the Gophers. Bryant missed his third straight game of 100 plus by one yard.

The game at Iowa kicked off before noon Central Time, and the Buckeyes won 31-10. Carter had the longest offensive play of the year, a 72-yard scoring strike, and had 121 yards in all. Greg Rogan plucked a fumble out of the air and returned it 31 yards for a score. Both of those big plays took place in the second quarter. Ten Buckeyes combined for 144 yards on the ground.

Carter scored for the fifth straight game and had his fourth straight game with over 100 yards receiving in the 30-9 win over Northwestern, a win despite being outgained 497-450. Workman ran for 123 yards and two touchdowns.

Carter scored for the sixth straight game and had his fifth straight game with over 100 yards receiving in the 30-17 win at Wisconsin. Carter set team records for touchdown catches and receiving yards in a season, and for career catches. Workman ran for 172 yards, and Tom Tupa relieved an injured Karsatos and went nine-for-13 for 125 yards.

The Buckeyes led Michigan 14-3, but lost 26-24 in the game where Jim Harbaugh guaranteed a win for the Wolverines. For the second straight year against Michigan, Carter brought the team within a field goal with a touchdown catch—a touchdown catch in his seventh straight game. The Buckeyes had a chance for the win with 1:01 left, but Matt Frantz' 45-yard field goal attempt was wide left. Workman ran for 126 yards, but Jamie Morris had 210 for Michigan. Spielman was credited with 29 tackles.

Earle Bruce broke out the suit and fedora in the 28-12 win over Texas A&M in the Cotton Bowl. The defense picked off five Aggie passes, with Chris Spielman and Michael Kee each returning one for a touchdown. For Spielman and Kee, these were the only scores of the year, and Spielman added another interception. Counting this game, in the last two bowl games, three of the Buckeyes' five touchdowns came on interception returns, and the defense had a total of nine interceptions and 11 forced turnovers. The two teams combined to throw eight interceptions and complete only 26 of 62 passes. The Buckeyes defense must have enjoyed playing in the Cotton Bowl stadium; in 1977, they had seven interceptions against SMU. Harris had 105 yards in receptions.

The Buckeyes' longest run was 11 yards, but they had pass plays of 34, 37, and 51 yards. Coach Bruce had announced that Tom Tupa would get some significant playing time, and he went three-for-eight passing in the second quarter.

FUN FACTS:
- The Buckeyes had a 1,000-yard rusher in Workman, and Carter finished with 1,127 receiving yards.

- Spielman had 105 solo and 100 assisted tackles, and his 205 were more than double that of the next defender.

- The edge in interceptions was 29-13.

- The defense had four interceptions for touchdowns.

- Four Buckeyes had a longer interception return than the opponents' long of 34 yards.

- The opponents had 49 more passes and 14 more receptions, but the Buckeyes had a 17-5 edge in passing touchdowns.

- Cris Carter's 11 touchdown catches were six more than the opponents' total.

- Jim Karsatos's total offense 16 touchdowns matched the 16 that the opponents scored.

- The Buckeyes beat Illinois and Indiana in consecutive weeks, the Buckeyes' 50th win against each.

1987 (6-4-1)

The defense made it 11 interceptions and three for touchdowns in the last two games, the Cotton Bowl and the 1987 opener, as they picked off six Mountaineer passes in the 24-3 win over West Virginia. The Mountaineers completed as many passes to the Buckeyes as they did to their own receivers. For Spielman, this was his second straight game with two interceptions. The total offense edge was only 213-197 in favor of the Buckeyes, but William White returned an interception—one of three on the day for him to tie a team record—29 yards for a score in the fourth quarter, and he flattened a cheerleader in the process. The defense added two fumble recoveries. West Virginia would play in the national championship game the next year against Notre Dame. The Mountaineers' quarterback Major Harris would play for the Columbus Thunderbolts in the Arena Football League in 1991 when I did the stats for the radio broadcasts.

The offense more than doubled to 435 yards, with Workman running for 162 and nine players recording a catch, in the 24-14 win over

Oregon. Workman was also the leading receiver with five for 63 yards. OSU's athletic director Rick Bay had had the same position at Oregon.

Earle Bruce wore his fedora in the 13-13 tie against LSU in Baton Rouge. In his 100th game, this was his only tie as a Buckeye. The start of the game was delayed when he refused to have the Buckeyes take the field before the Tigers. Chris Spielman, in Dick Fenlon's *Columbus Dispatch* story, said that his Tiger Stadium at Massillon was the real Tiger Stadium.

Jay Koch had a touchdown catch for the second straight game for the only Buckeye touchdown. While watching the game with me, my dad said the Buckeyes needed an interception. On cue, Greg Rogan picked off a Tommy Hodson pass with 27 seconds left, his second interception in the last 2:03. Matt Frantz had a 47-yard field goal attempt partially blocked on the last play. The defense picked off three LSU passes in the fourth quarter.

LSU's field is a dream come true for broadcasters and statisticians, with the 5 yard numerals (5, 15, 25, etc.) painted on the field. I have worked high school games where not even the 10 yard numerals were painted on the field; instead, there were orange folding markers on the sidelines that would easily get displaced.

The defense held Illinois to 54 yards rushing in the 10-6 win in Champaign. Tupa had minus two yards rushing but had the only Buckeye touchdown of the game on a 5-yard run. Future college coach Mark "Bo" Pelini had an interception for the Buckeyes.

This continued a pattern of seven games in eight years decided by seven points or less against the Illini:

- 1980: 49-42 win
- 1981: 34-27 win
- 1982: 26-21 win

- 1983: 17-13 loss

- 1984: 45-38 win

- 1985: 31-28 loss

The Indiana game was tied 10-10 at the half on a Matt Frantz 51-yard field goal with no time remaining, but the Hoosiers scored 21 unanswered in the 31-10 loss that Bruce called the darkest day in Ohio State football since he had been associated with it.

The Buckeyes had now scored a total of 33 points in the last three games.

The Buckeyes had a 17-0 halftime lead, but they needed a 50-yard Matt Frantz field goal with 3:10 left to beat Purdue 20-17 at West Lafayette. Bruce moved Workman to flanker, where he had four catches for 88 yards, with a 36-yard touchdown. The defense recorded a team record eight sacks.

Carlos Snow had his breakout game with four touchdowns—three on the ground and a 45-yard catch—as the Buckeyes broke open a 14-9 halftime game and beat Minnesota 42-9. He had the most rushing yards, the most receiving yards, the longest run, the longest reception, and the longest kickoff return in the game for the Buckeyes. Five Buckeyes had an interception. Jack would often punctuate his call on a Snow breakaway touchdown run with, "Adios, Carlos!"

Everett Ross caught a 79-yard touchdown pass from Tupa on the first play of the game, but the offense had only 68 yards, including two yards rushing, the rest of the game in the 13-7 loss to Michigan State. Ross's catch was 18 more yards than the passing yards for the Spartans.

The Buckeyes outgained Wisconsin 514-233, but they lost in Madison 26-24, the same score as the Michigan game the previous year. The Buckeyes turned the ball over six times in the second half and seven times in total. In the last two games, the defense had now allowed a total of 111 passing yards. The Badgers' quarterback was Tony Lowery from Groveport Madison High School. In 2016, I would broadcast his son Mike's high school games when he played at Gahanna Lincoln.

Coach Bruce was fired after the third straight loss, to Iowa 29-27, the three losses by a total of 10 points. Ross had four catches for 123 yards and two touchdowns on plays of 24 and 60. The Hawkeyes had the winning score on a fourth-and-23 pass play from the OSU 28 with six seconds remaining. They had also kicked a field goal as the first half ended.

I worked the stats for WOSU-TV in the 23-20 win at Michigan, the game where Bruce wore his suit and fedora and the players wore headbands with "EARLE" lettering. Ross and Snow had a touchdown for the second straight game, Ross with 1:36 left in the first half—giving him three in the last two games—and Snow on a 70-yard pass on the Buckeyes' first play of the second half. The Buckeyes trailed 13-0 before Ross's touchdown.

Tom Tupa's 1-yard run was the Buckeyes' last touchdown of the year and tied him for the team lead with four rushing touchdowns. He was injured in the fourth quarter, and Greg Frey came in for one play on third-and-nine and completed a 19-yard pass to keep the drive alive. In 1992, I would record some of Greg's post-game comments when he played for the Ohio Glory of the World League of American Football. A few years later, I would work the stats on televised games where Greg was the analyst. Matt Frantz, who missed a go-ahead field goal in the previous year's game and had missed the extra point after Tupa's run— his only miss in 53 career attempts—kicked the winning 26-yard field goal with 5:18 left.

For the second straight year, the losing team lost a lead of at least 11 points at home. Michigan's Jamie Morris ran for 130 yards, with 112 in the first half. I recall that Coach Schembechler was gracious in defeat, given Bruce's dismissal. Coach Bruce's last season was similar to his first in that he had a three point come-from-behind fourth quarter win at Ann Arbor.

This was the only win for the Buckeyes in my four times working in the press box in Ann Arbor, with the losses coming in 1983, 1985, and 1989. Adding in my four times sitting in the stands—1979, 1991,

1995, and 1997—the Buckeyes were only 2-6 in Ann Arbor, each of the two wins by three points. Spoiler alert: The 2000s would be much different.

FUN FACTS:

- The road games were decided by zero, 4, 3, 2, and 3 points.

- Seven of the 11 games were decided by six points or less.

- The total offense average difference was 10 yards per game in favor of the Buckeyes.

- The two longest pass plays—79 and 70 yards—came against Michigan State and Michigan, and each came on the team's first play of a half.

- The opponents had 34 more passes, but the Buckeyes had a 12-10 edge in passing touchdowns.

- Chris Spielman had 78 solo tackles and 78 assists. His 156 tackles were double that of the next closest Buckeye.

- Everett Ross had the longest reception and punt return.

- Two of Jay Koch's four receptions were for touchdowns.

- After this season, seven of the top eight single season punting averages and the top three career punting averages were by players named Tom—Skladany, Tupa, and Orosz.

- After beating Purdue and Minnesota in consecutive weeks, the Buckeyes had 25 wins against each.

1988 (4-6-1)

In January, I was at a car dealer shopping for a new car, and as the salesman and I headed to his office to negotiate, he gave me his business card. It had "VJ" in big letters, and below that, his name ... Vlade Janakievski! I had not seen him up close before and did not recognize him. He made the sale; this was shortly before he opened his delicatessen that would receive much publicity from Brent Musberger.

The spring game had a packed house, in anticipation of John Cooper's first year. I was able to attend the post-game interviews for WCVO-FM, and my hand appeared on the TV news that night. Trust me, it was my hand.

In the opening game, a 26-9 win over Syracuse, the team had no penalties and no turnovers. Like Coach Bruce, Coach Cooper's first game was against Syracuse. Snow scored for the third straight game, and the two teams combined for seven field goals, four by Pat O'Morrow. It was Syracuse's only loss in a 22 game span that straddled 1986 through 1988. The first touchdown in the John Cooper era was a pass to tight end Jeff Ellis; the first touchdown in the Earle Bruce era was a pass to tight end Ron Barwig.

Three years after last playing the Pitt Panthers, the Buckeyes scored 10 points again, but they gave up 42 in the 42-10 loss. The only highlight of this night game at Pitt was the 100-yard kickoff return by Snow to help him set a team record with 213 return yards in a game, and the team set an all-time team record of 256 return yards in a game. The penalties were seven and the turnovers were three. Pitt was coming off a bye week, having beaten Northern Iowa 59-10 in a battle of two Panther teams and in Earle Bruce's first game as the head coach of Northern Iowa.

The Buckeyes scored 16 points in the last two minutes to beat LSU 36-33, after the Tigers had taken a 33-20 lead with 4:29 left. LSU helped the Buckeyes by passing instead of keeping the clock running and taking an intentional safety. On the free kick, Bobby Olive had a 30-yard return, and Frey connected with Olive on a crawling 20-yard touchdown catch with 38 seconds left for the winning score—Olive's first scoring reception ever. Snow had two touchdowns, scoring for the fifth game in a row. Michael McCray's 23-yard return of a blocked punt for touchdown was the team's longest punt return of the year.

The official account states, "The game ostensibly ended at 7:19 P.M. but fans stormed the field as LSU tried to call a time out; the officials gave up at 7:21 P.M."

The only touchdown in the 31-12 loss to Illinois was Frey's 13-yard pass to Jeff Graham. John Spencer, Tim's brother, led the Buckeyes with five receptions, his only catches of the year. The Buckeyes lost despite having two more first downs. The Illini celebrated coach John Mackovic's 45th birthday and would replace Wisconsin as the thorn in the Buckeyes' side for several years.

For the second straight game, the Buckeyes had only one touchdown in the 41-7 loss at Indiana. Jaymes Bryant had the 8-yard scoring run and had 98 yards on the ground. Anthony Thompson of the Hoosiers, whom Coach Bill Mallory compared to Archie Griffin, ran for 190 yards and four touchdowns. Counting last year's matchup, Indiana had outscored the Buckeyes 72-17.

The losing streak was three after the 31-26 loss to Purdue, losing a 20-7 lead. Snow had missed the Illinois game and had little action in the Indiana game, but he returned with 128 yards, helping the Buckeyes to a 416-319 edge in total yards. Purdue took a 21-20 lead with a drive that started at the OSU 16 following a Buckeye fumble on a kickoff return. The Boilers' running back, Ernie Schramayr, caught 13 passes for two touchdowns.

During the game, Paul Warfield had the best line of the year. Twins John and Mike Sullivan collaborated for a tackle on defense, and Paul said, "Purdue has the Silver Twins, and the Buckeyes have the Sullivan brothers."

In two of the last three games, the opposing coaches were John Mackovic of Illinois and Fred Akers of Purdue. Akers had been the head coach at Texas, and Mackovic would eventually become the head coach of the Longhorns.

Snow scored for the second straight game, the only touchdown for either team, in the 13-6 win in a night game at Minnesota. The Gophers had a first-and-goal from the Buckeyes 1-yard line in the closing minutes—on first down, "Thompson vaults left no gain" in the play-by-play—but could not score. In this game and in the next two matchups between these teams, both quarterbacks were from Cincinnati—Frey from St. Xavier and Scott Schaffner, who had Ken Griffey Jr. as a teammate in both football and baseball, from Moeller High School. Both wore #15 in college.

For the second straight year, the Buckeyes scored on a pass play on their first possession against Michigan State, but that would be their only touchdown in a 20-10 loss. The game was tied at 10 at halftime.

Two Grahams—Jeff on a pass and Scottie on the ground—scored touchdowns in the 34-12 win over Wisconsin. Jeff had 121 yards on six catches.

Iowa scored the first 14 points and the last three on a field goal with 16 seconds left for a 24-24 tie. Scottie Graham scored for the second straight game. Iowa's miracle finish of last year almost had a replay, as they tried an onside kick after the field goal.

Mike Sullivan scored a touchdown on a 13-yard interception return for the Buckeyes. It continued a pattern of four games in five years that the Buckeyes had a defensive score against the Hawkeyes:

- 1984: Larry Kolic interception
- 1985: Sonny Gordon blocked a punt that resulted in a safety
- 1986: Greg Rogan fumble return

In the Michigan game, a 34-31 loss, the Buckeyes trailed 20-0 at halftime, a deficit matching the second quarter one in the Oklahoma game of 1977. Like that game, the Buckeyes took a lead, but they saw the opponent score last for the win. Carlos Snow ran for 170 yards and scored a touchdown on the team's first possession of the second half, as he did in 1987 against Michigan. Bill Matlock ran for his only two touchdowns of the year, and Bobby Olive had a diving catch for a score; including his only other score of the year, against LSU, both of his touchdowns were on diving catches.

The Buckeyes took a 31-27 lead with 2:02 remaining, but John Kolesar, an Ohioan who had the winning touchdown as a freshman, returned the kickoff 59 yards to the OSU 41 and caught the winning touchdown pass on the next play.

The Buckeyes' last possession reached the Michigan 39 but ended with an interception, with Coach Cooper waving his arms, pleading in vain for an incompletion ruling. The two teams combined for 968 yards in total offense, with the Buckeyes having one more yard on the ground. The Buckeyes had 353 of their 469 yards in the second half. For the third straight game in this series, a team had given up a lead of at least 11 points.

FUN FACTS:
- Greg Frey had all but four of the Buckeyes' pass attempts during the year.

- Frey's longest run was 14 yards, but he had a reception of 22 yards.

- Carlos Snow had the longest run (58 yards) and the longest kickoff return (100 yards) on the team. In each case, it was more than double the next longest of a teammate.

- John Sullivan led the team in tackles with 88 in '88.

- The offense averaged 27.5 points at home and 12.8 on the road.

- The OSU quarterbacks had eight touchdowns and 13 interceptions. The opponents had 13 touchdowns and eight interceptions.

1989 (8-4)

The Buckeyes led only 16-13 at halftime in the opening 37-13 win over Oklahoma State. Frey passed for 285 yards, and Kirk Herbstreit added 17 more, with nine Buckeyes having a catch. The Cowboys' quarterback was their eventual coach, Mike Gundy, and future Buckeye assistant coach and future opposing coach Larry Coker was a Cowboy assistant.

Pat O'Morrow (the official account has "O'Marrow") gave the Buckeyes a 3-0 lead heading into the second quarter at USC, but it was all Trojans after that in the 42-3 loss, giving up 491 yards on defense. The Buckeyes had given up four touchdowns on the ground to Sam Cunningham in the 1973 Rose Bowl and gave up four passing touchdowns in this game to Todd Marinovich. It was the second straight year not scoring an offensive touchdown and giving up 42 points in the second game, both on the road.

The Buckeyes led 24-0 and held on to beat Boston College 34-29. The defense stopped an Eagle run on fourth down from the 4-yard line with 45 seconds left. The two Grahams had huge scoring plays—Jeff 80 yards on a pass and Scottie 70 yards on a run. The two teams combined for 1,107 yards—602 by the Buckeyes, including 410 in the first half. Scottie ran for 151 and Snow for 147, and Jeff Graham had 101 receiving yards.

Jeff Graham had another big play, a 66-yard punt return for a score, but the Buckeyes lost at Illinois, 34-14, recording only 10 first downs and turning it over four times. It was the second year in a row that Graham had scored against the Illini.

The Buckeyes led Indiana 35-14 and held on to win 35-31, despite being outgained 444-290. Frey passed for only 37 yards, but he had scoring passes of two and four yards to Jim Palmer. Snow ran for 136 yards and Scottie Graham for 124, including a 60-yard scoring run. Anthony Thompson ran for 177 yards and three touchdowns, giving him seven against the Buckeyes in the last two years.

The running attack had 371 yards, 149 with two touchdowns by Snow, and the passing game had 57 yards in the 21-3 win over Purdue. The defense tied a team record of eight sacks, set in 1987 also against the Boilermakers, and the 62 yards in sacks set a new team record. In the last two games, the Buckeyes had nine completions for 94 yards. Coach Cooper said, in the postgame notes, "We need to do a better job of throwing the football," and would get his wish the next week.

Frey passed for 362 yards—with 18 of his 20 completions, 327 yards, and all three of his touchdowns in the second half—as the Buckeyes rallied from 31-0 down to beat Minnesota 41-37 in the Metrodome. Snow had three touchdowns, two on receptions. The last 15 points came in a span of 2:13, with Frey (#15) hitting Jeff Graham with a 15-yard pass with 51 seconds left. The smile on Frey's face after the go-ahead score was priceless. The play before Graham's catch was huge, with Jim Palmer breaking a tackle and gaining 34 yards, his longest gain of the year, to the 15.

Like last year, the Gophers had a pass into the end zone on their last play, as they had reached the Buckeyes' 22-yard line. At the time, the 31 point rally tied the biggest comeback in college football history, since broken. Minnesota's Scott Schaffner, a Cincinnati product, passed for two touchdowns and had the team's longest run of 18 yards.

Snow, Scottie Graham, and Dante Lee each had at least 100 rushing yards among the team's 456 yards on the ground in the 52-27 win over Northwestern. Lee was the leader with 157 and three touchdowns. Jaymes Bryant added 109 yards and two touchdowns on his two touches of the game—a 63-yard run and a 46-yard catch—in the span of 1:05 in the second quarter.

The 28-0 win over Iowa was Coach Cooper's first shutout, with the offense distributing their four touchdowns over the four quarters. Lee was a yard short of his second straight 100-yard game, and Scottie Graham scored on a run and a reception. In the postgame notes, Iowa coach Hayden Fry called it his most frustrating day in 38 years of coaching.

Scottie Graham ran for 152 yards, almost half of the team's 307, and two touchdowns in the 42-22 win over Wisconsin. Lee added 98 yards and two touchdowns on the ground. The Badgers tied a record that will never be broken: no pass completions, in eight attempts.

The offense had 200 yards rushing, 133 with two touchdowns by Scottie Graham, and 220 passing in the 28-18 loss at Michigan. It was the second straight year in this matchup that each team had at least 400 yards of total offense. As in the Minnesota game this year, both quarterbacks were from Cincinnati, as the Wolverines' Michael Taylor played for Princeton High School. The Wolverines' Todd Plate had two interceptions, leading to the newspaper headline, "Blue Plate Special."

The Buckeyes had a 14-3 lead over Auburn in the Hall of Fame Bowl in Tampa, but the Tigers rallied for their 31-14 win. Jeff Graham had 103 receiving yards, and Brian Stablein had his only touchdown catch of the year.

FUN FACTS:

- All 13 players who caught a pass averaged at least 10 yards per catch.

- Snow led the team with 990 yards rushing, but his longest gain of 25 was topped by four teammates, including a 45-yard run by safety Zack Dumas on a fake punt play against Illinois.

- Four Buckeyes had a longer run than the opponents' long of 40 yards.

- Frey improved from eight touchdown passes and 13 interceptions in 1988 to 13 touchdown passes and eight interceptions in 1989.

- The Buckeyes more than doubled their rushing touchdowns from 1988—from 14 to 30.

- The edge in rushing touchdowns was 30-17.

- Jeff Graham had the longest reception and punt return.

- Derek Isaman led the team with 88 tackles, the second straight year where the leader had 88.

- The Buckeyes had their best combined scoring output in consecutive games at Minnesota and Northwestern, in front of a combined attendance of 62,183. Every other regular season game had an attendance of at least 69,000.

CHAPTER 5

The 1990s
Oh, So Close, Part 2

THE 1990S WOULD SEE THE BUCKEYES come oh-so-close to beating Michigan in 1990, 1992, 1996, 1997, and 1999, and oh-so-close to being national champions in 1996 and 1998. Many fans will tell you that they prefer the former to the latter.

This was my last year calling high school games for WCVO-FM. As part of our halftime shows, I would record interviews with Bob Atha, Vlade Janakievski, Tom Skladany (I must have had a thing for kickers), and Jeff Logan—to give running backs a smidgen of equal time. Janakievski, Skladany, and Logan were easy to contact since I knew their business locations, but I used the White Pages (Do they still exist?)—I still have my 2008 edition—to find Atha. To prepare for his interview, I had researched my *1979 Ohio State Football Official Press Guide* and found that he "…was a conventional straight-on place kicker in high school but now has adopted a soccer-style kick." When I asked him about making the transition to a soccer-style kicker, he said, "I don't know where you got your information." I also used the visit to ask him for some advice on my minor running injury.

I broadcast the Gahanna-Worthington game that year and saw future Buckeye Dimitrious Stanley as the Worthington Cardinals' quarterback. Calling the game, I said, "Stanley has all the tools."

1990 (7-4-1)

Jeff Graham's 50-yard punt return in the fourth quarter was the winning score in the 17-10 opening win over Texas Tech. The halftime score was 3-0 in favor of the Red Raiders, meaning that the Buckeyes had gone their last four quarters without scoring. Robert Smith made his debut with 86 yards and the team's only offensive touchdown. The teams combined to lose seven fumbles.

Bobby Olive and Raymont Harris each had two touchdowns in the 31-10 win at Boston College. The two freshman running backs, Smith and Harris, ran for 102 and 96 yards, respectively.

The USC game in Columbus, a 35-26 loss, was "stopped with 2:36 left in the fourth quarter by mutual consent of coaches" and "declared completed due to weather conditions," as the official account shows. The game was played in a monsoon, and lightning was in the area at the end. Jeff Graham had 109 yards receiving and a score, and USC's Ricky Ervins ran for 199 yards and two touchdowns, with 164 yards in the first half.

Illinois scored the last two touchdowns in Columbus as they beat the Buckeyes 31-20. OSU had 243 yards on the ground, 118 by Harris, and 244 passing—outgaining the Illini 487-407.

Indiana scored the last ten points in Bloomington in the 27-27 tie. Smith ran for 127 yards, and each team had a touchdown bomb—65 yards to Jeff Graham, while the Hoosiers had one of 64 yards. The game ended with Tim Walton intercepting an Indiana pass, followed by three laterals, one of them illegal.

In the postgame notes, Coach Cooper predicted that the Big Ten championship could come down to the last game of the season. Hoosier coach Bill Mallory added that he was in favor of implementing overtime in college football. He would have to wait until the 1996 regular season.

The Buckeyes had scoring plays of 48, 58, 60, and 69 (a Robert Smith run) yards in the 42-2 win at Purdue. Jeff Graham had the 48- and 58-yard catches from Frey—he had 144 yards on the day—and returned the favor by throwing the 60-yard pass to Frey. Graham had been a quarterback at Kettering Archbishop Alter High School. The Boilers threw 54 passes, something that the Buckeyes had come to expect when playing Purdue, but the defense picked off five of them. Purdue had only four yards rushing.

The Buckeyes scored 38 in the first half—making it 71 points in the last four quarters against the Gophers—of the 52-23 win over Minnesota. Smith ran for 120 yards, and the total offense was 551 yards, to total 986 yards against Minnesota in the last two years.

The offense made it 142 points in the last three games in the 48-7 win over Northwestern, with a 462-174 edge in total yards. Smith ran for 128 yards, with 116 in the first half, and 11 players had at least one carry for the 274 yards on the ground.

In the 27-26 win at Iowa, Coach Cooper's 100th career win, the Buckeyes scored as time expired to end the first half and with one second left in the game to win it, on a 3-yard catch by Olive. It was Olive's second touchdown catch in the last seven minutes of the game. The Buckeyes benefitted from two huge breaks: the touchdown before halftime came on a deflected pass into the hands of Jeff Graham, and Iowa's Nick Bell dropped a pass that would have been a sure touchdown.

Graham and Olive combined for 204 of the Buckeyes' 223 receiving yards. It was Greg Frey's third miracle comeback in as many years—see LSU in 1988 and Minnesota in 1989. In those three games, he passed for 866 yards.

Jeff Graham had his second punt return for a touchdown of the year, for 81 yards, in the 35-10 win at Wisconsin. The score was only 14-10 heading into the fourth quarter, but Smith, who had 171 on the ground, had two touchdown runs before Graham's return. The Buckeyes outgained the Badgers 419-234.

Coach Cooper was right about the Big Ten championship coming down to the last game. It came down to the last play, and Michigan kicked a 37-yard field goal to win 16-13. Frey was stopped on fourth-and-one at the OSU 29, and J.D. Carlson, who had missed from 38 yards four minutes earlier, made his field goal. Michigan's Ricky Powers ran for 128 yards, more than half of his team's 248 total yards.

The Liberty Bowl game against Air Force was a 23-11 loss. The half-time score was baseball-like, Air Force ahead 6-5, and it was 13-11 with 2:47 left, but the Falcons kicked a field goal and returned an interception for a score on the next play from scrimmage. Smith had the only touchdown on a 29-yard run.

The Falcons proved Woody's theory, also proven in the 1972 Michigan game, by passing three times, completing one, misfiring on one, and having the third intercepted.

FUN FACTS:

- Kirk Herbstreit had more yards on kickoff returns (18) than on rushing (10) and passing (0) combined.

- Freshmen Robert Smith, Raymont Harris, and Butler By'not'e combined for 17 of the team's 22 rushing touchdowns and 1,884 of the team's 2,212 rushing yards.

- Seniors had 17 of the 20 touchdown receptions.

- Robert Smith had the longest run and kickoff return.

- Jeff Graham had the longest reception and punt return.

- Greg Frey had minus 97 yards rushing but 60 yards receiving on his one reception.

- Frey and Rich Huffman combined for two receptions, both for touchdowns.

- In 1990, opponents had 1,990 passing yards.

- The Buckeyes had three fewer plays than the opponents, but they had almost 800 more total yards and a 42-21 advantage in touchdowns from scrimmage.

- Opponents had seven more passes, but the Buckeyes had a 20-8 edge in passing touchdowns.

- The top 13 seasons for a quarterback in terms of yards all had occurred in the last 13 years to this point.

- For the second straight year, the Buckeyes had their best combined scoring output in consecutive games against Minnesota and Northwestern.

1991 (8-4)

Eight of 11 regular season games were in Ohio, including the Northwestern game in the old stadium in Cleveland.

The offense had 325 yards on the ground, 189 by Butler By'not'e and 105 from Jeff Cothran, and a 449-253 total offense advantage in the opening 38-14 win over Arizona. William Houston had three carries for three yards all year, and two of the three carries resulted in touchdowns in this game. New starting quarterback Kent Graham had minus 29 yards on the ground, but he had a 2-yard scoring run. Kent had transferred from Notre Dame, where he had some playing time in the 1988 national championship game. Carlos Snow, who had missed the 1990 season, broke the OSU record for kick return yards in a career. The attendance was a new stadium record.

Twenty-eight of the 38 points came in the fourth quarter in the 23-15 win over Louisville. The defense held Louisville to 27 yards on the ground and picked off three passes. The Cardinals' coach was Howard Schnellenberger, who led Miami to the 1983 national championship and had coached Archie's brother Keith with the Hurricanes.

Kirk Herbstreit got the start in the 33-19 win over Washington State as the offense ran for 321 yards and had 479 overall. Herbstreit had a 39-yard touchdown pass to Bernard Edwards, and Scottie Graham had the year's longest run of 65 yards. Steve Tovar had a rare (Spoiler alert: See the Iowa game) return of an extra point attempt 96 yards for two points with eight seconds remaining. Drew Bledsoe passed for 287 yards for the Cougars, but Roger Harper returned an interception 42 yards for a score, the only one of the year for the team.

The Buckeyes had more than twice as much possession time as Wisconsin in the 31-16 win in front of another new stadium record crowd. Raymont Harris scored twice in his seven carries, and Herbstreit's only carry was for 32 yards and a touchdown. Joey Galloway had his first reception as a Buckeye. The Badgers had 228 yards of total offense, with 28 on the ground, including 29 on one rush play. The Buckeyes were 4-0 for the first time since 1984.

Illinois had kicked a field goal on the final play to beat the Buckeyes in Champaign in 1985. This year, they did it with 36 seconds left in the 10-7 game. The teams were three points apart and eight yards apart in total offense, with the Illini rushing for only 84 yards. Galloway caught his first Buckeye touchdown pass for the longest Buckeye reception of the year, 44 yards, that tied the score with 3:10 left, a score that would last only two minutes and 34 seconds.

My sister Beverly and I went to the Northwestern game, a 34-3 win in Cleveland. A traffic delay around Mansfield caused us to be late and miss the first three touchdowns. Arriving in the stadium, we asked a worker wearing a "Browns Courtesy Staff" yellow jacket to help us find our section, to which he said, "I don't know." At least he was courteous!

Scottie Graham ran for 109 yards and three touchdowns. Four different Buckeyes combined to complete five passes, including one by punter Tim Williams for the longest Buckeye completion of the day, 21 yards on a busted punt play to Foster Paulk, normally a defensive back. Williams's two-handed pass would have made basketball coach Randy Ayers proud.

Snow had 169 of the team's 262 rushing yards in the 27-17 win over Michigan State in front of another new stadium record crowd.

The Buckeyes were outgained 440-221 in the 16-9 loss to Iowa. Broken record: it was a new stadium record crowd. For the second time this year, the Buckeyes returned an extra point attempt for two points, with Jason Simmons turning the trick.

Five different Buckeyes ran for a score among the team's 383 rushing yards in the 35-6 win at Minnesota. Herbstreit had the longest run of the game and the year for the team, 72 yards, breaking several tackles on the way. The players and fans experienced a novelty—watching replays of Herbstreit's run from several angles on the video board. The 72 yards were almost half of his 153 yards on the year.

The offense was on the short end of total yards, 356-225, but the Buckeyes beat Indiana 20-16. Snow had 124 yards, but his teammates combined for minus five. With this the last home game, the season attendance this year was a new record.

My entire family went to the Michigan game in Ann Arbor, a forgettable 31-3 loss in the rain. Somehow, the Buckeyes had a 19-13 edge in first downs. Three future ESPN broadcasters saw action. Desmond Howard had 96 yards on receptions, the 93-yard punt return, and the Heisman pose. Herbstreit was eight of 11 passing in relief and had the team's longest run and completion, but he was knocked out of the game in the fourth quarter on a roughing the passer penalty. Galloway had one reception for 11 yards. Tim Williams' 50-yard field goal was his longest of the year and his only attempt from at least 50 yards.

Tito Paul recovered a punt blocked by Steve Tovar to tie the score at 17 against Syracuse in the fourth quarter of the Hall of Fame Bowl, but the Orangemen connected on a 60-yard touchdown pass to win 24-17. Herbstreit started and played the entire game at quarterback, passing for 174 yards.

FUN FACTS:

- Carlos Snow led the team in touchdowns all four of his years.

- Similar to 1989, Snow led the team with 828 yards rushing, but his longest gain of 39 was topped or matched by four teammates.

- The team had a 28-9 advantage in rushing touchdowns.

- Snow's nine rushing touchdowns matched the opponents' total.

- Bernard Edwards and Brian Stablein each had 381 receiving yards to lead the team.

- The seven largest attendances through this year all occurred in 1991.

- The Buckeyes had 232 first downs, after 230 in 1990.

1992 (8-3-1)

The Buckeyes survived a two-point conversion attempt with 33 seconds left to beat Louisville 20-19 in the opener. As the Cardinals prepared for the conversion for the lead, Beverly asked me what I thought would happen, and I said, "History is on our side." Actually, it wasn't, based on losses to USC in the 1974 season and to Missouri in 1976 on two-point conversions. Dan Wilkinson pressured the Cardinals quarterback Jeff Brohm, the eventual Purdue coach, on the pass. Joey Galloway's only run of the year went 50 yards for a touchdown. Eddie George had the first carry of his Buckeye career and his only carry of the game, for three yards. The teams were separated by one point and eight yards on offense.

George scored the first touchdown of his Buckeye career against Bowling Green, a 17-6 win. Bobby Hoying had his first completion as a Buckeye, four yards to Galloway. Spoiler alert: The stats for this combination would escalate in 1993 and 1994. The score was only 7-6 at halftime. The Falcons had a 277-237 edge in total yards, but the Buckeye defense picked off four passes.

The day before the game, I was killing time at the Little Professor bookstore in the Northland Mall before the high school football game that I was working. I recognized a tall, red-headed man at a display of books—Steven Newman, the Ohio native who walked around the world in the 1980s and wrote the books *Worldwalk* and *Letters from Steven* about his adventure. Both books are compelling; I had devoured the 500 page *Worldwalk* in three days. He had stopped in the bookstore to offer to autograph copies of *Worldwalk*. We had a nice chat, and it happened that I had two extra tickets for the BG game. He accepted the tickets for himself and his lady friend, and along with Beverly, the four of us had dinner after the game. He shared stories about his journey, saying that the people of North Africa were among his favorites. He autographed his book for me, and I have a photo of the two of us.

The Buckeyes played Syracuse for the second time in the span of four games, dating back to the bowl game of last year, and beat the Orangemen 35-12 in a night game at the Carrier Dome. The scoring started in the first five minutes on a 46-yard pass from Herbstreit to Brian Stablein, his longest catch of the year. Eddie George scored three touchdowns on runs of one, one, and two yards. He would finish the season with five touchdowns. The defense had four interceptions for the second straight game.

I had joined the Buckeye Boosters Club for the season. The club would meet during the week, and Coach Cooper would talk about the upcoming game. Before the Wisconsin game, a 20-16 loss, he said, "… and we are staying in … where, Steve Snapp?" Snapp, the long-time Sports Information Director, let "Oconomowoc" roll off his tongue.

Stablein had a touchdown catch in the Wisconsin game among his nine receptions for the final score, and the Buckeyes' last drive ended inside the Badger 25.

Illinois scored half their points on a 96-yard return of an Eddie George fumble and a safety to win in Columbus, 18-16. Tim Walton had the Buckeyes' longest interception return of the year, 59 yards, to set up a Tim Williams field goal on the last play of the first half. For the second straight year and the third time in eight years, Illinois kicked a field goal (by two kickers named Chris—White and Richardson) in the fourth quarter for the win. The Buckeyes had a 342-270 edge in total yards and a 21-14 edge in first downs.

Raymont Harris scored three times—on runs of one, one, and three yards—in the 31-7 win over Northwestern. Eddie George ran for 97 yards, including a 60-yard run, all in the fourth quarter. Joe Metzger made the most of his only catch of the year, a 2-yard touchdown.

The Buckeyes liked the 27-17 win over Michigan State the previous year so much that they posted the same score this year. Herbstreit passed for 201 yards, and Stablein had 106 yards in receptions. Roger Harper had two interceptions.

Tito Paul scored on a blocked punt return for the second straight year, and Smith ran for 129 yards and two touchdowns in the 38-15 win at Iowa.

Smith had over 100 yards (119) and scored two touchdowns for the second straight game in the 17-0 win over Minnesota in front of a non-sellout home crowd. The offense had 244 yards on the ground and 217 passing.

Smith made it three games in a row with over 100 yards (175) and two touchdowns in the 27-10 win at Indiana. Coach Copper had called

Smith a home run hitter, with his ability to bust a touchdown run at any time, and one of his scores was a 64-yard job, the team's longest run of the year. The team also had its longest pass of the year, 54 yards to Chris Sanders.

The Michigan game, a 13-13 tie, was the last time that I sat in the stands in Ohio Stadium, as you will see shortly. Down 13-3 in the fourth quarter, Tim Williams kicked a field goal and Greg Beatty caught a 5-yard pass from Herbstreit on a fourth down play with 4:24 remaining. The Buckeyes had another possession a minute later, but they went three and out, and the game ended with OSU's Walter Taylor returning an interception 51 yards.

Herbstreit passed 46 times for 271 yards, and Stablein had 12 receptions for 111 yards. The two Wolverine quarterbacks, Elvis Grbac and Todd Collins, made the most of their three combined carries by each scoring a touchdown, but a missed PAT after Grbac's was instrumental in the tie score. In the postgame notes, both coaches described the turf as slippery; in fact, Greg Beatty slipped slightly before his catch.

A photo in the *Columbus Dispatch* the next day showed Kirk Herbstreit leaving the field in tears. This would be the last tie in the Michigan series, and in the last two tie games (1973 and 1992), the home team rallied from 10 points down. This would be the last game that my dad and I attended together. It would also turn out to be the last tie game in Ohio Stadium.

The Citrus Bowl in Orlando, won by Georgia 21-14, was billed as a battle between Robert Smith and the Bulldogs' Garrison Hearst. Smith ran for 112 yards and both touchdowns—he also had the longest pass play for either team of 45 yards—and Hearst ran for 163 and two scores. Each had 161 yards combined in rushing and passing. In his two bowl games, in 1990 and 1992, Smith scored all three Buckeye touchdowns.

The three losses this year came by a total of 13 points.

FUN FACTS:

- For the second straight year, the starting quarterback had four touchdown passes, and the backup quarterback had one touchdown pass.

- The Buckeyes and the opponents each had five touchdown passes, although the opponents had 85 more passes and 36 more completions.

- The Buckeyes had an edge of 26-14 in rushing touchdowns, 16-7 in field goals, and 19-7 in interceptions.

- Five Buckeyes had a longer run than the opponents' long of 37 yards.

- The two highest scoring outputs came on the road, at Syracuse and Iowa.

- Syracuse has had a 10-2 record three times in its history—1988, 1991, and 1992—and the Buckeyes played them each year, winning twice.

- The three best defensive efforts came at home.

1993 (10-1-1)

I received one of the best phone calls of my life on September 3 (9/3/93). The day before the opening game against Washington, about 24 hours before kickoff, D.C. Koehl, the long-time OSU Sports Information staffer, called to say that he needed someone to assist him keeping the game stats, and was I interested? In the words of Pat Paulsen on the *Smothers Brothers Comedy Hour*, "Sure, why not?"

My duties include: writing the yardage gained by the player on each play, pass attempts, scoring plays, punts, returns, first downs, interceptions, fumble information, penalties, score by quarter, the weather, the attendance, and more in a spiral notebook containing forms for each item.

One of the "other duties as assigned" is to record the start time and the end time of the game, hopefully remembering to check my phone once mobile phones came into use.

One play in particular keeps me busy—a touchdown pass. I keep my own play-by-play, so this entails jotting down the play on my notebook paper, updating the quarterback's stats, updating the receiver's stats, writing down the scoring play, and updating the first downs, if applicable. My stats on paper are strictly a back-up system to compare to what is keyed into the software.

For several years, it was just the two of us, with D.C. keying the plays on a computer, though for a while, a third staffer would check my math on the cumulative rushing yards for each player at halftime. These were the days before the media had stat monitors, and once the game was over, reporters—Rusty Miller was usually the first—would come to me to get a few stats.

Luckily, I do not need to record the tackles. As we added staff over the years to track tackles, I would hear them calling out, "Tackle by number 25…tackle by number 25…tackle by number 25… He's making all the tackles!"

In the early days, one of our biggest challenges was to calculate mentally the length of a play when it started on one side of the 50 and ended on the other. For example, on a play that went from the 35 to the opposite 29, I would add the two numbers and subtract from 100: 35+29=64; 100-64=36. D.C.'s method, and he would say it softly, was: "That's 15 on one side and 21 on the other, total of 36."

For each play in the official account, each team gets a one-letter code, typically the first letter of the college, to designate where the ball is on any play—for example, "Ball on the O20." This often invites fun on our crew when we call out the play, such as in a game with Rutgers: "Ball on the R2," would be followed by, "Insert *Star Wars* joke here." When we called out plays with players' numbers, we would have similar opportunities.

When in future years Dwayne Haskins passed to Austin Mack, we would follow the "Pass 7-11" play code with, "He's always open."

Stadium officials are stationed at the entrances to confirm credentials, of course. One year, officials used a dog to sniff our belongings for contraband. At one game, we had to wait for the dog to arrive before we could enter.

This was a breakout year for Coach Cooper, posting his best record to date of 10-1-1. He would use two quarterbacks during games, Bobby Hoying and Bret Powers—something that he would repeat in 1996 and 1997.

The offense had 207 yards rushing and 246 passing—144 from Hoying and 102 from Powers and a touchdown pass by each—in the opening 34-7 win over Rice. This was a breakout year for Joey Galloway, who would finish with 946 receiving yards, and he had three catches for 92 yards and a score in this game.

In the 21-12 win over Washington, a night game, Galloway had 104 receiving yards and a score, and Raymont Harris ran for 102 yards and a score. The Huskies' quarterback was future broadcaster Brock Huard.

Butler By'not'e needed only 10 seconds to return the opening kick-off 89 yards for a touchdown in the 63-28 rout of the Pitt Panthers in Pittsburgh. Galloway had four plays from scrimmage and scored on three of them—two catches and one run. Galloway would take off his helmet on the field after his touchdowns, a practice that was later forbidden. Eddie George had two touchdowns on five carries, playing in his home state. Keith Wilkerson's only carry of the year went for 24 yards and a touchdown, with Archie providing insight on the TV broadcast that Wilkerson was from Florida, and Eric Moss's only catch of the year was for nine yards and a touchdown. Eleven ball carriers contributed to the 307 yards on the ground, led by Travis McGuire's 78 yards. Terry Glenn led the receivers with three catches for 80 yards; he would be even more explosive when the team returned to Pittsburgh in 1995.

Five Buckeyes had at least one touchdown in the 51-3 win over Northwestern, and the total offense edge was 428-162. Ten players had carries, and nine had catches, led by Galloway with six for 119 yards. The defense had five interceptions that averaged 29 yards per return; Walter Taylor had two.

Coach Cooper talked about getting the Illinois monkey off his back after the 20-12 win on a windy day in Champaign, getting his first win over the Illini in six tries. Tito Paul did not recover a blocked punt for a touchdown as he had the last two years, but he caused a fumble by the punter that freshman Terry Glenn recovered for a touchdown. Galloway had the other touchdown on an 11-yard catch on the first possession. It was the second straight game where the defense gave up no touchdowns.

Galloway had three touchdowns on nine receptions for 186 yards, and Raymont Harris had the winning score with 1:06 left in the 28-21 win over Michigan State. For the second time, both Hoying and Powers each had over 100 yards passing, and Harris finished with 103 yards on the ground. The Buckeyes won despite five turnovers.

The Buckeyes had two defensive touchdowns—a 100-yard interception return by Marlon Kerner and a fumble recovery by Matt Finkes—in the 45-24 win at Purdue. Kerner's tied the team record set by David Brown in 1986, also at Purdue. The total offense was 486 yards, with 364 on the ground. Harris ran for 118 yards and two scores, George for 96, and B'ynote' for 95. The Buckeyes had a 16-play drive which tied a record that will never be broken—a 98-yard drive resulted in no points and did not have a field goal kick. Finkes's fumble recovery followed that drive.

On a snowy October 30, the Buckeyes held Penn State without a touchdown in the 24-6 win. I saw a regatta taking place on the Scioto River in the snow on the way to the game. The field was chewed up, and not just by Raymont Harris's 151 yards. The defense picked off four Nittany Lion passes, with Taylor getting two again. Ki-jana Carter ran for 123 yards for Penn State. I had called one of Carter's Westerville South high school games for WCVO-FM. It was the largest crowd to see Penn State play on the road, to date.

Galloway caught a 26-yard pass from Powers with 3:48 left to cap a 99-yard drive in the 14-14 tie at Wisconsin. The Buckeyes blocked a 32-yard field goal attempt to preserve the tie and keep the Buckeyes undefeated. I recall Coach Cooper saying that the blocked field goal was exactly how they had drawn it up. For the third time, both Hoying and Powers each had over 100 yards passing.

The total offense was 419-238 in favor of the Buckeyes, but they had to hold on to beat Indiana 23-17. Harris ran for 162 yards, Galloway had 115 receiving yards, and it was the fourth time that both Hoying and Powers each had over 100 yards passing.

Going into the Michigan game, in order for the Buckeyes to be ineligible to go to the Rose Bowl, three things had to happen: the Buckeyes lose to Michigan, Wisconsin win at Illinois, and Wisconsin win over Michigan State (a game played in Tokyo) a week later. You guessed it—the Buckeyes went 0-for-3 and settled for the Holiday Bowl against Brigham Young.

The 28-0 loss to Michigan was the only time between 1983 and 1997 that I did not go to Ann Arbor, and I was totally fine with that. I had already attended one 28-point loss, in 1991. Total offense was 421-212 in favor of the Wolverines, who intercepted four passes.

I missed the first half of the Holiday Bowl, a 28-21 win, because I was covering the Columbus Horizon basketball game in the Columbus Convention Center. Harris carried 39 times for 235 yards and three scores. Tim Patillo blocked a punt and returned it 20 yards for the first touchdown. This meant that the last two touchdowns that the Buckeyes scored against BYU had come from the defense or special teams, going back to the 1985 season bowl game. The Cougars had a first-and-goal at the OSU six following a 52-yard pass play with under 40 seconds, but they misfired on all four passes, with two of them dropped. Coach Cooper had guaranteed that his 11th-ranked Buckeyes would win their postseason game, and his prophecy came true.

FUN FACTS:

- Joey Galloway had 11 of the Buckeyes' 15 touchdown receptions.

- Galloway had the longest reception and punt return

- Butler By'not'e had the longest run and kickoff return; it was the second straight year he had the longest kickoff return.

- The Buckeyes had a kickoff return for a touchdown against Pitt in five-year intervals—Byars in 1983, Snow in 1988, and By'not'e in 1993.

- By'not'e's kickoff return for a touchdown extended the team's overall five-year interval feat to five, having accomplished it in 1973, 1978, 1983, 1988, and 1993. They had no other kickoff returns for touchdowns between 1978 and 1993.

- The edge in rushing touchdowns was 25-6.

- Harris had 12 rushing touchdowns to the opponents' six.

- Marlon Kerner's 100-yard interception return was one yard longer than the opponents' total of 99 return yards.

1994 (9-4)

As in 1986, the first two games were on the road, and they would lose to Alabama and Washington away from home during each season.

Joey Galloway returned for his senior year and had a 67-yard touchdown catch in the 34-10 win over Fresno State at Anaheim Stadium in front of only 28,513 fans on a Monday night. He misjudged where the goal line was and pulled up early due to the confusing yard lines on the baseball infield. He added an 8-yard touchdown run, and Eddie George ran for two scores. It was the second straight year that the Buckeyes scored 34 in the opener.

Mark and I went to the Washington game in Seattle, a 25-16 loss. The Huskies jumped out to a 19-0 lead in the first quarter, scoring three times in less than five minutes. A key play was when tight end D.J. Jones dropped a pass that he never controlled in the red zone, and it was ruled a fumble. George ran for 108 yards, but Napoleon Kaufman of the Huskies ran for 211. Hoying passed for 288, with Buster Tillman catching nine passes for 106 yards.

With real estate a premium, the parking lot had essentially bumper-to-bumper parking, which meant that we had to wait for others to leave before we could even move our car. At the time, I thought that the $66 per night rate at a downtown hotel was outrageous. The next day, we went to the Snoqualmie Falls (www.snoqualmiefalls.com) and to Roslyn, where the TV show *Northern Exposure* had its exterior scenes filmed. At a restaurant in Roslyn, I chatted with a group of motorcyclists, and one of them found it hard to believe that I would travel from Ohio to see a football game. Mark was living in Los Angeles at the time and said that he was enjoying the fresh air of Washington. While in Seattle, I did the usual sightseeing activities, including the Space Needle, Underground Seattle, and a ferry ride to Bainbridge Island. I wanted to go to a Mariners game, but I had two obstacles—the Kingdome had four 15-pound acoustic tiles drop 180 feet from the ceiling into choice seats behind home plate, and a little thing called a MLB work stoppage.

The offense rolled up 512 yards—126 on the ground for George and 217 passing for Hoying—in the 27-3 win over the Pitt Panthers.

The offense was over 500 yards again with 553—373 in the first half—in the 52-0 win over Houston on a hot day in Columbus. George ran for 105 on his birthday, and Jermon Jackson scored three times, his only game of the year where he scored. Ten ball careers combined for 312 yards.

Northwestern scored the first nine points and the last six, but the

Buckeyes scored 17 in the third quarter to win in Evanston, 17-15. The Wildcats scored with 5:01 remaining, but their rush attempt for two points was stopped by the Buckeye defense, which held the Wildcats to 212 yards. Eddie George had 229 of the team's 315 yards, with 206 on the ground.

Illinois scored the last 17 points in their 24-10 win, their fourth straight in Columbus. George ran for 124 yards, and Hoying passed for 229.

Eddie George had more than 200 rushing yards for the second time with 219 in the 23-7 win at Michigan State. The game had the longest run of the year, a 76-yard score by George, and the longest interception of the year, a 35-yard return by Greg Bellisari for a touchdown, the team's only pick for a score in the season.

Chris Sanders led the Buckeyes in receiving touchdowns on the year, and he had two in the 48-14 win over Purdue. Galloway topped him with three. Hoying had 290 yards passing and four touchdown passes in the first half as the Buckeyes led 41-0, finishing with five touchdowns and 304 yards. The five touchdowns tied the team record held by John Borton in 1952. The Buckeyes had an even 500 yards of total offense. The Boilers had the longest play of the game, a 90-yard scoring strike that was also the longest pass play in Ohio Stadium. The Purdue coach was former OSU assistant Jim Colletto.

The roof caved in in the 63-14 loss to #1 Penn State, as the Nittany Lions outgained the Buckeyes 572-214 and led 35-0 at halftime. Stanley Jackson ran for his only touchdown of the year. Coach Cooper and the rest of the Buckeyes quickly grew tired of the Lion sound effect on the PA system.

Chris Sanders had two more receiving touchdowns in the 24-3 win over Wisconsin, with 107 yards in all and the longest play of the year, 78 yards. George had 104 of the team's 204 rushing yards, and Hoying passed for 207. The defense picked off four passes, two by Kerner, and held the Badgers to 49 yards on the ground. The all-time attendance at Ohio Stadium broke the 30 million mark. The Badgers would play another Ohio team the next week, the Cincinnati Bearcats.

Galloway had a 93-yard kickoff return for a touchdown in the first quarter, and the Buckeyes broke open a 19-17 game after three quarters to win at Indiana, 32-17. Hoying had scoring passes to Rickey Dudley and Sanders in the fourth quarter, and George ran for 118 yards and two scores.

The Buckeyes were outgained 271-210 in Coach Cooper's first win over Michigan, 22-6. It was the first time in 111 games that the Wolverines failed to score a touchdown. The Buckeyes scored on a touchdown, safety, and field goal in the first half. Marlon Kerner blocked a field goal, and Luke Fickell, a defensive lineman and the least likely player to have an interception, had one in the fourth quarter. I had worked the stats for a high school game between DeSales and Beechcroft a few years before, seeing future Buckeyes Coach Fickell catch a touchdown pass for DeSales.

Galloway had two touchdown catches in the second quarter of his final game as a Buckeye, but Alabama scored the winning touchdown with 42 seconds left in the Florida Citrus Bowl to win 24-17. Although Galloway had eight catches for 146 yards, the Tide had a 521-276 edge in total yards. It was the only game of the year for the Buckeyes without a rushing touchdown.

The game was held up for several minutes when a dog—later identified as Leo, who lived four blocks away and was not owned by Tide quarterback Jay Barker—came onto the field. The TV cameras caught a clearly displeased Alabama Coach Gene Stallings, whose team was on the move. There was an account after the game that some fans had seen the dog heading to the stadium before the game.

FUN FACTS:

- Galloway scored on receptions, a run, and a kickoff return.

- Galloway had the longest kickoff return and punt return.

- Both Eddie George and Archie Griffin had 12

136

touchdowns in their junior year and would win the
Heisman Trophy the following year.

- The opponents had 45 more passes and 30 more
completions, but the Buckeyes had a 19-11 edge in
passing touchdowns.

- The two leading receivers, Joey Galloway and Chris
Sanders, each averaged 15.2 yards per catch.

- The Buckeyes averaged three more passing yards per game.

- Young players on the team included two with bloodlines
to players who had led the Buckeyes in rushing—Kevin
Griffin (Archie's nephew) and Shawn Springs (Ron's son).

1995 (11-2)

In 1995, I would go to three road games, of which two were wins. You can
probably guess which game was the loss.

I drove to the Kickoff Classic in New Jersey, with the Buckeyes facing Boston College. I had planned to go to Indiana, Pennsylvania, to see
Jimmy Stewart's hometown, but I got on the Pennsylvania Freeway by
mistake. After consulting a map—yes, a paper map!—at a rest stop, I saw
that I could check out Punxsutawney by continuing on and taking another
route. Talking with some of the locals in the city of Punxsutawney, I was
disappointed to learn that the movie *Groundhog Day* was not filmed there
but in Woodstock, Illinois. My next hiccup occurred when traffic ground
to a stop on I-80 east of the Penn State area. If I had done some research,
I would have learned that the Little League World Series was going on in
Williamsport. I was lucky to exit and hop on another route.

The Buckeyes beat BC easily, 38-6. Eddie George kicked off his
Heisman year with two touchdowns and 99 yards, his only game under
100 that year, and Terry Glenn had a breakout game with three catches

for 105 yards. After a BC field goal to make it 7-3, I thought that Coach Cooper probably wished he had faster kick returners. After Shawn Springs returned the kick 97 yards for a touchdown, I decided to stop second-guessing the coach. Eleven Buckeyes carried the ball, and nine had receptions.

Traffic was a minor issue at the Meadowlands, unlike when I returned there in 1999. Shopping for a hotel near the Meadowlands, I found the Mountain View Inn, which sounded like an idyllic spot in a secluded area, but learned that there is no such prospect in that locale. I stopped in Lancaster, Pennsylvania, on the way back to see my cousin Jim and his wife Kay.

The Buckeyes had 15 more minutes of possession in the home open- ing 30-20 win over Washington. Eddie George ran for 212 yards and two touchdowns. The Huskies had 10 penalties for 101 yards, the Buckeyes only one for eight yards.

I went to the Pitt game in Pittsburgh, a 54-14 rout, a game that was only 20-14 at halftime. If the BC game was a breakout game for Terry Glenn, the Pitt game was a shattering one with nine catches for 253 yards and four touchdowns. Hoying passed for 296 of the team's 421 passing yards and five of the team's seven passing touchdowns, and George ran for 122. It was the only game of the year without a rushing touchdown for the Buckeyes.

After 60 years, the Buckeyes and Notre Dame met again in Columbus, a 45-26 win. Notre Dame had interrupted their series with Michigan to play the Buckeyes in 1995 and 1996. I met a gentleman who had been at the 1935 game and asked him if it was true that the game had been played in black and white. There was some question if the Irish's Coach Lou Holtz would be on the field. He would be, walking slowly while wearing a neck brace.

After a scoreless first quarter, the Irish led 17-7 before Dimitrious Stanley made a twisting catch in the end zone for a score with 44 seconds left in the first half. Terry Glenn gave the Buckeyes a 28-20 lead with an 82-yard catch and sprint late in the third quarter. He finished with 128 receiving yards. Eddie George had his fourth career game of 200 plus yards with 207, a long of 61, and two touchdowns. Hoying passed for 272 and four touchdowns. The two teams combined for 980 yards, and it was the most points scored on a Lou Holtz Notre Dame team. My parking pass as a member of the stats crew allowed me to park a few steps from the stadium on the west side, so it was an easy exit. The game set an Ohio Stadium attendance record of 95,537; in '95, it was the first ever home game of at least 95,000.

The Buckeyes played at Penn State for the second straight year, trailed 10-0 for the second straight game, and won 28-25 on an Eddie George 6-yard run with 1:28 left. Hoying passed for 354 yards and three touchdowns, with Glenn accounting for 175 and two scores. George ran for 105 yards, and the team had a huge break when his apparent fumble was not recognized by the officials. The leading rushers were George, born in Pennsylvania, and Penn State's Curtis Enis, born in Ohio. Rickey Dudley had a huge game with a 25-yard touchdown catch and 97 yards in total.

The Buckeyes trailed Wisconsin 16-13 heading into the fourth quarter before two Eddie George touchdown runs, the last one 51 yards, produced a 27-16 win. The Buckeyes had 207 yards on the ground and 206 through the air. George finished with 141 yards and three scores.

George ran for 104 yards, and Hoying passed for 276 yards and three scores in the 28-0 win over Purdue. Terry Glenn had two touchdown receptions, setting the single season record with 12. The punt return team blocked two punts and tackled the punter on a third. Greg Bellisari had the longest run for either team, 27 yards on a fake punt.

The Buckeyes played a near-perfect first half, leading 56-0 just before halftime only to see Iowa score on the last play to make it 56-7, and the offense took the second half off in the 56-35 win. In the first half, George scored four times and Glenn twice, and Shawn Springs had a 60-yard interception return for a score. George finished with 110 yards, Glenn with 149, and Hoying with 273, all of those in the first half. Bellisari had two interceptions. Iowa had five more yards, 16 more plays, two more first downs, and 5:40 more possession time.

An unfortunate event during the 49-21 win over Minnesota in the Metrodome was Terry Glenn's leap for a catch and fall to the turf where he bounced like a basketball on the hardwood. As a result, he had to leave the game with a slightly separated shoulder. Prior to that unlucky incident in the game, he had three catches for 103 yards and a score, breaking the team season record for yards in a season. George had the longest run of the year, an 87-yard touchdown run on the first play of the second half, and 178 total on the ground plus eight catches for 86 more yards. Hoying passed for 287 yards and two scores, with 219 in the first half.

Eddie George jump started the offense in the second half with a 64-yard touchdown run on his way to setting the team's single game record of 314 yards in the 41-3 win over Illinois. He ran for two touchdowns and caught a pass for another, all in the third quarter. He also led the team with four receptions. Brent Musberger called him the Heisman winner, so you can pretty much take it to the bank. The defense gave up a season-low 160 yards.

Terry Glenn returned after a week off and caught two touchdown passes in the 42-3 win over Indiana. He had 103 yards, and George ran for 130 and two scores. Hoying passed for 203 yards and set the team single season record for passing yards, and the team set the single season record for most points. The defense held the Hoosiers to 168 total yards.

Mark and I went to the Michigan game in Ann Arbor, a 31-23 loss. Each team scored in each quarter. Trailing 31-15, the Buckeyes cut it to 31-23 with 6:33 left and advanced to the Michigan 34 before throwing an interception. Tim Biakabutuka, who had two carries for 15 yards in the 1993 game and two carries for three yards in last year's game, erupted for 313 yards for the Wolverines. George had 104 of the team's 106 yards on the ground, and Hoying passed for 286.

Rickey Dudley caught a 32-yard scoring pass in the fourth quarter to tie Tennessee at 14-14, but the Volunteers kicked two field goals to win 20-14 in the Citrus Bowl. Hoying out-passed sophomore quarterback Peyton Manning 246-182. George ran for 101 yards and Dudley finished with 106 receiving yards.

For the third time in OSU history (previously 1975 and 1979), the Buckeyes started 11-0 and lost in the bowl game. It was the Buckeyes' second straight Citrus Bowl in Orlando. I recall OSU President Gordon Gee saying that he wished Orlando Pace's mother had named him Pasadena instead of Orlando. Spoiler alert: Things would change in 1996.

FUN FACTS:

- Eddie George had 24 of the team's 29 rushing touchdowns.

- Eddie George's 24 rushing touchdowns were seven more than the opponents' total.

- George ran for 1,927 yards, and the opponents ran for 1,891.

- Terry Glenn's 17 touchdown catches were seven more than the opponents' total.

- The edge in passing touchdowns was 33-10.

- Tom Hoying completed two passes, both for touchdowns.

- The edge in interceptions was 24-13.

- Shawn Springs had the longest kickoff return and interception return, both for touchdowns.

- Alonzo Shavers's only catch of the year was for a seven yard touchdown.

- In OSU's first game on the road in 1992, 1993, 1994, and 1995, Eddie George had three, two, two, and two touchdowns, respectively.

- Eddie George and Archie Griffin each had one receiving touchdown in his career.

- Eddie George was second on the team with 47 receptions. He had none as a freshman and sophomore.

- Team members included Bobby and Tom Hoying, whose grandfather, Wally Post, played for the Cincinnati Reds, and Steve Wisniewski, whose great uncle, Kiki Cuyler, played for the Reds and is in the National Baseball Hall of Fame.

1996 (11-1)

Replacing the likes of Eddie George, Terry Glenn, Bobby Hoying and others would be a tough task, right? The Buckeyes re-loaded and came within a whisker of being national champions in 1996. Not even Urban Meyer's high-powered offenses would accomplish what the Buckeyes did in the first two games, scoring 70 and 72 points.

The offense had 317 yards on the ground and 315 passing in the 70-7 opening win over Rice. Freshman Michael Wiley had three touches for three touchdowns—a 49-yard run, a 60-yard catch, and a 51-yard catch. Pepe Pearson ran for 119 yards, and both Joe Germaine and Stanley Jackson passed for over 150.

The offense had over 600 yards again in the 72-0 win over Pitt, making it 126 points against the Panthers in the last two years. Joe Montgomery ran for 109 yards and Pearson for 103, and 11 Buckeyes caught a pass. Freshman David Boston had a 66-yard punt return for a touchdown—with only seven other teammates on the field.

Mark and I went to the game at Notre Dame, a 29-16 win to sweep the Irish in consecutive years. I flew to Midway Airport in Chicago, my flight being delayed an hour, making me nervous, and we drove to South Bend. On the airport shuttle, I saw former Groveport Madison coach

Bob Starr, who was on our stats crew calling the defensive plays for home games and was also on his way to the game. While in the Columbus airport, I saw the brother of a former co-worker, who asked me if I had seen the morning newspaper. I happened to have it with me and opened it to the local section to see an article about his sixth-grade niece who had performed the Heimlich maneuver on a classmate. She was quoted as saying that at first, she thought the kid "was fooling around because you know how little boys are."

Our seats were in the first row of an end zone, close enough to the field for us to shake hands with ESPN's Chris Fowler as he walked by. The stadium was being renovated to expand the capacity, with 59,075 at this game. Construction is visible in aerial shots. Our vantage point was perfect to see Dimitrious Stanley return the opening kickoff 85 yards coming right at us and perfect to see him run out of gas at the 13. Pearson ran for 173 yards and two touchdowns, and Stanley Jackson passed for two scores. Luke Fickell had an interception; he saved his for big games, having one against Michigan in 1994.

The fourth quarter had several big plays. On the opposite side of the field from our seats, Damon Moore made a one-on-one tackle on a fourth-and-11 play from the OSU 26 to stop the receiver two yards short of the first down. With the score 29-16 and with under four minutes left, the Irish returned a punt 90 yards for an apparent touchdown. As we were agonizing, behind us a lady listening to the radio broadcast on headphones matter-of-factly informed us: "There's a penalty flag on the field." The return was called back, and Rob Kelly intercepted Ron Powlus seven plays later. All six touchdowns were scored by Ohio natives. Notre Dame's Marc Edwards, a Cincinnati product, scored both of their touchdowns. I would have a chat with him a few years later when he played in a celebrity all-star basketball game. On the staff for the Irish was receivers coach Urban Meyer.

The Buckeyes outgained Penn State 565-211 in the 38-7 win. Pearson ran for 141 yards, both Jackson and Germaine passed for two scores, and Dimitrious Stanley had 105 yards receiving and two touchdowns.

Stanley had the big play the next week, a 48-yard reception for the winning score with 8:51 remaining in the 17-14 win over Wisconsin. He had 199 yards receiving, Stanley Jackson passed for 265 yards, and the defense held freshman running back Ron Dayne to three yards per carry and 65 yards.

Purdue jumped out 14-0 on touchdown passes of 86 and 55 yards, but the Buckeyes had 42 unanswered points in the 42-14 win in West Lafayette. The last three touchdowns were on plays of 63 yards or longer and three different ways—a 63-yard pass play to freshman running back Matt Keller, a 64-yard run by Pearson, who had 152 on the day, and a 79-yard fumble return by Rob Kelly. The defense picked off three passes.

Five Buckeyes scored a touchdown as the team had a 38-6 lead and won 38-26 at Iowa. Joe Montgomery ran for 160 yards and a score. Even defensive coordinator Fred Pagac marveled at the speed of the Hawkeyes' Tim Dwight, who had an 86-yard punt return for a score, 131 punt return yards in all, and a 19-yard run for another score.

The Buckeyes dominated Minnesota both on the scoreboard, 45-0, and in yards, 452-104. Pearson ran for 123 yards, and four passers, including Pearson with a 21-yard completion, combined for 222 yards, to eleven receivers. Freshman linebacker Andy Katzenmoyer returned an interception 42 yards for a score.

The defense made it back-to-back shutouts by blanking Illinois 48-0 at Champaign, scoring all their points in the middle two quarters. Counting the previous week, the total offense in the two games was 1,001 to 234. Pearson ran for 165 yards, with 160 in the first half, and two touchdowns. He had the team's longest run of the year of 76 yards.

The Buckeyes trailed Indiana 10-7 after three quarters but used two defensive touchdowns to beat Indiana 27-17 and clinch a trip to the Rose

Bowl. Matt Finkes returned a fumble caused by Katzenmoyer 45 (as in Katzenmoyer's jersey number) yards, and Damon Moore had a 28-yard interception return. Pearson ran for 130 yards, and Boston had 13 receptions for 153 yards and a score.

Joe Germaine had his only start of the year in the 13-9 loss to Michigan in Columbus. The Buckeyes dominated the first half, 220-62 in total yards, but they managed only three field goals. Pearson ran for 107 of his 117 yards in the first half. Like the Buckeyes' win in 1987, Michigan scored on a 70-yard drive on their first possession of the second half, scoring on the infamous slip by Shawn Springs that allowed Tai Streets to complete a 69-yard pass play from Brian Griese, whose high school was Christopher Columbus in Miami.

Fun Fact: OSU's John Lumpkin and Michigan's Tai Streets also played on their respective basketball teams.

David Boston scored the first and last touchdowns, the winner with 19 seconds left, in the 20-17 Rose Bowl win over Arizona State, exactly ten years after Coach Cooper's Arizona State team beat Michigan (quarterbacked by Jim Harbaugh) in the Rose Bowl. Dimitrious Stanley had the longest reception of the year, on a 72-yard pass from Germaine (playing a team from the state where he played in high school) in the third quarter, and had 124 yards in the game.

ASU's first touchdown was a 25-yard pass to Ricky Boyer—Did he catch it? Did Antoine Winfield interfere with him? The defense held ASU quarterback Jake Plummer to minus five yards rushing, but he Snaked his way 11 yards for the go-ahead touchdown with exactly 100 seconds remaining. Germaine led the 65-yard, 12-play winning drive that ended with Boston strutting five yards into the end zone with the catch. In the official account, one play is "complete to a button-hooking Stanley," and another is "lobbed incomplete."

Pearson ran for 111 yards—more than 100 for the fifth straight game—with a 62-yard run in the fourth quarter that led to a blocked field goal attempt. The defense held ASU to 75 yards rushing and 1.8 yard average.

It was the sixth straight year that the Buckeyes' bowl game had been decided by seven points or less. After the game, tight end John Lumpkin took off for Ann Arbor to play in the basketball game the next day and score two points against the Wolverines, in a 73-71 win. Not a bad few days for him, with two wins by a total of five points and his birthday on New Year's Eve.

FUN FACTS:

- The edge in rushing touchdowns was 27-8.

- Pepe Pearson's 17 rushing touchdowns were nine more than the opponents' total.

- The edge in passing touchdowns was 28-6, although the opponents had 26 more passes.

- Stanley (eight) and Boston (seven) had more receiving touchdowns than the opponents.

- The Buckeyes had a 288-29 edge in interception return yards.

- The Buckeyes scored more points in the second quarter than the opponents scored in the season.

- Seven defenders had an interception return at least as long as the opponents' long of 19 yards.

- Joe Montgomery, Jermon Jackson, and Michael Wiley averaged 6.8, 6.3, and 7.7 yards per carry, respectively.

- Stanley Jackson (12) and Germaine (15) had more touchdown passes than the opponents.

- Matt Calhoun and Michael Wiley each had six catches for three touchdowns.

- Dimitrious Stanley had the longest reception and kick-off return.

- Matt Finkes's two career touchdowns came in the state of Indiana.

1997 (10-3)

The opener, originally planned to be against Oregon but switched to Wyoming, was a 24-10 win on a Thursday night and a homecoming for Cowboy Coach Dana Dimel, who replaced Purdue-bound Joe Tiller and is a graduate of nearby Upper Arlington High School. Dimel was not the only Upper Arlington grad with coaching duties that day; Jon Tenuta was the Buckeyes' defensive backs coach. Stanley Jackson's longest run of the year was for 41 yards and the Buckeyes' first score of the year.

Sixteen days later, sophomores Michael Wiley and David Boston had two consecutive touchdowns each in the 44-13 win over Bowling Green—Wiley with a 100-yard kickoff return and a 7-yard run, and Boston with two short receptions. Wiley also completed a pass of 31 yards, one of four Buckeyes to complete a pass. The total offense edge was 428-169, as the defense held the Falcons to 36 yards rushing.

The Buckeyes led Arizona 28-0 after three quarters and held on for a 28-20 win, recovering an onside kick with 2:26 remaining. Four Buckeyes scored a touchdown, including Katzenmoyer returning an intercepted shovel pass for a score. Germaine and Jackson were both seven of eleven passing and over 100 yards, with Boston catching seven passes for 131 yards.

I went to the Buckeyes' 31-10 win over Missouri in Columbia. A highlight was Andy Katzenmoyer's hard tackle on Tiger quarterback Corby Jones, where Katzenmoyer came on an angle to Jones on a run and knocked him sideways. Germaine came in mid-game and passed for 186 yards and two touchdowns, both to Boston, who had over 100 yards receiving for the second straight game. The defense had three interceptions.

This was the year that Missouri lost to Nebraska in overtime on the same field, thanks to the Huskers scoring on the last play of regulation when Matt Davison made a diving catch of a tipped and kicked football thrown by eventual Cornhusker coach Scott Frost.

Traffic back to St. Louis on I-70 after the game was so slow that many drivers elected to take a shortcut by crossing over the grass shoulder on the right to a service road. On Sunday, undeterred by an announcement on the radio that it was a sellout, I went to the Cardinals baseball game, the last game of the season, and saw Mark McGwire, acquired mid-year, hit his 58th home run and Ryne Sandberg of the Cubs play his last game.

Stanley Jackson bounced back with a solid game the next week against Iowa, a 23-7 win. Pearson ran for 106 yards, and Wiley ran for two scores.

Mark and I went to the Penn State game in Happy Valley, a 31-27 loss, taking different flights. The closest hotel that I could find was 40 miles away in Clearfield. Penn State scored the first 10 points and the last 14, on runs of 51 and 26. In between, Joe Germaine came in for Stanley Jackson and went wild with 378 passing yards and two touchdowns. A key play before the 26-yard run was Ahmed Plummer getting his hands on a potential interception, but the receiver knocked it loose. Boston and Dee Miller combined for 302 receiving yards, Boston with 14 catches. The Buckeyes had a 565-445 advantage in total offense, but they gave up 211 yards on the ground to Curtis Enis. Each team had 26 first downs.

Similar to the Arizona game, four Buckeyes scored a touchdown with one on an interception in the 31-0 win over Indiana. Clinton Wayne scored on the pick in the second quarter, making it three defensive scores against the Hoosiers in as many quarters, dating back to last year. Gary Berry added two more interceptions. Total offense was 432-179 in favor of the Buckeyes.

The Buckeyes had not played Northwestern the past two years, the Wildcats having gone to the Rose Bowl in the 1995 season, so they took out their frustration in a 49-6 win, trailing 3-0 after the first quarter. Three quarterbacks combined for five touchdown passes—three by Germaine and one each by Jackson and Mark Garcia. Tom Hoying's only catch of the year was for 29 yards and a score, and Pearson ran for two scores. Total offense was 563-164 in favor of the Buckeyes, and first downs were 32-9.

The offense scored twice in the game, and Gary Berry scored twice on defense in the first quarter on an interception and a blocked punt return in the 37-13 win at Michigan State. The offense had 202 yards on the ground and 203 through the air, with Boston catching eight passes for 119 yards.

Germaine passed for 211 yards and three touchdowns, two to Boston, in the 31-3 win at Minnesota. The Buckeyes had a 359-157 edge in total offense and 18-6 in first downs. Berry had an interception for the second straight game.

Ahmed Plummer had the team's fourth and longest interception for a touchdown, 83 yards, in the 41-6 win over Illinois. Pearson ran for 111 yards, Dee Miller had 103 receiving yards, and Boston caught a touchdown pass from both Jackson and Germaine.

The Buckeyes had two offensive touchdowns to Michigan's one, a 252-189 edge in total offense, and held the Wolverines to 42 yards rushing but lost in Ann Arbor, 20-14. The defense held Michigan to 45 yards in the second half. Charles Woodson had a 78-yard punt return for a score and an interception in the end zone, and the Wolverines returned another interception for a touchdown. Jackson had no interceptions entering this game. David Boston caught a 56-yard touchdown pass, the team's longest of the season, from Joe Germaine in the third quarter, and Pearson scored on a 2-yard run with 13:08 remaining after Jerry Rudzinski recovered a fumble forced by Gary Berry. Of the five combined touchdowns, two of them were on drives of 62 and 72 yards, and the other three had a total offense of two yards.

Antoine Winfield was his usual terror on defense—he would win the Jim Thorpe Award the next year—to the point that Keith Jackson called it the Antoine Winfield Show. Rudzinski had the longest run of the game, 20 yards on a fake punt. Andy Katzenmoyer nearly returned a blocked PAT for two points and nearly had an interception with a clear route to the end zone in the fourth quarter. I had worked some of his Westerville South High School games where he was also a running back, mainly a blocking back.

The Buckeyes returned to the Sugar Bowl 20 years after losing to Alabama in 1977 and lost to Florida State 31-14 to drop to 0-3 overall against Bobby Bowden's Seminoles. Having faced Bear Bryant 20 years ago meant that the Buckeyes had matched up in the Sugar Bowl against two coaches who had the most all-time wins at some point.

The Buckeyes had a 21-18 edge in first downs, 20 more plays, and outscored FSU in the second half. John Lumpkin had the only touchdown on a 50-yard pass from Germaine. Perhaps the Buckeyes should have arranged more carries for Rudzinski, since his other carry in 1997 was for 24 yards in this game on another fake punt. The official account of the game played in the Superdome shows the wind as "None" and the Weather and Temperature as "Indoors."

The last two games of the year were against teams that were the national champions in 1997 (Michigan) and in 1993 and 1999 (Florida State).

FUN FACTS:
- Tom Hoying threw a touchdown pass in 1996 and caught one in 1997. Michael Wiley caught three touchdown passes in 1996 and threw one in 1997.

- The edge in passing touchdowns was 26-7, even though the opponents had 21 more passes.

- Boston had 14 receiving touchdowns, compared to the opponents' seven.

- Boston had the longest reception and punt return.

- Pepe Pearson had 10 rushing touchdowns, the same as the opponents.

- The longest pass for both Joe Germaine and Stanley Jackson was 56 yards, with both going to David Boston.

- For the second straight year, Germaine (15) and Jackson (eight) had more touchdown passes than the opponents (seven).

- In the two games with the smallest attendance, at Missouri and Minnesota, the Buckeyes scored 31 points in each.

- The defense had four interceptions for touchdowns.

- Antoine Winfield led the defense with exactly 100 tackles.

1998 (11-1)

After two years of sharing with Stanley Jackson, Joe Germaine had the quarterbacking position all to himself. Some wise guy said that with Reggie Germany and David Boston as receivers, Germaine would need a strong arm in order to throw to Germany and Boston.

For the night game opener at West Virginia on Labor Day weekend, a 34-17 win, I was in Louisiana on vacation. By coincidence, OSU's final touchdown was scored by Jonathan Wells, who was born in Louisiana. He was one of four Buckeyes to score a touchdown. The Buckeyes had a 549-310 edge in total yards. Wiley ran for 140 yards, Germaine passed for 301, and Boston and Dee Miller each had over 100 receiving yards and a score.

Reggie Germany had two receiving touchdowns, and the total offense edge was 512-194 in the 49-0 win over Toledo. Wiley had 151 yards on the ground, with two scores and his longest run of the year of 76 yards. Eleven Buckeyes carried the ball, five threw a pass, 10 had receptions, five defenders had an interception, and Germaine had three touchdown passes.

Wiley ran for 209 yards and two scores, and Boston had 112 receiving yards as the total offense advantage was 531-211 in the 35-14 win over Missouri, trailing 14-13 at halftime.

The defense held Penn State to 181 yards and nine first downs, Jerry Rudzinski scored on a fumble recovery, and Joe Cooper scored on a blocked punt in the 28-9 win over Penn State. Dee Miller had over 100 yards receiving against the Nittany Lions for the second straight year.

Five Buckeyes had a touchdown each, and the defense scored for the second straight game, on a fumble return by Na'il Diggs, in the 41-0 win at Illinois. Germaine passed for 307 yards and three touchdowns, and the total offense advantage was 518-199. The defense held the Illini to 43 yards on the ground. I was in Athens, Ohio, at the time seeing the Bobcats play Marshall and Chad Pennington. It was an impressive sight—Peden Stadium was filled with fans of both teams wearing green, and cars were parked anywhere they could.

The defense scored for the third straight game on a 60-yard interception return by Central McClellion, and the total offense edge was 586-271 in the 45-15 win over Minnesota. Wiley ran for 119 yards, and Germaine passed for 339, including 191 and two touchdowns to Boston.

I went to the Northwestern game in Evanston, a 36-10 win. Montgomery ran for 100 yards, and Germaine passed for 342 (231 in the second half) and three scores, with Boston catching eight passes for 171 and two scores. The total offense advantage was 524-238. Steve Bellisari was a defensive back as a freshman, though he would see some time at quarterback, and had one of the team's three interceptions.

Germaine passed for 351 yards, with 159 to Dee Miller and 110 and two scores to Boston (who had 153 yards at Indiana in 1996) in the 38-7 win at Indiana. The Hoosier quarterback was future NFL wide receiver Antwaan Randle El, who passed for 218 yards.

The Buckeyes were 9-0 and ahead of Michigan State, which would finish 6-6 on the year under Nick Saban, 24-9 with under 10 minutes left in the third quarter after a 73-yard interception return for a touchdown by Damon Moore. Moore's interception was so quick that, watching from the press box, I thought that the Spartans had completed the pass and the receiver was heading for the end zone, finally seeing that Moore was streaking the other way. The Spartans rallied for a 28-24 win, though the Buckeyes had a first-and-ten on the Spartan 15 with under two minutes left. There was no doubt in my mind that the Buckeyes would score, but Germaine misfired on all four passes, ending with an interception. The defense gave up only 22 points in the fourth quarter all year but gave up 10 in this game. MSU had also spoiled undefeated potential regular seasons for the Buckeyes in 1972 and 1974, with those games in East Lansing.

Joe Montgomery had the team's longest run of the year, 80 yards, and Mike Collins returned an interception for a score in the 45-14 win at Iowa. The Buckeyes dominated total offense, 627-180, with Montgomery running for 144 yards, Germaine passing for 319, and Boston recording 163 yards and two touchdowns in receptions.

It seemed as if Michael Wiley and David Boston were running at twice their usual speed in the 31-16 win over Michigan. Wiley had a 53-yard scoring run in the first three minutes, and Boston had 217 yards and two touchdowns, giving him three against Michigan in the last two years. Germaine passed for 330 yards and three touchdowns. Michigan had 24 more plays, and Tom Brady passed for 375 yards. The defense held the Wolverines to four (no typo) yards on the ground, sacking Brady seven times. This made Michigan's rushing total 46 yards in the last two matchups. Counting this game, the Buckeye defense had given up only two touchdowns in the last 13 quarters at home against Michigan, both by Tai Streets.

The Buckeyes played in the Sugar Bowl for the second straight year and beat Texas A&M 24-14, scoring all their points in the first half. Boston had 105 receiving yards, and the Buckeyes had a 432-283 edge in total yards. Kevin Griffin scored on a 16-yard blocked punt return

25 years after his uncle Archie had his only touchdown in a bowl game. In the two bowl games against the Aggies, three of the Buckeyes' seven touchdowns came from the defense or special teams. The Buckeyes raised their record to 4-0 against Texas A&M, with all four games either the first or last of a season.

It was the first time since 1982 that the Buckeyes had won the Michigan game and the bowl game in the same season. For the second time in three years, a four point loss at home to a team from The State Up North had denied the Buckeyes a shot at a national championship.

FUN FACTS:

- The Buckeyes had a 26-8 edge in passing touchdowns after a 26-7 edge the previous year. This year's advantage came even though the opponents had 34 more passes.

- Boston had 13 receiving touchdowns, compared to the opponents' eight.

- Six Buckeyes had a pass attempt.

- The Buckeyes scored more points in the first quarter than the opponents scored in the season.

- The edge in rushing touchdowns was 22-6.

- Wiley (10) and Montgomery (seven) had more rushing touchdowns than the opponents.

- For the second straight year, Dan Stultz scored 92 points. He missed one extra point and had 25 field goal attempts each year.

- For the second straight year, David Boston had the longest reception and punt return.

- David Boston's longest reception by year was 58, 56, and 58 yards.

- Dee Miller's longest receptions in his last three years were 43, 45, and 42 yards.

- The two players who would return in 1999 and had the most receptions in 1998 were Michael Wiley and Matt Keller, and they had 200 yards each in 1998.

- Thirteen defenders had an interception.

1999 (6-6)

I worked the spring game for TV, and while future spring games would draw 90,000-plus fans in Ohio Stadium, the Horseshoe was being renovated, and so this spring game was played at the practice field south of the Woody Hayes Athletic Center in front of a handful of fans. The broadcasters and I were on a scissors lift that swayed in the wind. The big question in this game was who would succeed Joe Germaine at quarterback—Steve Bellisari or Austin Moherman?

Beverly and I went to the opening game against Miami in the Meadowlands, flying into Philadelphia. On a hot day, the Hurricanes won 23-12. Moherman got the start, and the offense managed only 220 yards, with Wiley having a 69-yard run, his longest of the year. Hurricane assistant coaches included Larry Coker and Greg Schiano. Parking at the stadium was a free-for-all with no one directing the cars, and it was hard to find our rental car after the game.

Toledo had played in Columbus the year before, and Toledo appeared again this year—Coach Bob Toledo of UCLA. Moherman (who played high school ball in California) and Bellisari split the quarterback duties, with Bellisari passing for two touchdowns in the 42-20 win over the Bruins in a night game. Wiley ran for 119 yards, and Germany had 115 yards in receptions as the offense rolled up 507 yards. Wiley and Ken-Yon Rambo, both from California, each had two touchdowns in the game against a team from California, and UCLA's first touchdown was by Matt

Stanley—who played high school ball in Bexley, Ohio—on a 67-yard play off a deflected pass, his only score on a pass in his career. Bellisari had the team's longest pass and the longest run of the game, 39 and 30 yards.

OSU and Ohio were tied at 10 at halftime, but the Buckeyes scored 24 in the third quarter to win 40-16, with a 449-229 edge in total yards. Wiley ran for 98 yards and two touchdowns, Bellisari passed for 243, and Rambo had 181 yards in receptions and two scores.

The Buckeyes trailed 17-3 and were tied at halftime again with another Ohio team, 17-17 with the Cincinnati Bearcats, before winning 34-20. Four different Buckeyes scored, and Rambo had another monster game with 164 yards on three receptions. On the Bearcat staff was future head coach Jimbo Fisher.

The 1999 OSU-Wisconsin game was on the Big Ten Network recently as a Classic, and I was not recalling what the significance was. I was feeling good when the Buckeyes jumped out 17-0 but not so much when the Badgers poured it on to win 42-17. This was Ron Dayne's Heisman year, and he ran for 161 yards and four touchdowns. In Dayne's four years, the only two matchups with the Badgers were in 1996 and 1999 in Columbus.

Jonathan Wells ran for the winning score with 5:13 remaining to get the Buckeyes a 25-22 win at Purdue. Bellisari passed for 174 yards and ran for 96, including a 68-yard run. Each team had a touchdown on a trick play—Wiley threw a pass to Darnell Sanders, Sanders' only catch of the year, and Purdue's Vinny Sutherland had one to Drew Brees (heard of him?).

I was out of town for the game at Penn State and was spared seeing LaVar Arrington wreak havoc in the 23-10 Nittany Lion win. Arrington had three tackles for loss totaling minus 19 yards. The Buckeyes' only touchdown came on a fumble recovery by Gary Berry, as the offense managed only 143 yards. The Lions' Eric McCoo ran for 211 yards, the same as Curtis Enis had the last time that the Buckeyes visited Happy Valley.

Dan Stultz kicked 43- and 40-yard field goals in the fourth quarter, the last one with 1:15 remaining in the 20-17 win at Minnesota. Wiley ran for 118 yards and the two Buckeye touchdowns and completed the longest pass for the Buckeyes, 28 yards to Bellisari.

Bellisari passed for 240 yards and two touchdowns, and Rambo had 179 receiving yards in the 41-11 win over Iowa. The defense picked off three passes.

Michigan State had 30 more plays and held the Buckeyes to four first downs and zero net yards rushing in their 23-7 win in East Lansing. Wiley had the only touchdown on a 4-yard reception.

The first downs were even, and the total yards were only 12 apart, but the Buckeyes fell behind 19-0 and lost at home to Illinois 46-20. Wiley ran for 128 yards and two scores.

The Buckeyes followed their worst performance of the year with one of their better ones, even in losing to Michigan 24-17. The Buckeyes were up 17-10 and looking to add on when Jonathan Wells broke off a 76-yard run, the team's longest of the year, down the right sideline, but he cut toward the middle of the field at the end instead of keeping on a straight line. He was brought down at the Michigan 6-yard line, and Dan Stultz missed a 30-yard field goal after a bad snap. Both touchdowns were on unconventional pass plays—a 6-yard pass to tight end Kevin Houser, who had six receptions on the year, and a 1-yard pass to fullback Jamar Martin, his only touchdown catch and third reception of the year.

For the fourth straight year in this matchup, the Buckeyes had more total yards, 368-252, but were only 1-3 in those four games.

FUN FACTS:

- Ken-Yon Rambo had the longest reception and kickoff return.

- Entering the 1999 season, Michael Wiley had 1,999 career rushing yards.

- Michael Wiley was a perfect five-for-five in passing, for 123 yards and a touchdown.

- The edge in passing touchdowns was 15-14, even though the opponents had 53 more passes and 71 more completions.

- Jamar Martin and Darnell Sanders combined to catch four passes for two touchdowns.

- In 1998 and 1999, the Buckeyes had Percy King and Heath Queen on defense. Offensive lineman Isaiah Prince would come along in the Urban Meyer years.

- In each of his four years, the versatile fullback Matt Keller had a longer reception than a run.

CHAPTER 6

The 2000s
The Tressel Years

2000 (8-4)

I WORKED THE SPRING GAME, which was played at Crew Stadium—later renamed to Mapfre Stadium. Late in the game, Coach Cooper put player #8 at a wideout, and I said to myself, *Who is #8?* Coach Cooper had given Steve Bellisari a series at wideout.

The opening 43-10 win over Fresno State was in the renovated stadium, and it looked odd to see the sunken field and no track. The Buckeyes had four defensive touchdowns—two on fumbles and two on interceptions—with the first two scores of the game coming that way. David Mitchell had two of the scores on a fumble return and an interception, and the defense had a total of four interceptions. The game saw each team throw a touchdown pass in the last five seconds. After the Bulldogs scored, Coach Cooper had freshman Scott McMullen launch a 44-yard bomb to Ricky Bryant. Another freshman, Craig Krenzel, was two-for-five in relief of Bellisari. The Buckeyes were only +17 on total offense, first downs were 22 each, and time of possession was 30 minutes each. All six Buckeye touchdowns were scored by players who had never scored before.

Our stats crew location was now in a private room, with the visiting assistant coaches to our left. With a window separating them from us, the coaches would paper the windows with newspaper so that we could not see in. One year, I was able to peek through a tiny seam between the papers and catch a glimpse of Joe Paterno.

Mark, Beverly, and I went to the Arizona game in Tucson, a 27-17 Buckeyes win where they trailed 17-10 at halftime but blanked the Wildcats in the second half. Chad Cacchio became an extra receiving weapon, finishing second on the team with four touchdown receptions, and he had a 60-yard score in this game. The defense held Arizona to 194 yards, with nine sacks for minus 57 yards, and Bellisari passed for 240 yards and another score.

On one Wildcat pass play that was ruled a catch, the replays clearly showed the ball hitting the turf short of the receiver. The TV color announcer said something like, "Yeah, you can see that it's a catch," followed by the play-by-play announcer's diplomatic, "Well, I guess the camera lies sometimes." We could see a light rain in the stadium lights, but we could not feel it. It was as if the heat of the desert was evaporating it about 100 feet up.

We went to Old Tucson, which is, quoting https://www.visittucson.org/business/old-tucson, "one of Arizona's top Wild West attractions, featuring live action stunt shows, musicals and live entertainment ... walking the same streets made famous by movie legends such as John Wayne, Clint Eastwood, Elizabeth Taylor and Kurt Russell. Immortalized in more than 400 films and commercial productions."

The game against the Miami RedHawks was tied at 10 at halftime before the Buckeyes pulled away, 27-16. Going back to the 1999 season, it was the third straight game against an Ohio team that was tied at halftime. Derek Combs ran for 142 yards and Jonathan Wells for 113, and Rambo had six catches for 100 yards—the only time in OSU history that a receiver has had exactly 100 yards in a game. Miami quarterback Mike

Bath ran and passed for all but 27 of their 368 yards. Three Buckeye defenders picked off one of his passes.

Six different Buckeyes scored a touchdown in the 45-6 win over Penn State. The defense held the Nittany Lions to 213 yards, and Mike Collins scored on an 11-yard fumble return.

Beverly and I went to the Wisconsin game in Madison, a 23-7 win. Derek Combs finished with 122 yards on the ground and did his best Keith Byars impersonation, losing a shoe on his 80-yard touchdown run, the team's longest run of the year. Bellisari fooled the Badgers by concealing the ball then throwing a 20-yard touchdown pass to Darnell Sanders. The defense had its second game of recording nine sacks.

The next day, we checked out the National Mustard Museum in nearby Middleton. We had flown to Madison through Detroit, and I can tell you that the Detroit airport had the best French Fries.

October 14 was the Homecoming game, and ironically, it was a homecoming for Minnesota Coach Glen Mason, a former Buckeye player and assistant coach who would be a candidate to follow Coach Cooper the next year. He would celebrate with a 29-17 win, giving the Buckeyes their first loss. The offense mustered only 200 yards—no reference to the National Mustard Museum.

I listened to the Iowa game, a 38-10 win, on the radio on my way to Upper Sandusky, where I was the color announcer for Time Warner's broadcast of the Pumpkin Bowl, a doubleheader of games between eighth-grade teams. Five different Buckeyes scored a touchdown, and the total offense advantage was 446-246, with the defense recording eight more sacks and holding the Hawkeyes to 13 net yards on the ground. Bellisari passed for 315 yards, with Rambo collecting 130 receiving yards and Germany 123, each with a score.

The Buckeyes had a 20-10 lead after three quarters, but they gave up three touchdown passes by Drew Brees in the fourth, including a 64-yard score with 1:55 remaining, to lose 31-27 at Purdue. Nate Clements had an 83-yard punt return for the 20-10 lead. It was the same score as the loss at Penn State in 1997, where the Buckeyes also gave up a ten-point lead. The Buckeyes intercepted Drew Brees four times, three in the first half. He passed for 455 yards, with 307 in the second half, three Purdue receivers had at least 100 yards, and the Boilers had a 486-278 edge in total yards. The only consolation in this result was that Purdue also beat Michigan this year.

Brent Musberger punctuated Purdue's winning touchdown pass with "Holy Toledo!" and called it an instant classic. Spoiler alert: He would revise his exclamation in the matchup in two years.

The Buckeyes trailed Michigan State 13-3 heading into the second quarter, but they blanked them the rest of the way in the 27-13 win. Combs ran for 153 of the team's 157 yards, with 105 in the second half, and Mike Doss had a 73-yard return of a fumble for a score.

In the 24-21 win over Illinois in Champaign, Dan Stultz kicked a 34-yard field goal at the final gun, his fourth of the game. Fifteen years earlier in the same stadium, the Illini had a similar finish as time expired—a 38-yard field goal to win 31-28. Eighteen years earlier in the same stadium, the Buckeyes kicked a field goal with three seconds remaining to break a 21-21 tie and beat the Illini. Stultz has the distinction of attempting a field goal in five seasons. Jonathan Wells ran for 131 yards, and Bellisari passed for 251, with both of his touchdown passes going to Darnell Sanders, who led the team with five catches for scores on the year.

In the Michigan game, the Buckeyes led 9-0, fell behind 31-12, rallied to 31-26, but fell 38-26. It was the fifth straight game in the rivalry where the Buckeyes had more total yards, with a record of 1-4. Bellisari passed for 251 yards, same as last week, and Wolverine quarterback Drew Henson passed for 303. Henson would later play third base for the Columbus Clippers minor league baseball team from 2001 through 2003.

The Buckeyes trailed only 10-7 after three quarters in the Outback Bowl in Tampa, but they lost to South Carolina and Coach Lou Holtz,

24-7. These two teams had a combined record of 6-17 in 1999, with South Carolina going 0-11. The Buckeyes' only touchdown came when offensive lineman Mike Gurr recovered a Jonathan Wells fumble in the end zone. Ryan Brewer, an Ohioan from Troy, scored all three touchdowns for South Carolina; he entered the game with one previous touchdown.

This was Coach Cooper's last game. I would later work the stats for a few televised high school games where he was the color announcer. Coach Cooper and Coach Holtz were the two coaches inducted into The National Football Foundation & College Hall of Fame in 2008.

FUN FACTS:

- Nate Clements led the team with 513 yards on punt returns. The only punt that he did not return went for a loss of three yards.

- For the second straight year, Ken-Yon Rambo had the longest reception and kickoff return.

- Six players attempted a pass, including punter B.J. Sander and punter/place kicker Dan Stultz.

- Dan Stultz, who had 92 points in 1997 and 1998, had 91 points.

- The defense gave up 111 points in each half.

2001 (7-5)

I was happy with the choice of Jim Tressel to be the next coach. In one press conference, he quizzed Steve Bellisari on what is the most important play in football—Bellisari did not know that the answer was the punt.

Jonathan Wells ran for 119 yards and two touchdowns, including the first of the Tressel era, in the opening 28-14 win over Akron. Bellisari passed for 246 yards, with 106 going to Michael Jenkins, and the total offense edge was 525-248. Chris Gamble joined Jenkins in having his first career reception as a Buckeye. The Akron quarterback was future Cleveland Brown Charlie Frye. On a Buckeye pass interference call, I saw Coach Tressel waving his hand over his head, the first time that I had seen a motion for an uncatchable pass.

The Buckeyes were idle the next week due to 9/11, and two weeks later, they lost to UCLA at the Rose Bowl, 13-6. The offense managed only 45 yards passing and 166 total. This was the first glimpse of a feature of Tressel-ball, scores by special teams and defense, as the Buckeyes' only score came on a return of a punt—the most important play in football—blocked by Mike Doss and scored by Ricky Bryant. Bryant would score both of his OSU touchdowns against teams from California, having caught a pass in the Fresno State game last year.

Mark, Beverly, and I went to the Indiana game, a 27-14 win where freshman Lydell Ross ran for 124 yards and two touchdowns. We experienced the infamous traffic snail's pace leading to Bloomington and arrived after kickoff. It was impossible to find a hotel room, even in Indianapolis. I finally found one in downtown Bloomington. One hotel employee told me on the phone that they were on "lockdown" due to an auto race.

Jonathan Wells ran for 179 yards and three touchdowns—one of them 71 yards, the team's longest of the year—as the Buckeyes jumped out 38-7 and beat Northwestern 38-20 in a night game. Mike Doss had a 30-yard fumble return for a score.

The Buckeyes led 17-7 at halftime, but they went scoreless in the second half in the 20-17 loss to Wisconsin in Columbus. This was the third straight year the visiting team won the game between the two teams.

October 20 was to have been a bye situation, but the San Diego State game from September 15 was moved to this date. The Buckeyes trailed 12-6 at halftime before winning, 27-12. Derek Ross had two of the team's four interceptions. Krenzel missed the game to attend his sister's wedding.

The Buckeyes led Penn State 27-9 in the third quarter on three big-play touchdowns—a 66-yard reception by Michael Jenkins, a 65-yard run by Wells, and a 45-yard interception return by Derek Ross—but lost 29-27 in Happy Valley. The big play for the Nittany Lions was a 69-yard missed-tackles run by quarterback Zack Mills. Wells ran for 143 yards, and Jenkins had 172 on four receptions, including another for 68 yards to the Penn State 1-yard line, where the Buckeyes had to settle for a field goal by Mike Nugent. Do the math in this two point loss! Nugent had a 34-yard attempt blocked with 2:55 remaining. Ross had a second interception, and Cie Grant also had one.

Chris Vance put on a show with five catches for 101 yards and a score in a 31-28 win over Minnesota in the Metrodome. Wells ran for 152 yards and two scores.

Vance had another circus catch, a one-handed snag in the back of the end zone in the 35-9 win over Purdue. Vance finished with 138 yards, Bellisari passed for 263, and Wells had his third straight game of 100 plus with 101 yards. Total offense was 429-211 in favor of the Buckeyes. Four different Buckeyes scored a touchdown, and the defense recorded two safeties.

Bellisari was suspended for the next two games, so Scott McMullen got the start, and Craig Krenzel relieved him in the 34-22 loss to Illinois, a loss despite having 40 more yards of offense. The Buckeyes had led 22-21 heading into the fourth quarter. Wells had another big game with 192 yards, Jenkins had 10 receptions for 155 yards, and Vance had a score in his third straight game.

In the 26-20 win at Michigan, 310 days after Tressel became the coach, Wells had three touchdowns in the first half—giving him five against Michigan in the last two years—including a 46-yard run on a fourth-and-one play. He finished with 129 yards, outgaining the Michigan team by 12 yards. Krenzel played the entire game, and the team had only one turnover, compared to five by the Wolverines. The defense had four interceptions, including Doss with returns of 35 and 36 yards inside the Michigan 10-yard line, and freshman Dustin Fox ended the game with his only pick of the year. For Doss, they were two of his three interceptions for the year, and for Tim Anderson, it was also his only pick of the year. The Buckeyes benefitted from a safety on a botched snap to the quarterback and a dropped pass that would have been a touchdown.

The Buckeyes re-matched with South Carolina in the Outback Bowl, fell behind 28-0 in the third quarter, tied it up at 28 with 1:54 remaining, but lost 31-28 on a field goal on the final play. It was the same score and same finish as the 1985 Illinois game. In that game, the coach's son kicked the winning field goal. In this game, the coach's son, Skip, was an assistant on his staff. Lou Holtz could not beat the Buckeyes while at Minnesota or Notre Dame, but he went 2-0 at South Carolina.

In the halftime interview with the score 14-0, Coach Tressel said "We're going to play better in the second half." With the score 28-0, the Buckeyes had been outscored 48-3 going back to the Michigan game. South Carolina completed a two point conversion to make it 28-0; an unsuccessful result would have produced a different outcome.

Cie Grant had given the Buckeyes another chance with an interception to put the ball at the Buckeyes' 18-yard line with 1:12 remaining, but Bellisari was intercepted to set up South Carolina's winning field goal. If Coach Tressel had a crystal ball to foresee his success in overtime the next two years, would he have played that possession more conservatively?

Craig Krenzel started, but he had a total of six runs and passes and gave way to Bellisari, who passed for 320 yards (269 in the second half) and two touchdowns to Darnell Sanders and ran for another. Spoiler alert: The next time Krenzel would play in a losing game as a starting quarterback would be in October of 2003. Jenkins, playing in his home city of Tampa, had eight receptions for 152 yards, with 118 yards in the second half. Bellisari is a Florida native, and Lydell Ross, another Tampa native, had the team's longest run of 13 yards on his only carry.

The Buckeyes did not lose consecutive games in 2001 and finished 7-5, with four of the five losses by seven points or less, which shows how close they came to going 11-1. The combined record was 21-15 over the last three years. Spoiler alert 2: Things would change in 2002.

FUN FACTS:
- The 26-20 score of the Michigan game was virtually identical to the Buckeyes' average for the year—26.0 on offense and 20.3 on defense.
- The fumble and interception returns for touchdowns were by Ross (Derek) and Doss (Mike).
- The Buckeyes were 2-0 in front of the two smallest attendances, at Indiana and Minnesota.
- The edge in rushing touchdowns was 25-14.
- Jonathan Wells's 16 rushing touchdowns were two more than the opponents' total.
- Derek Ross had 194 interception return yards, compared to the opponents' total of 175.

2002 (14-0)

A scene before the season would even start is one of my all-time favorite memories: Mike Doss's press conference where, in tears, he said that he was returning for his senior year to win a national championship.

The opening 45-21 win over Texas Tech on an 83-degree "pleasant" (according to the official account) day was Maurice Clarett's debut, and he ran for 175 yards and three touchdowns, two of them 59 and 45 yards, adding four receptions to lead the team. The TV camera caught Coach Tressel trailing Clarett down the sideline on one of his scoring runs. The defense held the Red Raiders to 31 yards on the ground. The Texas Tech quarterback was Kliff Kingsbury, the eventual Arizona Cardinals coach. Dustin Fox had an interception in his second straight regular season game.

The *Columbus Dispatch* story the next day included a line that the fans were yelling, "Maurice! ... or was it 'more ice!'?"

Clarett had only 66 yards, but he had a rushing and a receiving touchdown in the 51-17 win over Kent State. Mike Doss and A.J. Hawk had pick-six interceptions, with Hawk failing to hand the ball to an official, breaking one of Coach Tressel's rules. Chris Gamble had six receptions to lead the team, and Andy Groom took the day off from his punting duties. Kent State had a 22-17 edge in first downs, and their quarterback was future Cleveland Brown Joshua Cribbs, who had 254 yards in total offense.

The Buckeyes trailed Washington State 7-6 at halftime before winning, 25-7. Clarett ran for two touchdowns and 230 yards, with 194 in the second half. The defense held the Cougars to 17 yards on the ground, with a long of 18. Coach Tressel—Gasp!—was not wearing his iconic sweater vest.

An injury forced Clarett to sit out the 23-19 win over Cincinnati, a game that I witnessed at Paul Brown Stadium, with Krenzel scoring the winning touchdown on a twisting 6-yard run with 3:44 remaining. Lydell Ross filled in for Clarett with 130 yards. It was a hot day, but not hot enough for Coach Tressel to shed his sweater vest. A friend of mine told me later that he had consumed six bottles of water. It was a big weekend in Cincinnati. With the Reds' final series in the old ballpark and Oktoberfest going on, the city was expecting a half million people in downtown. The game notes show that the game set attendance records for Paul Brown Stadium and for any sporting event in the Cincinnati area. We should have known that this was a good omen, playing in a stadium named for the coach who brought OSU its first national championship, 60 years ago—a coach also in his second year at OSU.

Late in the game, the Buckeyes had a defensive back wearing number 7, and I said to myself, *Who is number 7?* I was not alone, as the broadcasters were surprised, too. This was the first appearance of Chris Gamble as a defensive back, and he picked off a Bearcat pass in the end zone. All three Bearcat turnovers were in the fourth quarter, with both interceptions in the end zone.

The Bearcats had four cracks at the end zone from the OSU 15, but they misfired on all four passes, with Will Allen intercepting in the end zone—the exact same yard line and sequence as in the Buckeye loss to Michigan State in 1998. The Bearcats had a 415-292 edge in total yards.

Clarett returned for the 45-17 win over Indiana and ran for 104 yards and three touchdowns. Gamble had the longest run of the game, 43 yards for a score, the longest of his three carries on the year. The defense held the Hoosiers to 56 yards on the ground. Jenkins caught a touchdown pass from both Krenzel and McMullen, who was a perfect seven-for-seven.

I went to the Northwestern game in Evanston, a 27-16 win, somehow being able to buy a ticket at the game. This was the game in which Maurice Clarett had 140 yards and two touchdowns, overcoming three fumbles. Wildcat fans felt that they were robbed when an apparent touchdown pass to Mark Philmore, a Reynoldsburg High School grad, was ruled a no-catch.

The total offense was 567-265 in favor of the Buckeyes in the 50-7 win over San Jose State. Clarett ran for 132 yards and two touchdowns, Krenzel passed for 241 and three scores, and Jenkins had seven catches for 136 and a score. San Jose State had zero yards rushing.

As the Buckeyes had another nail-biting 19-14 win at Wisconsin, I was on my way to Massachusetts on a vacation to see the Naismith Memorial Basketball Hall of Fame in Springfield. In the Columbus airport, I hoped to catch part of the game on a TV. However, the TV at a bar had the Florida Gators game on. I asked the bartender if he would switch to the Buckeyes game, and I had to ask myself if I was really in Columbus when he replied, "No. These guys (motioning to men sitting at the bar) want to see the Florida game!"

The game-winning drive was 88 yards, capped by a 3-yard pass to Ben Hartsock. Gamble had an interception in the end zone on the Badgers' next possession, with 7:09 remaining. Clarett ran for 133 yards, and Jenkins had 114 in receptions—including a 45-yard catch on the winning drive—and a touchdown. This was the fourth straight year in the matchup where the visiting team won.

Gamble (#7) intercepted Zack Mills (#7) and zig-zagged 40 yards for a touchdown in the 13-7 win over Penn State, and DID hand (more like, flip) the ball to an official. Of his seven career interceptions, this was the only one with return yards. Gamble had 31 receptions on the year without a touchdown, so his second and last touchdown of the year was most timely. The defense held the Nittany Lions to 179 yards—58 in the second half and 352 fewer than last year—with two other interceptions, one by end Will Smith for his only pick of the year.

In the 34-3 win over Minnesota, the defense held the Golden Gophers to 53 net yards on the ground, with 51 in losses, and 59 passing yards, giving up a total of 291 in the last two games. Chris Vance had a touchdown reception against Minnesota for the second straight year.

For the Craig Krenzel-to-Michael Jenkins "Holy Buckeye" (Brent Musberger had exclaimed "Holy Toledo!" in the 2000 Purdue win) 10-6 win at Purdue, I was at a conference in San Diego and saw none of the game. I asked a Buckeyes fan at the conference if he knew the outcome, and he raised his arms in the O-H formation with the good news. However, he gave the wrong account of the ending, saying that the Buckeyes led 10-3 and that Purdue kicked a late field goal. The 37-yard pass came with 1:36 remaining, with Jenkins (#12) beating Purdue's defender #12. Jenkins also blocked a punt in the game.

The defense held Purdue to 56 yards on the ground, with a long of seven yards by quarterback Brandon Kirsch, while Krenzel's 15-yard run was the longest of the game. Gamble had an interception at the OSU 11-yard line with 45 seconds left to seal it. Dustin Fox had a pick in the end zone on Purdue's first possession. Jenkins and Gamble combined for 138 of the team's 173 receiving yards and combined for all 46 of the team's punt return yardage, with Gamble having the longest of the game, 22, and the most yards, 35.

Calling that game, Brent Musberger swore that the Buckeyes did not get the kick off in time as the first half wound down for the field goal, but he ate his words when he saw the replay.

After the game, Boiler fans serenaded the team with "Overrated!" to which the team responded, "Undefeated!"

The Illinois game the next week was ending as the high school play-off game that I was working was starting at Grove City High School. We could see fans listening to the Buckeyes game in their cars, then scurrying into the stadium after the Buckeyes pulled out another win. For the second straight week, the Buckeyes had no touchdowns in the first half. The Illini's John Gockman kicked a 48-yard field goal as time expired to force the overtime, and Maurice Hall had the winning touchdown in overtime. Krenzel had a 14-yard scramble on third-and-ten to set up Hall's score. Tim Anderson knocked down the Illini's last pass to seal the win.

In the first quarter, Krenzel stretched the ball to the end zone pylon, but he was not given the touchdown. After three false start penalties, they had to settle for a Mike Nugent field goal. Jenkins had six catches for 147 yards (of the team's 176) and a 50-yard touchdown. Jenkins (#12) had the only touchdown in regulation of win #12 on Krenzel's 12th touchdown pass. The 23-16 score meant that OSU gave up 16 points twice in 2002 to the two teams based in Illinois, with both games in the state of Illinois and in the two lowest attended games of the year.

Friends ask me what my favorite Michigan game is, and my answer is this 14-9 win, since it seemed as if every play was crucial, and it led to a national championship.

Clarett (#13) had the first touchdown of two yards in game #13, and Hall had the winning one of three yards. This was the third straight game of the season in which all the touchdowns were scored by Jenkins or a player named Maurice, with Maurice Hall scoring the winning touchdown for the second straight game. For the fourth straight year in the rivalry, the losing team had more total yards. Krenzel was 10 (as in Big 10) for 14 (as in 14 points in the game and 14 wins on the year) in passing. The Buckeyes had only 17 plays in the first half, nine of them on the touchdown drive.

Will Allen's interception on the last play was the only one for either team in a combined 62 passes. His two interceptions on the year that sealed the wins over Cincinnati and Michigan netted no return yards, but no one was complaining. The only two turnovers of the game were Michigan's fumble with 2:02 remaining and Allen's interception. For the second straight year, the Michigan game ended with the Buckeyes intercepting. In the 2001 and 2002 Michigan games, the Buckeyes' edge in turnovers was a combined seven to one.

This was Clarett's 10th game of the year. He rushed for 119 yards, exactly 10% of his 1,190 yards to that point, in the game to win the Big 10 championship. He had the longest run for either team, 28 yards, and the longest reception for either team, 26 yards on a wheel route. He had a touchdown run in the south end zone, just as Archie had 30 years ago as a freshman in the win over Michigan when the team also scored 14 points.

It was the same score as the 1981 Michigan game and had the same scoring pattern: Michigan up 3-0, OSU up 7-3, OSU up 7-6, Michigan up 9-7, OSU wins 14-9.

Our booth in the press box has a huge, heavy sliding glass window that muffles the crowd noise. After this game and after every win over Michigan, we open the window. Going from quiet to the roar of the crowd is amazing! In later years, the fans would sing along to *Sweet Caroline*, perhaps earning an entry in the Guinness World Records book?

Mark and I went to the Tostitos Fiesta Bowl national championship game against the Miami Hurricanes in Tempe, the 31-24 win in double overtime. As an OSU employee, I was in a lottery for tickets, and it took a third drawing before I won the right to buy tickets. I was on my way home from the OSU-Duke basketball game in Greensboro, North Carolina, when I saw the email with my good fortune.

The day after the title game, we went to the Suns-Lakers game, which the Suns won 107-93. Kobe Bryant scored 37 points, Shaquille O'Neal had 25, and Whitehall product Samaki Walker had five for the Lakers.

It was warm enough in Tempe that I could have gone swimming in the hotel's outdoor pool. The official account of the game lists the weather as "beautiful." We saw Jack Tatum before the game and had our picture taken with him. Our seats on the 45-yard line in the upper deck were incredible. Looking up behind us in the VIP section, we saw that Governor Bob Taft and his wife were seated on the 40-yard line. How did we rate a better location than the governor? We had sat in the first row of an end zone at Michigan State in 1975, at Washington in 1994, and at Notre Dame in 1996, so this more than balanced out those locations. A co-worker later said that he had great seats "right on the 10-yard line." I held my tongue. One perk at the game was the all-you-can-eat Tostitos and salsa.

The Buckeyes were playing Miami for the third time in 25 years, none of them in Miami, and I was at all three. Miami was #1 and OSU #2, and Larry Coker had won the national championship in his year #1 (2001), and Jim Tressel would win his in his year #2 (2002). This was the third straight year where the opposing coach was a former OSU assistant coach.

On the Buckeyes' punt on their first possession, Keith Jackson alerted us to how dangerous Miami's Roscoe Parrish was as a punt returner; we would find out on the last punt of the game. Cie Grant left with a bruised rib on the first possession on defense, but he returned shortly. Spoiler alert: He would make a big play with the game on the line. In the previous bowl game, he also was shaken up in the first half and came back with a big play near the end.

Krenzel's only completion in the first quarter was 12 yards to Jenkins (#12) and gave the quarterback exactly 2,000 yards to that point. You can see red-shirted Troy Smith in uniform on the sideline congratulating Jenkins on the catch. It was the Buckeyes' first first down of the game and came with less than 30 seconds left in the quarter.

Gamble had the longest play of the game on offense—and the Buckeyes' longest reception of the year—a 57-yard catch in the third quarter on a third-and-15 play before the Sean Taylor interception in the end zone where Clarett ripped the ball away on the return. Branden Joe coming out of the backfield was uncovered on the play, but Krenzel tried to hit Ben Hartsock in the end zone. It would have been Joe's second touch of the year; he had one carry for one yard otherwise. Clarett hustled to make the play after picking himself off the ground from making a block, and Woody Hayes would have scolded Taylor for carrying the ball in his inside arm. Nugent kicked a 44-yard field goal (an OSU record 25th in a season) to make it 17-7, meaning that the scoring run in bowl games the last two years for the Buckeyes was 45-10. If the 57-yard pass had not been a tad underthrown so that Gamble did not have to wait on it, he may have scored.

Nugent missed a 42-field goal—shorter than the one that he had made—with 6:36 left in regulation. He was 25 of 27 on field goals on the season before this one.

Andy Groom and Mike Doss combined on a touchdown-saving tackle on Roscoe Parrish's

50-yard punt return with 2:02 remaining in regulation. It reminded me of the 1993 Holiday Bowl, where Ty Howard made a touchdown-saving tackle on a 52-yard pass play on BYU's last possession. Larry Coker was an OSU assistant coach in that Holiday Bowl. Both Howard (Briggs) and Groom (Bishop Hartley) attended high school in Columbus. For Groom, this was his only assisted tackle of the year. Simon Fraser, another central Ohio product, recorded his only tackle of the game two plays later, sacking Ken Dorsey.

Miami's Todd Sievers kicked a 40-yard field goal on the last play to force overtime. It was the second straight bowl game with the opposing kicker kicking a field goal on the last play of regulation, and the kickers had similar names—Weaver and Sievers. For some reason, the official account shows the field goal good with one second remaining. It does show the time as three seconds when the play begins after three timeouts, so, apparently, the kick was in the air for only two seconds. When interviewed on TV at halftime, similar to his halftime prediction in the previous bowl game, Coach Tressel had said, "It's going to be down to the final seconds."

It also meant that the opponent kicked a field goal as time expired to force overtime in two of the last three games of the 2002 season, including the Illinois game. Keith Jackson was 0-for-2 winging it on his recollection of the Oklahoma game of 1977, 25 years ago, when he could not recall Uwe von Schamann's name and thought that his field goal was 43 yards. In fact, it was 41 yards.

During the timeout before the fourth down play that resulted in the pass interference call in the end zone on the pass to Chris Gamble, Dan Fouts said that Jenkins and Ben Hartsock were the first two options. However, Krenzel immediately went to Gamble, the lone receiver on the right side, outside the hash marks—more on hash marks later. The full-game replay of the game does not capture the premature fireworks and streamers in Miami's colors.

Regardless of whether Miami fans agree with the pass interference call by official Terry Porter on the play to Gamble, it had to be a case of karma. Replays showed Kelly Jennings grabbing Gamble's jersey on a pass play before the punt and showed that Gamble may have caught the ball inbounds anyway. TV analyst Dan Fouts was more emphatic about the Chris Gamble penalty play ("Bad call ... bad call") than he was about the obvious grab of Gamble's jersey previously. The first overtime drive took 11 plays to cover the 25 yards.

In the second overtime, Krenzel hit Jenkins with a short pass that could have been intercepted. Clarett scored the winning touchdown from five yards out, making it the third straight game that a player named Maurice scored the Buckeyes' winning touchdown. Maurice Hall had also scored the last touchdown of the game against Minnesota, making it four of the last five games where a Maurice had scored the last touchdown.

Similar to the 1997 Rose Bowl (see David Boston), a freshman scored the winning touchdown in the north end zone, it was a five yard play in each case, and it was his second touchdown of the game. Each player has two syllables in his first and last name.

On Miami's second overtime possession, Matt Wilhelm floored Ken Dorsey and knocked him out of the game for a play. It turned out that Wilhelm's family was staying at our hotel, and at breakfast the next day, we had a chat with his brother.

Miami's Quadtrine Hill had no touches in the game until their last possession, when he caught a third down pass from the backup quarterback and had a carry for no gain on third-and-goal from the 1-yard line. Cie Grant bind-side pressured Ken Dorsey on 4th-and-goal from the 1-yard line, and Donnie Nickey knocked down the pass to close out the win. Grant had a late big play in the bowl game last year, an interception with 1:12 remaining, and is from New Philadelphia, Ohio. Woody, who coached there, must have been smiling.

The two overtimes had a total of three defensive penalties in the end zone, one of them declined when Kellen Winslow had the go-ahead touchdown, and Gamble was involved in the last two, one as a receiver and one as a defensive back. The Buckeyes had almost three more minutes of possession time in the game, including seven more after the first quarter. They had 14 first downs and 14 incompletions in win #14.

The scene of Tim Anderson consoling Dorsey after the last play is one of my all-time favorite images of sportsmanship. Another magic number was 34—this broke Miami's 34 game winning streak, and it was the Buckeyes' first national championship won on the field in 34 years.

Each team was six of 18 on third downs. The Buckeyes were two of three on fourth down (matching their success rate for the season)—scoring their first touchdown, the pass to Jenkins in the first overtime, and unsuccessful on a fake field goal. Miami was one for two on fourth down—successful to keep the drive alive on their last possession and unsuccessful on the last play of the game.

The Hurricanes had more total yards, 369-267, but the Buckeyes had the longest reception and the longest run. The longest run for OSU was 11 yards, by Krenzel, and for Miami was 10 yards. For the second straight bowl game, the longest Buckeye run was by a quarterback, with Bellisari having the longest in the previous season. Both of Krenzel's interceptions came on passes inside the hash marks. All seven Buckeyes receptions were completed outside of the hash marks. All seven receptions against a team from Florida were by natives of Florida—Jenkins, Gamble, and Vance. Krenzel did attempt passes to Clarett, Hartsock, Branden Joe, and Bam Childress, but they are from Ohio, so that would have spoiled the story. In the previous year's bowl game, Jenkins, Vance, and Gamble, playing in their home state, combined for 15 of the 22 receptions.

Four of the five Miami turnovers were claimed by players from Ohio: Clarett, Will Allen, Dustin Fox, and Mike Doss. Fox and Doss had the two interceptions, each on a third-down play, and each is from Canton. The fifth turnover was caused by Kenny Peterson, another Canton native.

Three of Jenkins's four receptions gained first downs—including the one for 17 yards on fourth-and-14 (there's that number 14 again) to set up the score in the first overtime—and the one that did not gain a first down did put the ball on the Miami 5-yard line, with Clarett scoring the winning touchdown on the next play. Clarett had only 47 yards, but 40 of them came after halftime. Six of Krenzel's seven completions gained first downs, and the two longest completions (57 and 17 yards) came on 3rd-and-15 and 4th-and-14 plays.

For Simon Fraser, it meant that for the second time in three seasons he had played on an undefeated championship team, adding to his state title at Upper Arlington High School in 2000, that team going 15-0. For Mike Doss, it made three championships in six years, including his two state titles with Canton McKinley in 1997 and 1998. Cities named Utica were good to the Buckeyes—Krenzel is from Utica, Michigan, and Will Smith, tied for the most solo tackles in the game with six, was from Utica, New York. In last year's bowl game, Smith led the Buckeyes in assisted tackles with six. Krenzel led all rushers with a career high 81 yards, 16 more than Miami had as a team. His seven completions netted 122 yards, matching the 122 that Kellen Winslow had by himself, and his 203 total yards matched the digits of the calendar year of the game. The Buckeye defense gave up five rushing first downs per game in the 2002 season, and held Miami to only three.

The five Buckeyes scores came on "drives" of 17, 14, 1, 25, and 25 yards, with the two longest ones taking place in the overtimes. This was similar to the Buckeyes' second-half performance in their previous national championship game against USC in the 1968 season, where the last two touchdowns came on drives of 21 and 16 yards. As in the win over USC, the defense recorded five turnovers.

Six of the seven touchdowns were in the south end zone; the only one in the north end zone was the winning one. Both field goals were in the north end zone, and all four interceptions—two by each team—were thrown with the team going toward the north. Miami's four punts were 43, 43, 43, and 44 yards. Miami had scored at least 26 points in each regular season game.

In his book *One and Done*, Maurice Clarett writes that the night before the Michigan game, Coach Tressel had Clarett and Cie Grant room together for the first time. Think of that — they were the players who made the last big play on offense and on defense against Miami.

In three games this season, the opponent had a first down inside the Buckeyes 16-yard line and four plays on their last possession to keep the game alive. To me, that more than made up for the 1998 loss to Michigan State, when the Buckeyes had four plays at the Spartan 15-yard line on their last possession.

- Cincinnati: from the Buckeyes' 15-yard line
- Illinois: from the Buckeyes' 11-yard line
- Miami: from the Buckeyes' 2-yard line

Listing some of the "what-ifs" … if any of these had gone otherwise, the outcome would have been different, and would we have called this one of the best games of all time?

- What if the Buckeyes had kicked a field goal instead of running on a fake?
- What if the 57-yard pass to Gamble had not been a tad underthrown?
- What if on the pass intercepted by Sean Taylor in the end zone, Krenzel had thrown to Branden Joe, wide open outside the hash marks, instead of throwing to Ben Hartsock inside the hash marks?
- What if Sean Taylor, intercepting about five yards deep in the end zone, had not decided to bring it out? When he caught the ball, his momentum was toward the center of the field, though he quickly pivoted to the left sideline.
- What if Sean Taylor had carried the ball in his outside arm following his interception?

- What if Nugent had made his 42-yard field goal? He had only one other miss in the season between 40 and 49 yards, out of 11 attempts.

- What if the obvious grab of Gamble's jersey had been called, or if his catch along the sideline had been ruled a completion?

- Miami had used the shotgun formation a few times in the game. If they had had Ken Dorsey in the shotgun instead of under center on the last play, would Cie Grant have blitzed, or if he did, would Dorsey have seen him? Miami had both of their touchdown passes with the Buckeyes blitzing.

I compare the 2002 season to the 1969 season of the New York Miracle Mets.

- Both teams made a dramatic improvement over the year before.

- The Buckeyes played the national champions of the previous year, and the Mets played the team (Baltimore) that would win the World Series the next year. Both the Hurricanes and the Orioles have orange as one of their colors.

- Jim Tressel and Gil Hodges (same number of syllables) were in the second year of leading his team.

- Both teams made huge defensive plays in the championship game/series.

- Both teams won with offenses in unconventional ways. The Buckeyes won with their quarterback using his legs. The Mets won both games of a doubleheader in the regular season by 1-0 scores where the pitcher drove in the only run.

FUN FACTS:

- Seven of the team's last 11 wins were by seven points or less. In those seven games, the defense gave up no touchdowns and a total of three field goals in the fourth quarter.

- Texas Tech, Kent State, Cincinnati, and Indiana, which had a combined record of 22-30, each scored as many points or more in regulation against the Buckeyes than Miami did.

- Chris Gamble had the Buckeyes' longest reception, longest kickoff return, longest punt return of the year, and the most interceptions.

- Gamble's longest reception of 57 yards and Jenkins's longest of 50 yards came in the two overtime games. No other Buckeye had a reception longer than 37 yards.

- Gamble's longest reception of 57 yards and longest run of 43 yards add up to 100.

- Gamble had the longest punt return for the second straight year.

- Gamble had all four of his interceptions in games decided by seven points or less, and all four were in the second half.

- Three of Gamble's four interceptions ended up in an end zone—two in the opponent's end zone and one on a return against Penn State.

- The leaders in kickoff returns and punt returns—Hall and Gamble—had a different jersey number in 2001.

- For the second straight year, the leaders in interceptions—Derek Ross and Chris Gamble—wore #7 and had an interception for a touchdown.

- The edge in interceptions was 18-7.

- On October 26, Will Smith had an interception for no return yards. On the corresponding weekend 15 years earlier, on October 24, David Brown had an interception for no return yards. Each is from Utica, New York.

- Andy Groom averaged 44.95 yards per punt, after averaging 44.98 yards last year.

- The edge in rushing touchdowns was 31-5.

- Clarett (16) and Lydell Ross (six) had more rushing touchdowns than the opponents had in total.

- Clarett had 222 carries for 1,237 yards and a 5.6 average per carry in his only year with the Buckeyes. The 222 carries matched the number that Keith Byars had in his first year (1983) of significant action with the Buckeyes, when he had 1,199 yards and a 5.4 average. Each had two touchdowns in the bowl game that year, in the same stadium, against a team currently in the Atlantic Coast Conference.

- In the wins over Cincinnati, Purdue, and Miami—where the combined scoring difference in regulation was eight points—Krenzel had the team's longest run.

- Chris Gamble and Scott McMullen had a combined seven rushes and two touchdowns.

- In a 14-game season, the Buckeyes and the opponents had 14 passing touchdowns, even though the opponents threw 166 more passes and had 142 more completions.

- In a 14-game season, the Buckeyes averaged 14 yards per reception.

- In a 14-game season, the Buckeyes scored 14 against Michigan.

- In a 14-game season, the Buckeyes scored 14 in overtime against Miami.

- Opponents averaged only 77.7 rushing yards and five rushing first downs per game.

- The Buckeyes had exactly 3,000 yards on rushing plays before losses were factored in.

- The Buckeyes had only two more first downs than the opponents on the season. The 2001 team, with a record of 7-5, had 14 more first downs than the opponents.

- In the last four games, the opponents had 83 first downs to 56 for the Buckeyes.

- The Buckeyes averaged 38 points per game in the first seven games (no overtime games) and 18 points per game in regulation in the last seven games.

- The average winning margin was 23 points in the first seven games, and seven points per game (inflated by a 31-point win over Minnesota) in regulation in the last seven games.

- The defense gave up its most points in the first and last games of the season.

- The Buckeyes doubled their wins from the previous year,

not unusual for Coach Tressel, who had four seasons at Youngstown State with at least twice as many wins as the season before.

- The only opponents to score exactly seven points were "State" universities—Washington State, San Jose State, and Penn State.

- The attendance of 77,502 at the national championship game was exactly 1,000 more than in the Buckeyes' last bowl win, in the Sugar Bowl of the 1998 season.

- In the last four games, the Buckeyes' total offense yards were 267, 321, 264, and 267. The opponents' total offense yards were 341, 358, 368, and 369. Total: 1,119 for the Buckeyes and 1,436 for the opponents.

2003 (11-2)

During the season, Jim Tressel was asked by a reporter why the offensive numbers were so low, and he replied that it is hard to gain yards when you're scoring off turnovers and giving the ball back. It's hard to dispute that logic!

I went to a pre-season media event where Tressel said that Santonio Holmes, yet to play a game, was as good a receiver as anyone in the country. For some reason, broadcasters would have trouble with Holmes's first name—*Santanio* and even *San Antonio*, perhaps because he would eventually play in a bowl game in San Antonio.

In the opening 28-9 win over Washington in a night game, Maurice Hall had the first touchdown of the game, which meant that in the last three games of the previous season, a player named Maurice scored the Buckeyes' winning touchdown, and now this Maurice score kicked off the new season. The defense held the Huskies to seven yards on the ground with a long of nine. Troy Smith made his Buckeye debut with one carry for two yards. For the second straight game, Krenzel had the team's longest run.

Simon Fraser had a sack, prompting Keith Jackson to paraphrase Howard Cosell, "and down goes … the other guy." A few years ago, I saw Fraser in a grocery store and asked him if he would like to be my broadcast partner for my high school football games. Unfortunately for me, it did not work out for him.

Without Maurice Clarett, the Buckeyes' offense sputtered often, but the team made up for it with defensive scores. One such game was the following week, when they scored no offensive touchdowns against San Diego State, using a Will Allen 100-yard interception return and three Mike Nugent field goals in a 16-13 win. This meant that I had witnessed two of the three 100-yard interception returns in OSU history, seeing the David Brown one in West Lafayette in 1986, but not the one by Marlon Kerner at Purdue in 1993. The Aztecs had a 20-10 edge in first downs, and one of their receivers had six catches, compared to the total of five for the Buckeyes.

Against North Carolina State, a 44-38 win in three overtimes, the Buckeyes led 24-7 in the fourth quarter, only to see Philip Rivers lead the Wolfpack rally to a tie with 21 seconds left in regulation. Counting this game, in the first down category in the last two games, the Buckeyes had a 48-25 deficit. Krenzel had 37 yards rushing, and no other Buckeye had more than five. The two teams combined for 65 rushing yards and a one-yard per rush average. Rivers passed for 315 yards, with 217 after halftime. Krenzel ran or passed for five of the six touchdowns.

Each team scored touchdowns in the first and second overtime, and Krenzel threw his third overtime touchdown—to three different receivers—for a 44-38 lead. The Buckeyes could not convert on the required two-point conversion, which meant that a touchdown and two-point conversion would win the game for the Wolfpack. NC State had a first down on the OSU 4-yard line, and their first three plays were a Rivers 2-yard rush, an incompletion, and a Rivers 1-yard rush. After the last rush, TV color announcer Ed Cunningham had a classic succinct analysis, given that the Wolfpack had a quarterback who would go on to a stellar NFL career. After a pause and with little emotion: "What are you doing?" When the Buckeyes stopped the fourth down rush for the win, I had a déjà vu moment—the Miami game eight months earlier—and was sure that the Buckeyes would never lose an overtime game. Spoiler alert: See 2004, Northwestern.

Krenzel missed the Bowling Green game, a 24-17 win, and for the third straight game, the opponent had more first downs. Maurice Hall ran for 107 yards, Scott McMullen passed for 118, and the defense held the Falcons to 40 yards on the ground. The Buckeyes were like animals on defense—Fox and Hawk had interceptions.

Krenzel missed the 20-0 win over Northwestern, too. McMullen passed for 166 yards and had the team's longest run of 16 yards.

Krenzel returned to action and connected with Jenkins to tie the game at 10-10 with 6:09 remaining in Madison, but backup quarterback Matt Schabert hit Lee Evans, from Bedford, Ohio—are all Badger receivers from Ohio?—with a 79-yard pass play to give Wisconsin a 17-10 win. It was Evans's only catch of the game. For the second straight week, the Buckeye quarterback had the team's longest run, on Krenzel's 18-yard effort.

Defense and special teams led to 16 of the 19 points in the 19-10 win over Iowa, the second time in six games without an offensive touchdown. Jenkins had a 54-yard punt return, Donte Whitner scored on a blocked punt, and the defense recorded a safety. On the Iowa touchdown, Tressel tugged on his sweater vest to demonstrate to the officials that the Hawkeyes were holding. Again, the opponents had more first downs, and again, Krenzel had the longest Buckeye run, a whopping nine yards. The two teams combined for 122 yards on the ground, an average of 1.5 yards per carry. Troy Smith had a kickoff return of 16 yards.

Santonio Holmes had a breakout game of six catches for 153 yards and two touchdowns in the 35-6 win at Indiana. Lydell Ross, who ran for 124 yards two years previous in Bloomington, ran for 167 and three scores, and Krenzel and McMullen combined for 383 passing yards, with 11 Buckeyes with a catch. The defense held the Hoosiers to minus 12 yards on the ground, with a long of six. It's not often that a freshman being redshirted gets interviewed on TV during a game, but that's what took place as the sideline reporter had a chat with Anthony Gonzalez.

McMullen filled in for an injured Krenzel during the game and threw the winning touchdown pass to Jenkins with 1:35 remaining in the 21-20 win at Penn State. Ross was over 100 yards again, with 110. Jenkins had only 20 yards on three receptions, but two were for scores. The Nittany Lions had only 33 yards on the ground. The Buckeyes had a huge break when a pass that Ben Hartsock never came close to catching was ruled a catch. It was a break similar to the Eddie George non-fumble in Happy Valley in 1995. Penn State's 60-yard field goal attempt on the final play was short of the mark.

Ross had 125 yards, his third straight game over 100, in the 33-23 win over Michigan State. The rush defense topped the previous week's performance by holding the Spartans to five net yards, with a long of nine. Mike Nugent kicked four field goals, and Krenzel had three touchdown passes to three different receivers whose last name started with the letter *H*—Hartsock, Holmes, and Ryan Hamby—in the span of less than 15 minutes. He could have joined the 4-H organization if only he had connected with Roy Hall.

The Buckeyes had their second 16-13 win of the year and their second overtime win in the game with Purdue. In both 16-13 games, the offense had no touchdowns; Mike Kudla recovered a fumble in the end zone in the fourth quarter in this one. Jenkins had six catches for 123 yards. Mike Nugent made his field goal in overtime, and the Boilers' Ben Jones missed his. For the second straight year, the Buckeyes had an overtime game the week before the Michigan game.

Against Michigan, a 35-21 loss, the Buckeyes trailed by 21 points twice, rallied to 28-21, and had a chance to tie it after Chris Gamble intercepted a pass in the fourth quarter; however, they could not score again. The Buckeyes were held to 54 yards on the ground, but they passed for 329, with McMullen filling in for an injured Krenzel after Krenzel threw two touchdown passes to Holmes. Holmes had 121 receiving yards, and Jenkins had 132. Krenzel had the team's longest run of 14 yards.

Mark and I went to the Fiesta Bowl game against Kansas State, flying into Las Vegas on New Year's Day. On New Year's Eve, I was at the Columbus Blue Jackets game, getting player interviews for a buddy of mine. Interestingly, I transmitted those interviews to a company in Phoenix.

Flipping the script from the Michigan game, the Buckeyes had a 21-point lead twice, winning 35-28. A Buckeye wearing #13 was instrumental in this game, too; John Hollins returned a punt blocked by Harlan Jacobs (#13) for the first score. Krenzel threw two touchdown passes to Jenkins, and both of his completions to Holmes went for touchdowns, the last one with inches to spare in the back of the end zone. Like the win over Miami, receivers from Florida (Jenkins and Holmes) made the key receptions. Krenzel was 11 for 24 for 189 yards, 20 years after Mike Tomczak completed less than half of his passes in the bowl win over Pittsburgh in the same stadium. The Buckeyes had all four of their offensive touchdowns on passes, and the Wildcats had all four of their touchdowns on the ground. In the previous year's win over Miami, all four Buckeye touchdowns were on the ground. Like the Miami game, two Buckeyes had two offensive touchdowns each.

For the Buckeyes, Branden Joe had 46 of his season's 99 rushing yards in this game. The Wildcats' Ell Roberson passed for 294 yards, completing only 20 of 51 passes. For the second straight bowl game, the Buckeyes won despite being outgained—a combined 747 to 604 yards. In the last two bowl games, the opponents had 44 first downs combined to 29 for the Buckeyes. For the second straight bowl game, the defense gave up 14 passing first downs.

In the game, Mike Nugent's two solo tackles matched those of Chris Gamble and Simon Fraser, and were more than those of Will Smith (1), Darrion Scott (1), Quinn Pitcock (1), and Tim Anderson (0).

After the game, the band played *Carmen Ohio* only when Coach Tressel nodded to the director that yes, the team was ready. Wildcats' assistant coach and future Wisconsin head coach Bret Bielema shows up on the replay.

The 2002 team had won seven games by seven points or less, and the 2003 team won six games by seven points or less.

FUN FACTS:

- The defense held opponents to 62 rushing yards per game and two yards per carry.

- For the second straight year, the defense gave up five rushing first downs per game.

- The opponents had 27 more first downs than the Buckeyes. Over the previous two years, the Buckeyes had a combined record of 25-2, but the opponents had a 490-465 edge in first downs.

- All three games in which the defense gave up less than 10 points were home games.

- In each overtime game, the Buckeyes had 15 first downs. The opponents had a combined 52 first downs to 30 for the Buckeyes in the two overtime games.

- For the second straight year, Michael Jenkins's longest reception came in an overtime game.

- For the second straight year, Ben Hartsock had two touchdown receptions and a longest reception of 20 yards.

- Both Craig Krenzel and Scott McMullen averaged one touchdown pass per 10.2 completions.

- In six of the 12 regular season games, the Buckeye quarterback had the team's longest run.

- The Buckeyes had a 20-14 edge in passing touchdowns, even though the opponents had 149 more passes and 90 more completions.

- The Buckeyes gave up 14 passing touchdowns for the second straight year.

- Jenkins had the longest reception and punt return.

- Chris Gamble had two of his three interceptions in the last two games.

- Gamble and Dustin Fox led the team with three interceptions each for a total of six return yards.

- The two leaders in solo tackles were animals—Fox and Hawk.

- For the second straight year, a defensive back who had an interception return for a touchdown—Allen in 2003 and Gamble in 2002—wore a different jersey number the year before.

- Three times, Santonio Holmes had two touchdown receptions in a game.

- The last eight touchdowns of the year were scored by players whose last name ended in the letter S—Holmes, Ross, Jenkins, and Hollins.

- Ten of the 12 regular season games had an attendance of at least 104,000.

- Troy Smith had 83 yards on kickoff returns, 14 yards on

three rushes, and no pass attempts. Spoiler alert: Things would change.

2004 (8-4)

I was working the stats for the high school playoffs in Canton and heard someone say, "Steve Basford?" It was Jack Kramer, whom I had not seen since 1990. He was there to broadcast games for teams in western Ohio, and we reminisced about the WOSU-TV days. I said, "Those were the days," and that they were the best ten years of my life, based on working the stats in home games, taking a few plane trips, and working the stats in eight of the ten conference press boxes.

It took Coach Tressel four years before he would have back-to-back losses. The Buckeyes won their first three and lost the next three, but they rebounded to finish 8-4.

In the 27-6 opening win over Cincinnati, the Buckeyes had a 462-238 edge in total offense, with Ross rushing for 141 and Justin Zwick passing for 213. Ted Ginn's debut was not auspicious—one catch for minus one yard, where he tried to use his trademark fancy feet to avoid tackles, and another for seven yards. The defense held the Bearcats to 76 yards on the ground.

Tied at 21, the game against Marshall appeared to be headed to over-time, but Mike Nugent kicked a 55-yard field goal on the last play of the game for a 24-21 win. Zwick passed for 324 yards and three touchdowns, with all three scores and 255 yards in the first half, two to Holmes for 80 and 47 yards. Holmes finished with ten catches for 224 yards, with 199 in the first half.

Nugent was the story the next week, too, when I went to the North Carolina State game in Raleigh, a 22-14 Buckeyes win. Nugent was five-for-five on field goals, three of them between 46 and 50 yards, impressing a Wolfpack fan sitting next to me. He was further amazed when I told him that Nugent was only seven-of-14 on field goals as a freshman. The only touchdown came after Donte Whitner returned an interception to the 3-yard line. The Wolfpack outgained the Buckeyes 256-137.

The 33-27 loss at Northwestern in a night game was the Buckeyes' first overtime loss, but I was happy for Jeff Backes, an honor student at my alma mater, Upper Arlington High School, where he, along with the Buckeyes' Simon Fraser, played on the Golden Bears' 15-0 state championship team in 2000. In that 2000 playoff season, Upper Arlington beat Cincinnati Colerain, coached by eventual OSU assistant Kerry Coombs. Backes had the only interception for Northwestern, and another Franklin County product, Mark Philmore of Reynoldsburg, had 11 receptions for 134 yards and a score. Backes had four receptions on offense in the 2002 matchup with the Buckeyes.

The Buckeyes rallied from ten points down to tie it at 27 with 1:54 remaining in regulation, but Nugent finally missed a field goal in overtime. The Wildcats were the only team to have more than one rushing touchdown (two) against the Buckeyes all season, and it took overtime to do it. The Buckeyes scored 27 points for the second straight meeting in Evanston.

Coach Tressel's first back-to-back loss experience came to Wisconsin, 24-13. Ted Ginn's 65- yard punt return was the only touchdown, and for the second time in four weeks, Mike Nugent kicked a 55-yard field goal to end a half, making it 14-13 at halftime. Nugent's second 55-yard field goal in 2004 gave him two of the three 55-yard field goals by a Buckeye in Ohio Stadium, the team record. The Buckeyes mustered only 224 yards in total offense and were minus 13 minutes in possession time.

The Buckeyes avoided a shutout on a 23-yard pass from Troy Smith to Rory Nicol with 2:19 remaining in their third straight loss, 33-7, at Iowa. Smith had the longest run of 13 yards; the team's next longest was five. This was the fifth straight game in which the Buckeyes rushed for less than 100 yards—they had 27—as they were outgained 448-177.

Two freshmen shined in the 30-7 win over Indiana: freshman Ted Ginn caught a 59-yard scoring pass from new starting quarterback Troy Smith on the first possession. Smith had another touchdown pass to Holmes in the first quarter, and freshman Antonio Pittman ran for 144 yards and a score.

For the second straight game, Ted Ginn jump-started the scoring with a 67-yard punt return in the 21-10 win over Penn State. Tyler Everett had a 24-yard interception return for a score also in the first quarter, making it the seventh straight game in this series in which one team or the other had a defensive touchdown. Maurice Hall had the longest kickoff return of the year for 62 yards to set up Branden Joe's touchdown run. The two teams combined for only 448 total yards, with 128 yards passing.

For the third straight game, Ted Ginn had the first score, and he scored three different ways—on a 17-yard run, a 60-yard punt return, and a 58-yard reception—in the 32-19 win at Michigan State. The reception came with 1:37 remaining in the game and the team trailing 19-17 before the score. A.J. Hawk followed with an interception, and Maurice Hall had his longest run of the year, 51 yards for the final score. The Spartans had 100 more yards in total offense.

The Buckeyes rallied from down 17-3 to tie it at 17 on a Troy Smith 5-yard run—the TV feed froze when he was close to the end zone—but the Buckeyes lost at Purdue 24-17 on a score with 2:17 remaining. Two freshmen and a sophomore—Ginn, Pittman, and Smith—accounted for all but five of the 146 rushing yards.

I listened to the game while returning from Upland, Indiana, after having worked the stats for the Ohio Dominican radio broadcast of the game against Taylor. This was Ohio Dominican's first football team, and they would lose all ten games. If you have not heard of Taylor University, perhaps you have heard of two of their alumni: Buckeyes basketball coach Chris Holtmann and Akron basketball coach John Groce, who played there and later served as an assistant.

Ohio Dominican's 0-10 record matched the 0-10 record that the Columbus Thunderbolts of the Arena Football League posted in 1991 when I worked the stats for radio. Somehow, these were not held against me, and I kept on getting hired for stats work.

The 37-21 win over Michigan seemed to come out of nowhere, the Buckeyes coming off the loss to Purdue and the 37 points being five more than any other output that year to that point. The Buckeyes exploded on their first possession with Anthony Gonzalez catching a 68-yard pass from Troy Smith, raising his arms in celebration as he scored. Ted Ginn's 82-yard punt return was another highlight play—touchdown #7 on the year for #7. He started on the right sideline and flew to the left before sprinting down the left sideline for the score. Santonio Holmes caught a 12-yard touchdown pass from Smith, which meant that the four players who scored touchdowns were freshmen or sophomores, with Smith running for a score. Smith ran for 145 yards and passed for 241, accounting for all but 60 of the team's 446 yards.

When Gonzalez was recruited, there was speculation that he would play as a defensive back. Having seen film of him as a receiver, I was hoping that would be his spot.

The game had a statistical oddity that must have confused the fans. In the second quarter, OSU had the ball inside the Michigan 1-yard line, and Troy Smith scored on a sneak. So, why does the box score show a 2-yard run? Stay with me on this, if you like. A few plays earlier, the ball was between the 10 and the 11 with a Buckeyes first down. The rule is that we record the line of scrimmage as the next closer line (the 10), UNLESS the team can gain a first down without scoring, which was the case. So, this series had to start statistically at the 11. When the ball was inside the 1-yard line, the Buckeyes barely did not have enough yardage for a first down. We could not say that the line of scrimmage was the one, because that would have been 10 yards from the previous 11 and meant a first down. But the Buckeyes did not have a first down, so the line of scrimmage had to be the two. Got it?

Mark and I went to the Alamo Bowl, a 33-7 win over Oklahoma State, flying into Houston. We felt right at home having lunch on the way in Columbus, Texas, off Route 71. We did the Riverwalk boat ride, recognizing the scenery from the 1984 movie *Cloak & Dagger*.

It was impressive to see the Alamodome filled half with Scarlet and Gray fans and half with Cowboy fans. Troy Smith had been suspended, and Justin Zwick had a solid game with 189 yards passing. The broadcasters gave Ginn credit for Gonzalez's 23-yard touchdown catch from Zwick for the first score, as he drew the attention of the Cowboy defensive backs, clearing out space for Gonzalez. Zwick would become hobbled during the game, and the TV camera caught Todd Boeckman on the sideline, with the commentators saying that Tressel would do anything to avoid putting him in and losing his redshirt year. Enter Ted Ginn, Jr. in the wildcat, and he scored on a 5-yard draw play. He would also have an insane, reversing run of 28 yards.

The Buckeyes had balance with nine first downs rushing and nine passing, and the Cowboys had balance with seven first downs rushing and seven passing. Gonzalez had eight receptions on the year; his first four receptions gained 31 yards, and his last four gained 138 and two touchdowns, one each in the last two games. Mike Nugent broke Pete Johnson's all-time OSU scoring record with the help of four field goals.

After the game, I heard frequently that Cowboy Coach Les Miles was a hot commodity for more major coaching positions, and he would become the LSU coach the next year.

The 37 and 33 points that the Buckeyes scored in the last two games were their two biggest outputs of the year.

Jim Tressel was known as The Senator, and a few days later, I saw a coach who would become a senator, Tommy Tuberville of Auburn.

After returning to Columbus and spending one night at home, I was back on a plane to New Orleans. Stan Anderson, who keyed plays into the software for the official stats, had the job of supplying the stat monitors for the Sugar Bowl game between Virginia Tech and undefeated Auburn, and he arranged for me to help. I took the bus on a foggy New Year's Eve from the New Orleans airport to downtown, where the bus dropped me off a few blocks from the hotel connected to the Superdome. This was eight months before Hurricane Katrina.

My pass allowed me into all the media events. While waiting for a press conference in a lobby, Virginia Tech coach Frank Beamer came in and sat caddy-corner from me on a couch. I was able to eavesdrop on his laid-back chat with his Sports Information staff. Seven years later on a sidewalk in Atlanta where I went to see the Virginia Tech-Georgia Tech game, I would see Coach Beamer again.

I went to a media event where players were available for one-on-one interviews and asked VT kicker Brandon Pace if he was looking forward to kicking in a dome and if he had watched Mike Nugent kicking in a dome a few days ago. If he noticed that I was not taking notes or recording his comments, he was very gracious.

In the hotel lobby on New Year's Day, I watched the Iowa-LSU Capital One Bowl, which the Hawkeyes won on a 56-yard pass on the last play of the game after the Tigers went ahead with 46 seconds left. A Hawkeye fan walked by and said, "You've got to cheat ... to beat ... the Hawkeyes!" Later in the Superdome, I got word that Texas had beaten Michigan on a field goal on the last play in the Rose Bowl.

At the Sugar Bowl game, I was watching the local news on TV in the press box dining area when the sports anchor whom I had just seen on the air came in and sat down. I did not have an assigned seat in the press box, but I found one and jotted down the plays as if I were a media person, never getting busted.

Auburn won the game 16-13 to finish 13-0, making it the second time in three years that I had gone to a bowl and the winning team finished undefeated. After the game, we collected the monitors, and Stan wrapped them in a gigantic shrink-wrap and placed them on a skid to be transported back to their home. On the day after the game, I went to a press conference where Archie Manning spoke.

FUN FACTS:

- The Buckeyes and the opponents each had 25 touchdowns from scrimmage, but the Buckeyes had a six to one edge in scores on returns.

- Thanks to Ted Ginn and Santonio Holmes, the Buckeyes had almost three times as many punt return yards as the opponents.

- The Buckeyes had almost four times as many interception return yards as the opponents.

- Only six yards separated Zwick's (1,241) total offense and Smith's (1,235) total offense.

- Four Buckeyes had a longer run than the opponents' long of 41 yards.

- Four Buckeyes had a longer reception than the opponents' long of 46 yards.

- The four highest scoring outputs came in the last six games.

- The running game averaged 98 yards per game in the first six games and 193 in the last six.

- The two biggest scoring games in the regular season came against the two Teams from The State Up North.

- As in 1987, the Buckeyes had a three-game losing streak, including consecutive losses to Wisconsin and Iowa, but beat Michigan.

2005 (10-2)

Taking over as the starting tailback, Antonio Pittman ran for 100 yards in the opening 34-14 win over the Miami RedHawks. With Troy Smith still ineligible, Zwick started and tossed a scoring pass to Holmes. Boeckman in relief threw one to Ginn. Donte Whitner—like Smith and Ginn, a Cleveland Glenville product—had a 26-yard interception return for a score.

Troy Smith was reinstated for the Texas game, a 25-22 Longhorn win in Columbus, but Coach Tressel gave the start to Zwick. I arrived at OSU early to avoid traffic, parked at a lot across the Olentangy River from the stadium, and walked to the AMC Lennox theater, where I saw *I Heart Huckabees*. To this day, I have no idea what the plot or purpose of the movie was. Director David O. Russell would go on to better things—see *Silver Linings Playbook*.

In the second quarter, Smith came in and threw a 36-yard touchdown pass to Santonio Holmes. All 22 points would be by Buckeyes whose last name started with the letter *H*, with Josh Huston kicking five field goals. The Buckeyes might have had another score by an *H* player, but a pass to Ryan Hamby in the end zone was broken up. The defense had Vince Young bottled up in the first half, but he threw the winning touchdown, confirmed after video review, with 2:37 remaining.

Antonio Pittman led the Buckeyes with 75 rushing yards, and Billy Pittman led the Longhorns with 130 receiving yards. Unlike three years ago, Field Judge Terry Porter would not have a significant role in this big game. Texas would win the national championship this year, snapping USC's 34-game win streak. When the Buckeyes won the 2002 national championship, they snapped Miami's 34-game win streak. USC's coach was former OSU assistant Pete Carroll, and Miami's coach was former OSU assistant Larry Coker.

The defense held San Diego State to three first downs—only two after throwing an 80-yard scoring pass on the game's first play—and 13 yards rushing, with a long of six, in the 27-6 win. Smith ran for two touchdowns and led the team with 87 yards on the ground.

The defense topped their performance from the previous week by holding #21 ranked Iowa to minus nine on the ground, with a long of seven, and 137 yards total in the 31-6 win. Smith accounted for all four touchdowns, running for 127 yards and two touchdowns again, and passing for 191, connecting on two scores with Gonzalez. Pittman ran for 171.

The Nittany Lions slowed Smith down a bit in their 17-10 win at Happy Valley, though he did run for the team's only score. The two teams combined for only 425 total yards, even less than last year's 448.

Halftime of the Michigan State game, a 35-24 win, was also the halfway point of the regular season, and that is when the Buckeyes turned the game and their season around. With the Spartans leading 17-7 and lining up for a 35-yard field goal, Nate Salley blocked the kick and Ashton Youboty returned it 72 yards as time expired, causing Spartan Coach John L. Smith to gnash his teeth in his chat with the TV reporter on the way to the locker room. The Buckeyes had three other huge scoring plays, with passes of 46 and 51 yards to Holmes and a 57-yard pass to Ginn. Smith passed for 249 yards, Pittman ran for 101, and Holmes had five catches for 150. The defense set an OSU record with 12 sacks. With all the Buckeye big plays, the Spartans had almost 22 more minutes of possession.

The defense held Indiana to 137 yards, only 42 on the ground, in the 41-10 win at Bloomington. It was Smith, Pittman, and Holmes again, with 281 yards total offense, 133 rushing, and 104 receiving, respectively. Ginn had the team's longest punt return of the year, 62 yards for a score, and Brandon Mitchell had the team's longest interception return of the year, 57 yards for a touchdown.

Minnesota racked up 578 yards and had a 17-17 tie at halftime, but the Buckeyes scored four times in the second half in the 45-31 win in Minneapolis. Smith passed for 233 yards and three touchdowns, two to

Holmes, Pittman ran for 186 (134 in the second half), and Ginn had a 100-yard kickoff return for a score.

The only glitch in the 40-2 win over Illinois was a returned fumbled PAT attempt for two points by the Illini, as the defense held Illinois to 160 yards, 68 on the ground. Smith passed for 298 yards and three touchdowns (two to Holmes for the second straight game), with Ginn catching four for 138 yards and a score.

Smith ran for 75 yards and two scores, but he rested his arm for next week with only 12 passes in the 48-7 win over Northwestern, the fourth straight game with at least 40 points. Pittman ran for 132 yards, and Hawk returned a blocked punt for a score.

The Buckeyes beat Michigan 25-21 on a touchdown by Antonio Pittman with 24 seconds left, scoring 13 points in the fourth quarter to rally from a 21-12 deficit. Each team lost a nine-point lead in the game. The defense held the Wolverines to 32 yards on the ground, with a long of seven.

Bobby Carpenter injured his right leg on the first defensive play of the game and was replaced by James Laurinaitis, or as Brent Musberger said, "Jim Laurinaitis." Musberger recounted Tressel's speech in the Schottenstein Center on the day that he was hired. He said that Tressel had stated that the Buckeyes would play Michigan in 306 days instead of 310 days. He almost could be forgiven for this, as he was wearing maize and blue colors.

Santonio Holmes caught a touchdown pass and was flagged for a celebration penalty for diving into the end zone to avoid a tackle, as he had done last year against the Wolverines. Seriously? The key play on the winning drive was Anthony Gonzalez's acrobatic 26-yard catch to the Michigan 4-yard line on a scramble by Smith, much like Mike Lanese's key catch against the Wolverines in 1984. The sideline official threw his hat to signify that Gonzalez had gone out of bounds before the catch, but he assured Gonzalez, "You're all right; you're all right," since he had been forced out of bounds. Gonzalez and Lanese both have high intellects—Lanese was a Rhodes Scholar—so there must have been a connection.

Smith passed for 300 yards, prompting Mark May on ESPN—perceived as an OSU hater, based on the Buckeyes roughing up his Pitt Panthers over the years—to say that after two years of facing Troy Smith, Lloyd Carr must be looking over his shoulder, worrying, "Where's Troy Smith? Where's Troy Smith?"

Mark and I went to the Fiesta Bowl game, a 34-20 win over Notre Dame, our third trip to Tempe in four years and the last Fiesta Bowl to be played in Tempe. With scoring plays of more than 50 (56, 68, 85, and 60) and topping what they did against Michigan State, the Buckeyes rolled up 617 yards, and according to the post-game press conference, impressed even Coach Tressel. Ginn had two of them, a 56-yard catch and a 68-yard run. Santonio Holmes had an 85-yard reception for a score and was flagged for a celebration penalty for raising his arm to signal #1 before scoring. Seriously?? Pittman sealed the win with a 60-yard scoring run.

A key play in the game was one of the best dropped passes in OSU history. In the third quarter, Anthony Gonzalez bobbled a pass which Notre Dame's Tom Zbikowski returned 89 yards for an apparent touchdown, only to have replay overturn it as an incomplete pass. The scene of Gonzalez celebrating on the bench with his arms in a touchdown-like pose is a classic.

Smith passed for 342 yards, with Ginn and Holmes combining for 291, and Pittman ran for 136. The defense held the Irish to 62 rushing yards. Both quarterbacks were from Ohio, with Dublin Coffman's Brady Quinn passing for 286 yards. His future brother-in-law, A.J. Hawk, sacked him twice, and Mike Kudla added three sacks. The other A.J., punter Trapasso, pretty much took the game off, punting only once.

For the past several years when I am at a baseball game or watching one where Jeff Samardzija is pitching, I like to stump my friends by asking, "Can you remember the first time that you saw Samardzija play?" and trick them with the fact that he was a receiver in this game. It was the second straight bowl game where both teams had the same record entering the game—7-4 the previous year and 9-2 in 2005.

On the flight home, we sat in front of Jay Richardson's mother and had a chat with her. I told her that I had worked the stats on TV for one of Jay's games when he played for Dublin Scioto High School.

I got home in time to see the end of the Texas-USC game for the national championship, won by the Longhorns 41-38 on Vince Young's run with 19 seconds left. I felt that Vince Young deserved the Heisman that year over the Trojans' Reggie Bush. Bush would later forfeit the award.

FUN FACTS:

- The six highest scoring outputs came in the last seven games.

- All seven of Antonio Pittman's touchdowns came in the last five games.

- Pittman had 1,331 rushing yards compared to the opponents' 881.

- The consecutive games at Indiana and Minnesota were the only two regular season games with an attendance under 104,000 and had two of the Buckeyes' three highest scoring outputs.

- The Buckeyes had a 424-63 edge in punt return yards.

- The Buckeyes had a 5-0 edge in touchdowns on returns, after 6-1 the previous year.

- The edge in passing touchdowns was 18-8, even though the opponents had 103 more passes and 50 more completions.

- Santonio Holmes's 11 touchdown receptions were three more than the opponents' total.

- Ted Ginn had the longest run, kickoff return, and punt return.

- The defense had six interceptions, with two of them returned for touchdowns.

2006 (12-1)

Ted Ginn had the first two touchdowns on receptions in the 35-12 opening win over Northern Illinois. He finished with 123 yards, Pittman ran for 111, and Smith passed for 297, giving him 939 in his last three games. A.J. Trapasso was super rested again, as in the Fiesta Bowl, with only one punt. The Huskies' Garrett Wolfe ran or caught passes for 285 of their 343 yards.

I nearly missed the game. I had checked myself into the Ohio State University Hospital Emergency Room with extreme exhaustion the night before. I called D.C. and informed him that I could miss the game. Doctors kept me overnight, so my main concern was whether or not I would be released in time for the game. Luckily, the game had a 3:30 start, and I walked the short distance to the stadium. The late Dave Railsback worked in our booth for many games, relaying information to the TV production staff, and he and I had a routine every game. Dave, a high school football official, would ask me, having done stats every Friday night, "Where were you last night?" On this occasion, my answer was, "University Hospital."

Mark and I went to the Texas game in Austin, a 24-7 win in the largest crowd to see a game in the state of Texas. Smith passed for 269 yards, dropping a perfect 29-yard pass into Ginn's hands coming right at us in the northwest corner of the end zone with 16 seconds remaining in the first half. That came 99 seconds after the Longhorns' only touchdown, which came after a borderline roughing the passer call on Jay

Richardson on a third down play at the Buckeyes' 9-yard line. Gonzalez had 142 yards on eight catches and the first score.

Buckeyes' linebacker James Laurinaitis had a phenomenal game, forcing a fumble at the OSU 2-yard line and returning an interception 25 yards. I had worked the stats for some games for WBNS-TV sports anchor Jeff Hogan, so a few days later, I emailed him to say that his lead-in should be, "Longhorns Suffer from a Severe Case of Laurinaitis." He replied that he wished that I had shared that earlier!

The defense held the Cincinnati Bearcats to minus four yards on the ground in the 37-7 win. Smith distributed 203 yards to 11 receivers, with two touchdown passes to Ginn. Laurinaitis picked off a pass again, one of three for the defense.

Malcolm Jenkins and Antonio Smith returned interceptions—61 and 55 yards—1:24 apart in the fourth quarter of the 28-6 win over Penn State, although Jenkins may have deposited the ball short of the goal line. These were the two longest interception returns of the year. The Buckeyes had only five more yards of offense, with Pittman running for 110. Laurinaitis intercepted for the third straight game,

The Buckeyes had more than twice as much possession time in the 38-7 win at Iowa, with Gonzalez catching two of Smith's four touchdown passes and Pittman running for 117 yards. Laurinaitis intercepted for the fourth straight game, one of three for the defense.

The Buckeyes had only 48 more yards of offense in the 35-7 win over Bowling Green. Ginn had 10 catches for 122 yards and a score, and Pittman had two scoring runs of eight yards each.

Ginn had a 60-yard punt return in the 38-7 win over Michigan State, giving him five scores in his three games against the Spartans. Smith passed for 234 yards and two scores, and Gonzalez had seven catches for 118 and a touchdown.

Rory Nicol had two catches, both for touchdowns, with one of them thrown by Ted Ginn in the 44-3 win over Indiana. The balanced offense had

270 yards on the ground and 270 in the air, with Pittman running for 105. The defense held the Hoosiers to seven yards on the ground and 165 overall.

The defense had a similar performance in the 44-0 win over Minnesota, holding the Gophers to 47 yards on the ground and 182 overall with three interceptions. Pittman ran for 116 yards and two touchdowns, and A.J. Trapasso took the game off, as no punting was needed.

The offense generated only 224 yards at Illinois with only 29 in the second half, leading 17-0 at halftime and hanging on to win 17-10. The Illini scored with 1:40 to cut it to seven and got the ball back with only four seconds left after a Trapasso punt to the Illinois 2-yard line. Trapasso, who had had no punts the week before, had a season-high seven punts.

Seven different Buckeyes—Brian Hartline twice, Pittman, Brandon Mitchell on an interception, Ginn, Gonzalez, Chris Wells, and Boeckman—scored touchdowns in the 54-10 win at Northwestern. Freshman Chris Wells gave a glimpse of his future with 99 yards, and factoring in Pittman and the Wildcats' Tyrell Sutton, those three from Akron had 236 of the 299 rushing yards.

Bo Schembechler passed away the day before the 42-39 win over #2 Michigan. Six different Buckeyes—Roy Hall, Pittman, Ginn, Wells, Gonzalez, and Brian Robiskie—scored a touchdown each as the teams combined for exactly 900 yards. Wells did a 360-degree turn in the backfield on the way to his 52-yard touchdown, his longest run of the year. Pittman also had his longest run of the year, a 56-yard run for his score, and finished with 139. Ginn had 104 yards in receptions, and Smith passed for 316, giving him 857 total passing yards in three contests against the Wolverines. One of my favorite plays was when Coach Tressel had the team hurry to the line of scrimmage with Ted Ginn at tight end, catching Michigan off-guard and resulting in a 39-yard touchdown pass from Troy Smith.

Mark and I went to the national championship game in Glendale, Arizona, the brutal 41-14 loss to Florida. On the flight leg from Denver to Phoenix, I could not get my T-Mobile Sidekick phone to shut down, but luckily it went undetected. We saw Cornelius Greene outside the stadium before the game, and I informed him that I worked the stats with him on the WOSU-TV broadcasts 25 years ago.

Ginn had the 93-yard opening kickoff return, but he was injured in the celebration. A misconception is that he was done for the game, but he was in on the next series and was the target of an incomplete pass. His kickoff return meant that he averaged 73 yards on his three touchdowns in the last two bowl games, both in the Phoenix area. Ginn had the first touchdown in the postseason game the year before. Pittman had the only offensive touchdown against Florida and had the last touchdown in the previous year's postseason game.

Watching the game on replay, I thought that the Buckeyes defense played well. After Florida's first drive, their last six scoring drives averaged 27 yards. The Buckeyes were in the game down 21-14 when the roof caved in. Even though the Buckeyes trailed 34-14 at halftime, I thought that they could come back. Our seats in the end zone allowed me to observe the lateral speed of the Gators' skilled players, especially Percy Harvin, from left to right, which the TV angle from the 50-yard line does not capture well.

I recall Gators Coach Urban Meyer saying after the game that he did not run up the score in the second half out of respect for his home state and for the university where he earned his master's degree. At the time, I said to myself, "Yeah, right." Also, at the time, I could not fathom how Earle Bruce could spend so much time with him, being unaware that Coach Meyer considered Coach Bruce his mentor.

Not-So Fun Fact: The defense gave up 86 points in the first 11 games and 80 in the last two.

FUN FACTS:

- Total offense was one yard short of 5,000 yards.
- Ted Ginn scored on receptions, a kickoff return, and a punt return, and threw a touchdown pass.

- Ginn had the longest reception, kickoff return, and punt return.

- All 31 touchdown passes were thrown by Smith (30) and Ginn (one), teammates at Cleveland Glenville High School.

- The edge in passing touchdowns was 31-10, even though the opponents had 75 more passes and 21 more completions.

- The edge in rushing touchdowns was 25-9.

- Pittman had 14 rushing touchdowns, compared to the opponents' nine.

- Pittman was Mr. Consistent, with exactly one less carry in 2006 than in 2005.

- Return yardage was 342 on 21 interceptions for the Buckeyes, and zero on six interceptions for the opponents.

2007 (11-2)

Some wise guy noticed that the not too compelling first four games were against Youngstown State, Akron, Washington, and Northwestern … and that the first letter of each spelled YAWN.

Five different Buckeyes—Chris Wells, Dane Sanzenbacher, Brandon Saine, Trever Robinson, and Taurian Washington—scored touchdowns in the 38-6 opening win over Youngstown State. Brian Robiskie had nine receptions for 153 yards, and the defense limited the Penguins to 176 total yards. Crossing the footbridge over the Olentangy River after the game, I heard the biggest cheer of the day coming from north of the stadium—from fans watching Michigan losing to Appalachian State.

It was a baseball score at halftime, 3-2 against Akron, with a final score of 20-2, as the Zips finished with three first downs, three yards rushing, and 69 total yards. Chris Wells ran for 143 yards, and total offense in the second half was 248-20 in favor of the Buckeyes.

As the Buckeyes were playing Washington in Seattle, I was in Nashville to see the Vanderbilt-Mississippi game. Luckily, the Buckeyes' game, a 33-14 win, was on a big screen TV outside the stadium. For the second straight week, the offense had only three points in the first half, trailing 7-3, but it had 304 yards in the second half. Wells ran for 135, Boeckman passed for two touchdowns, and Robiskie had 107 receiving yards, including the longest scoring catch of the year, 68 yards. Laurinaitis had two of the team's three interceptions, his only two of the year. Counting this game, in their last three trips to Seattle, the Buckeyes had scored a total of three points in the first half.

The defense pitched a shutout, with the special teams giving up a 99-yard kickoff return in the 58-7 win over Northwestern. Chris Wells ran for 100 yards, and Boeckman threw four touchdown passes, three to Robiskie. The defense held the Wildcats to zero net yards on the ground. After four games, the defense had given up only two touchdowns, both to Washington.

Chris Wells ran for 116 yards and had two touchdowns in the first quarter in the 30-7 win at Minnesota. Robiskie had 99 reception yards, with another huge scoring play of 52 yards. The Gophers had only 45 yards on the ground.

The defense came with ten seconds of recording a shutout in the 23-7 win at Purdue, facing 60 passes by Curtis Painter. Boeckman passed for 200 yards and two touchdowns, and the defense held the Boilers to four net yards on the ground.

Brian Hartline had a 90-yard punt return for a score, breaking the 57 year-old record for the longest in OSU history, and Donald Washington had a 70-yard interception return, the team's longest of the year, in the 48-3 win over Kent State. It was the fourth time in seven games that the defense had not given up an offensive touchdown. Ten receivers caught a pass, and Hartline added another touchdown.

Chris Wells exploded for 221 yards, and the Buckeyes led 24-0 in the 24-17 win over Michigan State. Again, the defense did not give up an offensive touchdown. The Spartans scored on an interception and a fumble return. The Buckeyes had a 422-185 edge in total offense.

Malcolm Jenkins—one of four Buckeyes to score a touchdown—had a pick-six for the second straight year against Penn State in the 37-17 win. The Buckeyes had a 453-263 advantage in total offense. Chris Wells ran for 133 yards, and Boeckman passed for 253 and three scores.

By a nearly identical score as the previous week, the Buckeyes beat Wisconsin, 38-17, rallying from down 17-10 in the third quarter. Chris Wells had three of the four comeback touchdowns on runs of 31, 30, and 23, and finished with 169 yards. The defense limited the Badgers to 12 yards on the ground, with a minus 84 in losses and 10 sacks.

The bid for an undefeated season ended with the 28-21 home loss to Illinois. Chris Wells and Maurice Wells scored the three Buckeyes touchdowns, but the Illini's Juice Williams passed for touchdowns to four different receivers, one of them to Jacob Willis, son of former OSU receiver Lenny Willis. Illinois may have caught a huge break when an apparent fumble at the OSU 3-yard line was not detected. The Buckeyes had the ball for only three plays and 1:14 of the fourth quarter, as the Illini held the ball for the last 8:09, covering only 48 yards. In the last two games of this Illibuck series, each team had 38 points.

Chris Wells had 222 of the team's 279 yards and both touchdowns in the 14-3 win at Michigan, as the defense held the Wolverines to 15 yards on the ground and 91 total, with only 14 in the second half. At halftime, Lloyd Carr described the precipitation as a wet rain. Michigan's backup quarterback Ryan Mallett saw some action, and the Buckeyes would face him again in three years, playing for Arkansas in the Sugar Bowl.

Mark and I went to the national championship game in New Orleans, which LSU won 38-24. I put to good use my new toy from Christmas—a stand-alone GPS! Before the game, we went to the radio pre-game show hosted by Jeff Logan. He put me on the air, and one of his questions was, "What is the OSU record for most rushing yards by a running back in a postseason game?" Put on the spot, I incorrectly said, "Tim Spencer with about 160 yards in the 1982 Holiday Bowl." Once off the air, I realized that it was Raymont Harris in the 1993 Holiday Bowl, looked up the number using my T-Mobile Sidekick, jotted it down on a piece of paper and handed it to Jeff.

Like last year's national championship game, the Buckeyes had an explosive touchdown in the beginning—a Chris Wells 65-yard run on the game's first series—and led 10-0 in the first quarter, but the Tigers ran off 31 unanswered points. I have seen accounts that say that LSU won in a rout, but I point out that the Buckeyes had 353 total yards to 326 for LSU. The Buckeyes had the leading rusher, Wells with 146; the leading passer, Boeckman with 208; the leading receiver, Hartline with 75 yards; the longest run; and the longest pass. The Tigers had more total yards than the Buckeyes when the Buckeyes won in 1988 and in the tie in 1987. Even though LSU was playing in their home state, I still was impressed by the noise level of their fans.

The loss to Coach Les Miles, from Elyria, meant that the Buckeyes' last three losses were to coaches who were Ohio natives, following Urban Meyer of Ashtabula and Ron Zook of Illinois, a Loudonville native. Also on the Tigers staff were Youngstown native/former OSU player/future head coach Bo Pelini and future OSU assistant Greg Studrawa from Fostoria. In six of the last eight bowl games, the opposing coach—Lou Holtz twice, Larry Coker, Miles twice, and Meyer—was either born in Ohio, had assisted at OSU, or both.

Our flight home was from Baton Rouge to Memphis to Detroit to Columbus.

FUN FACTS:

- The defense gave up 166 points, the same as in 2006.

- The defense had three straight games giving up seven points in each and three straight games giving up 17 points in each.

- The ground game had 2,553 yards, and passing yards were 2,565.

- The defense held the opponents to 82.8 yards per game on the ground.

- Chris Wells ran for 1,609 yards, compared to the opponents' total of 1,077.

- The edge in rushing touchdowns was 21-3.

- Chris Wells had 15 rushing touchdowns, compared to the opponents' three.

- Maurice Wells' three rushing touchdowns matched the opponents' total.

- Both of Chris Wells' games of over 200 yards (222 and 221) came against the Teams from The State Up North.

- The edge in passing touchdowns was 26-13, even though the opponents had 76 more passes.

- The edge in punt return yards was 472-90. The Buckeyes had as many yards on one punt return (90 by Hartline) as the opponents had on the year.

- The last six regular season games had an attendance of at least 105,000.

2008 (10-3)

The biggest buzz in the off-season was where high school phenom Terrelle Pryor would commit to play in college. When he appeared at a basketball game with Jim Tressel, the fans recognized him, as he was hard to miss at 6'6".

He made his debut in relief of Boeckman in the opening 43-0 win over Youngstown State and scored on an 18-yard run. The worst outcome was Chris Wells injuring his right foot in the third quarter after rushing for 111 yards. The defense held the Penguins to minus 11 on the ground and 74 overall, with the offense recording 495. Boeckman, Pryor, and Joe Bauserman combined for 244 yards passing, distributing to 11 receivers. Ryan Pretorius and Aaron Pettrey combined for five field goals, with each successful on one of at least 50 yards.

Without Wells, the Buckeyes trailed the Ohio Bobcats 7-6 at half-time before winning 26-14. The total offense advantage was only 272-254, with four Buckeyes picking off a pass and Ray Small returning a punt 69 yards with 5:57 remaining to seal it.

The Buckeyes travelled to Los Angeles and led USC 3-0, but that was it in the 35-3 loss. Pryor, in relief of Boeckman, was successful enough with his mobility to avoid sacks except for once, had 40 yards rushing and the team's longest run of 13 yards, and was seven-for-nine passing to earn the start next week and for the rest of the year.

The Buckeyes played the Trojans again (Troy University), and four of Pryor's ten completions were for touchdowns, two to Hartline, in the 28-10 win over these Trojans, who had a 315-309 edge in total yards. Kurt Coleman had two interceptions.

The Buckeyes had a 34-6 lead and beat Minnesota 34-21. Chris Wells returned with 106 yards, and Pryor ran for 97 and two touchdowns. Both Pryor and Boeckman threw scoring passes to Robiskie, and the defense held the Gophers to 81 yards on the ground.

The Buckeyes scored first and last in the 20-17 win at Wisconsin, with Pryor scoring on an 11-yard run with 1:08 remaining to cap a 12-play, 80-yard drive. Wells scored on a 33-yard run on the opening series and had a 54-yard run later, finishing with 168, and Malcolm Jenkins intercepted on the Badgers' last possession with under a minute remaining. The Buckeyes had one more yard in total offense.

The Buckeyes were outgained in total offense 298-222 but beat Purdue 16-3, scoring a touchdown only on Etienne Sabino's 20-yard return of a blocked punt on the Boilers' first possession. After throwing 60 passes in the game last year, the Boilers' Curtis Painter had only 51 in this game. Malcolm Jenkins intercepted for the second straight game, and the defense held the Boilers to 70 yards on the ground.

I was at the Wake Forest-Maryland game in the DC area during the Michigan State game, but I caught the second half of the 45-7 win. Chris Wells ran for 140 yards and two touchdowns, and in the fourth quarter, Thaddeus Gibson had a 69-yard fumble return and Jermale Hines had a 48-yard fumble return for scores. The Buckeyes had a 5-0 advantage in turnovers. For the Spartans, two future NFL quarterbacks would see action—Kirk Cousins and Brian Hoyer.

Pryor passed for 226 yards, but Penn State scored 10 points in the fourth quarter in Columbus to win 13-6. Pryor's last pass from the Penn State 43 was intercepted in the end zone with 27 seconds remaining. The two teams were seven points apart and six yards apart. The two quarterbacks were Pryor from Pennsylvania (Jeannette) and Daryll Clark from Ohio (Youngstown).

Chris Wells ran for 140 yards and two touchdowns, and Pryor passed for three scores, including two to Robiskie in the 45-10 win at Northwestern. The Wildcats' quarterback Mike Kafka ran or passed for 260 of their 294 yards.

Four Buckeyes had a touchdown each, and Malcolm Jenkins blocked a punt for a safety in the 30-20 win over Illinois. Pryor rested his arm for the next week with only 10 passes, but he ran for 110 yards, with Chris Wells running for 143, part of the team's 305 yards on the ground. The Illini outgained the Buckeyes, 455-354, the third straight year that they had more yards.

The score was only 14-7 at halftime, but the Buckeyes scored 28 unanswered to beat Michigan 42-7, outgaining the Wolverines 416-198. Chris Wells ran for 134 yards and a touchdown, making it into the end zone all three years against Michigan. In his last game at Ohio Stadium, Boeckman threw an 18-yard scoring pass to Hartline. Between Pryor and Boeckman, three of the eight completions went for scores, two to Hartline and one to Robiskie.

The Buckeyes played in the Phoenix area for the fifth time in seven years, losing to Texas 24-21 in the Fiesta Bowl after leading 6-3 at halftime. Both Buckeye touchdowns were scored in the fourth quarter by freshmen, Pryor as a split end catching a 5-yard pass from Boeckman, and Dan Herron on a 15-yard run for the lead with 2:05 remaining. Texas followed Herron's score with a 78-yard drive, with the winning touchdown pass of 26 yards from Colt McCoy with 16 seconds remaining. The Longhorns' fourth down conversion two plays earlier was by inches, as the official account shows: "Spot was reviewed and confirmed."

Chris Wells ran for 106 yards, and Robiskie had half of the team's ten receptions for 116 yards. Colt McCoy was 41 for 58 passing for 414 yards. He had minus 15 yards on the ground, but he danced into the end zone from 14 yards for their first touchdown. The defense held the Longhorns to 54 yards on the ground. The Longhorns' previous lowest scoring game had been 28 against another OSU—Oklahoma State.

FUN FACTS:
- The highest combined scoring in consecutive games was the 75 against Northwestern and Illinois on the road, in front of the two smallest crowds of the year.

- Freshmen Pryor and Herron combined for 12 of the 21 rushing touchdowns, and freshman Pryor threw 12 of the 17 passing touchdowns.

- The edge in passing touchdowns was 17-12, even though the opponents had 173 more passes and 93 more completions.

- Opponents averaged five yards per game in punt returns.

- The Buckeyes had 14 more yards on one punt return (80 by Ray Small) than the opponents had on the year.

- For the second straight year, Donald Washington had the longest interception return.

- The edge in rushing touchdowns was 21-7.

- Playing in 10 games, Chris Wells had eight rushing touchdowns, compared to the opponents' seven.

2009 (11-2)

In 2009, I went to the Rose Bowl, but did not go to the Rose Bowl. Say what? In August, I took the Diamond Baseball tour of the West Coast, where we saw six games in six days in six ballparks—Los Angeles, Oakland, San Francisco, Anaheim, San Diego, and Phoenix. The first day in Los Angeles, we visited the Rose Bowl stadium. A guy on the trip from Oregon told me that the Oregon Ducks, whom the Buckeyes would play in six months, had a new coach, Chip Kelly.

The Buckeyes led Navy 20-7 at halftime in the opener, but they were facing a possible tie as Navy lined up for a two point conversion with 2:23 remaining. Brian Rolle intercepted the pass and returned it for two points in the 31-27 win, almost the identical score as the 1981 Liberty Bowl win (31-28) over the Midshipmen. The 27 points would be the most scored by any opponent this year.

In front of a new stadium attendance record at night, the Buckeyes lost to USC, 18-15. The Buckeyes led 15-10, but the Trojans scored with 1:05 remaining. The two teams combined for only 206 rushing yards, 88 by the Buckeyes. Going back to the Fiesta Bowl of last year, those last two losses were by three points each in the closing moments. Like the 2005 loss to Texas, this was a three point loss in a non-conference night game in Ohio Stadium.

Pryor had 372 yards of total offense—110 on the ground with a score and 262 passing with three touchdowns—in the 38-0 win over Toledo in Cleveland, with the Rockets as the home team. Dane Sanzenbacher, a native of Toledo, had a breakout game with five receptions for 126 yards and two scores, and the total offense was 522-210 in favor of the Buckeyes. The defense held the Rockets to 13 yards on the ground, with a long of eight.

The defense held Illinois to 170 yards in the 30-0 win. Sanzenbacher had another touchdown reception, and the defense picked off three Illini passes.

Brandon Saine ran for 113 yards, and Pryor tossed touchdowns to three different receivers in the 33-14 win at Indiana. The defense held the Hoosiers to 18 yards on the ground, with a long of nine.

Wisconsin had exactly twice as many total yards, 368-184, an edge of 89-40 in plays and 22-8 in first downs, and an advantage of 42:47 to 17:13 in time of possession, but the Buckeyes scored three touchdowns on defense and special teams—Kurt Coleman on an 89-yard interception return, Jermale Hines on a 32-yard interception return, and Ray Small on a 96-yard kickoff return—in the 31-13 win. It was the only game of the year in which the Buckeyes had an interception for a score, and the only game in which the Buckeyes had a kickoff return for a score. The defense had six sacks of Badger quarterback Scott Tolzien.

The Buckeyes turned the ball over five times in the 26-18 loss at Purdue, trailing at one point 23-7. Down 26-10 with 7:14 remaining, Pryor hit Posey with a 25-yard pass and scored a two point conversion to cut it to eight, but the Buckeyes could not score on their last possession. The Boilers had 24 more plays, 12 more first downs, and 12 more minutes of possession time, and passed 52 times, making their total 163 in the last three years against the Buckeyes. Pryor passed for 221 yards, but the ground game had only 66 yards.

The offense had 509 yards in the 38-7 win over Minnesota. Pryor ran for 104 yards and a score, also passing for 239 and touchdown plays of 62 and 57 yards to DeVier Posey, who had eight catches for 161 yards.

The defense held New Mexico State to 62 yards and two first downs, both in the first half, in the 45-0 win. The Buckeyes failed to score in the first and fourth quarters, but Pryor accounted for three touchdowns in the second quarter with an 8-yard run and passes to Dane Sanzenbacher of 19 and 39 yards. Brian Rolle scored on a fumble recovery, and Dan Herron scored on the longest run of the year, 53 yards. Ten ball carriers totaled 310 yards.

Pryor accounted for all three touchdowns in the 24-7 win at Penn State—a 7-yard run, a 62-yard pass to Posey, and a 6-yard pass to Brandon Saine. The defense held the Nittany Lions to 201 yards and nine first downs. Ray Small had 130 yards on punt returns, while Penn State had zero.

The Buckeyes had a 24-10 lead on Iowa in the fourth quarter, but they needed overtime to win 27-24. Devin Barclay, who had switched jersey numbers from 12 to 23 during the year, kicked a 39-yard field goal after the defense forced the Hawkeyes out of field goal range on their over-time possession. Iowa started their comeback with a 99-yard kickoff return for a touchdown. Brandon Saine ran for 103 yards and two touchdowns, and Anderson Russell had two of the Buckeyes' three interceptions.

I was at the Virginia-Clemson game in South Carolina when the Buckeyes won at Michigan 21-10. All three touchdowns were unconventional—Cameron Heyward recovered a fumble in the end zone, Saine scored on a 29-yard counter run, and Herron scored on a 12-yard middle screen pass. Kurt Coleman had two interceptions, and the team had three interceptions in the fourth quarter, with Devon Torrence picking one off at the goal line. The Buckeyes had only nine more yards of offense but a 251-80 edge on the ground. It was the second straight 11-point win in Ann Arbor.

Pryor had been "limited" to 17 passes in each of the previous three games, but he came out firing—passing eight times in the first series—and finished 23 of 37 for 266 yards and two touchdowns in the 26-17 Rose Bowl win over Oregon. He ran or passed for 338 of the team's 419 yards. Sanzenbacher had nine receptions, and Posey had eight for 101 yards, but the key catch was Jake Ballard's only one of the game for 24 yards on a third-and-13 play, a leaping jump-ball catch to keep a fourth quarter drive alive. Both Pryor and Ballard are 6'6" former basketball players. The catch led to Posey's 17-yard scoring catch that made it a two-score game. Devin Barclay and Aaron Pettrey combined to go four-for-four on field goals. Each hit one in the last 1:05 of the first half; Pettrey's 45-yarder came on the last play, following Ross Homan's interception.

The Buckeyes had a 41:37 to 18:23 advantage in possession time; 419-260 in total offense; 26-12 in first downs; 89-53 in plays; and 11/21 to 2/11 in third down conversions. Like the Rose Bowl win of the 1968 season, the combined score was 43 points.

FUN FACTS:

- The defense held opponents to 90.8 rushing yards per game.

- Rushing yards in the last three years were 2,553 in 2007; 2,502 in 2008; and 2,540 in 2009.

- Pryor's eight passes on the first drive of the Rose Bowl matched the Buckeyes' total in the entire Rose Bowl game of the 1973 season.

- Ray Small had the longest kickoff and punt return.

- Opponents averaged less than four yards per game in punt returns.

- The edge in rushing touchdowns was 20-8.

- The edge in passing touchdowns was 19-10, even though the opponents had 101 more passes and 52 more completions.

- The Buckeyes averaged two more passing yards per game than did the opponents.

- The edge in interceptions was 24-11.

- Twelve defenders had an interception.

- The last five regular season games had an attendance of at least 104,000.

- The two lowest attendances were in the state of Indiana, and the combined attendance was less than the smallest crowd at any OSU home game.

- All 12 regular season games were in Ohio or a bordering state.

CHAPTER 7

The 2010s and Beyond
Urban Renewal and a New Day

2010 (12-1)

MARK, BEVERLY, AND I went to the basketball game in West Lafayette on January 12, the game where Evan Turner led a huge comeback for the win. On the way back, I saw the newsflash that the opening game against Marshall would move to a Thursday night.

In that 45-7 win over Marshall, the Buckeyes had a 529-199 edge in total yards. Brandon Saine ran for 103 yards; Pryor passed for 247—giving him 513 in the last two games—and three touchdowns, two to Posey, and Sanzenbacher had 113 receiving yards. Brian Rolle had a 30-yard interception return for a score. The defense held the Thundering Herd to 44 yards on the ground.

The Miami Hurricanes scored 24 points, the same as in the championship game of the 2002 season, as the Buckeyes won in Columbus, 36-24. Pryor ran for 113 yards and passed for 233, and Posey had 105 receiving yards. The defense had four interceptions for 124 yards, with Cameron Heyward returning one for 80 without scoring. Devin Barclay made five of his six field goal attempts, the five tying the OSU record. Miami had an 88-yard kickoff return and a 79-yard punt return for scores.

The Buckeyes had a 439-162 advantage in total yards and almost 16 more minutes of possession in the 43-7 win over the Ohio Bobcats. Pryor and Joe Bauserman distributed 281 passing yards to 10 receivers.

Twelve receivers—including Pryor catching a 20-yard scoring pass from high school teammate Jordan Hall—combined for 303 yards and six touchdowns, with Sanzenbacher scoring four times in the 73-20 beatdown of Eastern Michigan. Pryor passed for 224 yards and four touchdowns, adding 104 yards and another score on the ground. Joe Bauserman made it three Buckeyes to throw a touchdown pass, with a 17-yard toss to Jordan Hall. Ten ball carriers combined for 342 yards. The defense held Eastern Michigan to 40 yards on the ground.

The Buckeyes led only 17-13 with 1:49 left in the game before Dan Herron scored on a 6-yard run for the final 24-13 score at Illinois. Pryor ran for 104 yards, including his longest run of the year of 66 yards.

Pryor passed for 334 yards and three touchdowns as the Buckeyes jumped out to a 38-0 lead in the 38-10 win over Indiana. Posey had 103 receiving yards and a score, and the defense held the Hoosiers to 210 yards, picking off three passes.

Wisconsin scored the first 21 points—including the opening kickoff for 97 yards—and the last 10 in their 31-18 win in Madison to give the Buckeyes their only loss of the year. Herron scored the team's two touchdowns. It was the only game of the year where the Buckeyes did not have both a rushing and a passing touchdown, and the only game where the opponent had more than one rushing touchdown.

Pryor passed for 270 yards, and 11 different receivers had a catch, with four receivers catching a touchdown pass, in the 49-0 win over Purdue. The Buckeyes had a 489-118 edge in total offense. Kenny Guiton threw the only completion of his freshman year. Spoiler alert: He would play a key role in 2012, especially against Purdue, and in 2013.

During timeouts in this game, movie director and OSU alumnus Don Handfield filmed scenes for his film *Touchback*. A camera operator and two actors in football uniforms hustled onto the field near the north end zone for clips of a quarterback calling signals under center.

I went to the Minnesota game in Minneapolis, a 52-10 win in their year-old TCF Bank Stadium. Herron ran for 114 yards, and Posey had 115 receiving yards. In the second half, Zach Domicone recovered a blocked punt, and John Simon returned a fumble 30 yards off a quarterback sack for scores. Total offense was 507-232 for the Buckeyes.

The Buckeyes trailed Penn State 14-3 at halftime, but five different players scored in the second half to win 38-14. Herron ran for 190 yards, as the Buckeyes had 306 of their 453 yards in the second half. As in the 2006 Penn State game, the defense returned two interceptions for touchdowns, by Devon Torrence and Travis Howard.

The Buckeyes trailed 17-10 in the fourth quarter, but Herron scored with 1:47 remaining to pull out the 20-17 win at Iowa. Sanzenbacher had 102 receiving yards, and Reid Fragel had his only touchdown catch of the year for the team's other score. Pryor had 273 yards in total offense and was the team's leading rusher with 78 yards.

After a scoreless first period, the Buckeyes scored 24 in the second and beat Michigan 37-7. Four different Buckeyes scored a touchdown, with Jordan Hall answering the Wolverines' only score with an 85-yard kickoff return. Herron had 175 yards and the team's longest run of the year, an 89-yard carry from the OSU 2-yard line to the Michigan 9-yard line. Pryor passed for 220 yards, with scoring passes to Sanzenbacher and Posey. It would be the last regular season game for Jim Tressel and for coach Rich Rodriguez at Michigan.

Terrelle Pryor was to bowl games as Troy Smith was to Michigan games, as the Buckeyes finally beat a SEC team in a bowl game. In the 31-26 Sugar Bowl win over Arkansas, his total offense was 336 yards, after posting 338 in last year's Rose Bowl. The Buckeyes led 28-10 at halftime and 31-13 in the third quarter. Arkansas recorded a safety on a ruling after it appeared that Dan Herron's forward progress had taken him out of the end zone.

After a blocked punt that gave the Razorbacks the ball at the OSU 18-yard line, defensive lineman Solomon Thomas intercepted a Ryan Mallett pass with 58 seconds remaining, the only pick for either team. Posey had a touchdown catch for the second straight bowl game.

The two teams combined for 848 yards, though the Buckeyes had 338 of their 446 in the first half. The two punters drew rave reviews from the broadcasters when they combined to record "In20"s (Inside the 20) on six of their 11 punts.

FUN FACTS:

- Pryor, Herron, Saine, Posey, Sanzenbacher, and Jaamal Berry each had a play from scrimmage of at least 60 yards.

- Jordan Hall had a 70-yard punt return and an 85-yard kickoff return, and Cameron Heyward had an 80-yard interception return.

- Jordan Hall scored on a run, a reception, and a kickoff return, and threw a pass for a touchdown.

- Fourteen players had an interception.

- The defense held opponents to 96.7 rushing yards per game, the second straight year under 100.

- The edge in rushing touchdowns was 27-9.

- Herron had 16 rushing touchdowns, compared to the opponents' nine.

- The edge in passing touchdowns was 30-9, even though the opponents had 36 more passes.

- Dane Sanzenbacher had 11 receiving touchdowns, compared to the opponents' nine.

2011 (6-7)

In Luke Fickell's first game as interim head coach on a 93-degree day, Jake Stoneburner caught three touchdown passes from Joe Bauserman in the 42-0 win over Akron. Bauserman added a score on the ground, and he and freshman Braxton Miller combined for 293 passing yards to 11 different receivers, as the total offense was 517-90 in favor of the Buckeyes. The defense held the Zips to 35 yards on the ground.

Playing another Mid-American Conference team, the Buckeyes trailed Toledo 22-21 in the third quarter before Carlos Hyde's second touchdown of the game produced a 27-22 win, with neither team scoring in the fourth quarter. Stoneburner had his fourth touchdown catch in two games, and Chris Fields had a 69-yard punt return for a score. Fields's return was the only touchdown on the year that would not come from the offense. Toledo outgained the Buckeyes 338-301, with 292 of the Rockets' yards coming through the air.

The Buckeyes traveled to Miami Gardens and managed only two Drew Basil field goals in the 24-6 loss to the Miami Hurricanes. Bauserman and Miller combined to complete only four passes out of 18 attempts for 35 yards. Counting this game, in the last four games between the two teams, Miami scored 23, 24, 24, and 24 points. In the five games between the two teams, each team scored 95 points. This was the fourth different venue in the five matchups between the two teams.

The Buckeyes had only 22 more total yards, but they easily beat Colorado in Columbus, 37-17. In his first start as quarterback, Braxton Miller threw two touchdown passes to Devin Smith and ran and passed for 83 yards each. Jordan Hall had a 90-yard kickoff return that led to a Carlos Hyde 5-yard touchdown run.

The Buckeyes managed only a 33-yard touchdown pass from Bauserman to Evan Spencer with ten seconds remaining in the 10-7 loss to Michigan State in Columbus. For the Spartans, future NFL players Kirk Cousins passed for 250 yards, Le'Veon Bell of Groveport Madison High School ran for 50 yards, and B.J. Cunningham of Westerville South High School had 154 receiving yards and their only touchdown. MSU's defense sacked Bauserman and Miller nine times.

The Buckeyes had a 27-6 lead in the third quarter at Nebraska before losing 34-27. Hyde ran for 104 yards and two touchdowns, and Miller added 91, but Bauserman and Miller combined to complete only six passes out of 18 attempts, with Miller connecting on a 32-yard scoring strike to Stoneburner.

Miller had only one completion in four attempts in the 17-7 win at Illinois, but he made it count with a 17-yard scoring pass to Stoneburner. Dan Herron ran for 114 yards and scored the other touchdown.

Facing another future NFL quarterback in Russell Wilson, the Buckeyes beat Wisconsin 33-29 in an Instant Classic, with each team scoring a touchdown within a minute in the last 1:18. The Buckeyes had a 26-14 lead with 3:48 left before the Badgers scored twice to take a 29-26 lead with 1:18 remaining. Miller had only 89 yards passing, but he threw the winning pass of 40 yards to Devin Smith, Smith's only catch of the game, with 20 seconds remaining. Miller came dangerously close to the line of scrimmage on his heave to Smith, but video review confirmed that it was a proper pass. Herron ran for 160 yards and Miller for 99 with two touchdowns, including one of 44. The Buckeyes had 104 yards and three points in the first half, and 253 yards and 30 points in the second. The teams scored 52 of the 62 points in the second half.

After a 13-13 tie at halftime, the Buckeyes beat Indiana 34-20 in Columbus. Three Buckeyes ran for 100 plus yards—Herron with 141, Miller with 105 and an 81-yard scoring run, and Carlos Hyde with 105.

A blocked PAT kick after a Buckeye touchdown with 55 seconds remaining kept the score tied and produced overtime at Purdue, where the Boilers won 26-23. Jordan Hall had two touchdown receptions, the last one on a fourth down Miller scramble. Drew Basil had a 33-yard field goal in overtime, but Purdue had a touchdown to win it.

All the scoring was in the first half as Penn State won in Columbus, 20-14. Miller ran for 105 and a score, and he passed to Stoneburner for the other. The two teams combined for 171 yards passing.

Miller had 335—100 rushing and 235 passing—of the team's 372 yards in the 40-34 loss at Michigan. Corey Brown had a 54-yard reception for the first score, the Buckeyes' longest completion of the year, and four Buckeyes each had a touchdown. On the Buckeyes' last possession, Miller overthrew a wide open DeVier Posey, all alone streaking down the left sideline. On third down, Miller misunderstood the signal from Coach Fickell and spiked the ball; on the next play, he was intercepted, the Buckeyes' only turnover of the game.

I did not watch this game. I was at the Marshall vs. East Carolina game in Huntington, West Virginia, where I saw the Thundering Herd receiver Aaron Dobson make a catch that ESPN ranked as one of the best of the year and was described on the Marshall website as "a leaping, backhanded 13-yard TD grab just before halftime that became a viral social media sensation almost immediately." The East Carolina offensive coordinator that day was Lincoln Riley, the eventual Oklahoma head coach.

Neither team had 300 yards, though the Buckeyes had more yards and more first downs in the Gator Bowl Classic, where Florida won 24-17 in a contest between two teams with a 6-6 record and with a coach (Will Muschamp at Florida) in his first year at the head of a FBS team. Down 24-10, Jordan Hall caught an 11-yard touchdown pass from Miller with 57 seconds remaining, but the onside kick was unsuccessful. Similar to the OSU-Miami game the year before, the team from Florida scored 24 points and had two non-offensive touchdowns, the Gators scoring on a 99-yard kickoff return and a blocked punt return.

Despite the 6-7 record, the team never gave up, as evidenced by the fact that after the first quarter, the Buckeyes outscored the opponents 267-174. They scored the last touchdown of the game against Michigan State, Purdue in regulation, Michigan, and Florida. Six of the seven losses were by seven points or less, which meant that the Buckeyes easily could have had a record close to 12-1. Ten years earlier, in Coach Tressel's debut, the Buckeyes easily could have gone 11-1. Spoiler alert: Next year would be different.

FUN FACTS:

- Half of Jake Stoneburner's 14 receptions were for touchdowns.

- The Buckeyes averaged 10 yards per punt return, but they had six games with zero yards on punt returns.

- Interception return yards were 128 for the Buckeyes vs. one for the opponents.

- Both the Buckeyes and the opponents had 18 touchdown passes, even though the opponents had 107 more passes and 89 more completions.

2012 (12-0)

When the rumors flew that Urban Meyer could be the new coach, a friend called me to ask if I thought it could happen. I said, "No way," based on the 2010 *Sports Illustrated* story on his tenuous health issue. Remind me again that I am no expert!

Coach Meyer described the offense of 2011 as a "clown show." The three leading receivers had only 14 receptions each. Corey Brown was one of them, and he would explode for 60 receptions in 2012.

Seven Buckeyes scored touchdowns, two by Carlos Hyde, in the opener against the Miami RedHawks, a 56-10 win. Trailing 3-0 after the first quarter, Devin Smith's one-hand catch for a score started the landslide. The offense had 538 yards, and the defense held Miami to minus one on the ground, with a long of six yards. Miller ran for 161 yards and passed for 207, Bradley Roby recovered a fumble for a score, and Travis Howard had two interceptions.

In a battle between two universities among those with the largest student enrollment, Miller accounted for all four touchdowns in the 31-16 win over Central Florida. He ran for 141 and three scores and passed for 155 and another to Stoneburner. The defense picked off future NFL quarterback Blake Bortles three times.

With the score tied at 28, Miller found Devin Smith all alone down the right sideline, and the 72-yard pass play, the team's longest of the year, was the winner in the 35-28 win over California. Again, Miller accounted for all the touchdowns, passing for 249 and four scores. Smith had five catches for 145 yards and two touchdowns, and Stoneburner had two scores. The Bears' Brendan Bigelow carried only four times, but he had scoring runs of 59 and 81 among his 160 yards.

The Buckeyes trailed the University of Alabama at Birmingham 9-0 in the second quarter after a blocked punt return for a score and a field goal, and trailed 12-7 later, but they had three touchdowns in that quarter and won 29-15. Jordan Hall ran for 105 yards, but the Blazers outgained the Buckeyes 403-347 and had two more first downs and seven more minutes of possession time.

The Buckeyes would have only four of the 12 games on the road, and the first was a 17-16 win over Michigan State. Miller ran for 136 yards and passed for 179, connecting with Devin Smith—they must have liked the right sideline—for the 63-yard go-ahead touchdown in the third quarter. Coach Meyer called this game the turning point of the season. The last two games in this series were decided by a total of four points.

Bradley Roby had two of the team's three interceptions, including one of 41 yards for the first touchdown, in the 63-38 win over

Nebraska in a night game. The Cornhuskers would have leads of 14-7 and 24-21. Miller ran for 186 yards, and Carlos Hyde for 140 and four touchdowns, as the Buckeyes rolled up 371 yards on the ground and the two teams combined for 935 total yards. Coach Meyer called the crowd noise "an inferno."

Mark, Beverly, and I went to the Indiana game in Bloomington. Scoring over 50 for the second straight game and third time in seven games, the Buckeyes won 52-49 in a game that spanned two days, starting at 8 p.m. and ending after midnight. The two teams combined for 1,059 total yards and five touchdowns on plays of at least 46 yards. Each team scored in each quarter, and the Buckeyes had an 18-point lead twice in the fourth quarter. Corey Brown scored the first touchdown and recovered the onside kick with 1:05 remaining. Noteworthy is the fact that the Hoosier coach was eventual OSU offensive coordinator Kevin Wilson. Hyde ran for 156 yards, Devin Smith had 106 receiving yards, and Miller ran for 149 and passed for 211. Bradley Roby recovered a punt blocked by Jordan Hall for a touchdown, scoring in the second straight game.

For the second straight year, the Purdue game went into overtime, with the Buckeyes winning 29-22. The Boilers' first two touchdowns came on an 83-yard pass play on the first play of the game and a 100-yard kickoff return. The Buckeyes blocked the PAT kick after the first touchdown, and the Boilers had blocked the Buckeyes' PAT kick after the last touchdown the previous year, significant events in games that went into overtime. The Buckeyes also blocked a 34-yard field goal attempt. With Miller injured late in the third quarter, Kenny Guiton led the last drive of the game, seven plays for 61 yards. With the Buckeyes down 22-14, Devin Smith had the longest Buckeye catch of the game, 39 yards, and Chris Fields had the shortest catch of the day for either team, two yards, with three seconds remaining for the touchdown. I was surprised that it was not reviewed, as he seemed to catch it inches off the turf. Fields had three of his four receptions on the year in this game, and it was his first career touchdown catch. Another Fields catch in the third quarter was for 35 yards to the Purdue 2-yard line, where Carlos Hyde scored. Jeff Heuerman caught the conversion pass to tie it at 22, and Hyde had the winning touchdown in overtime. Coach Meyer called Guiton the Old Righthander, coming in from the bullpen to pull the win out.

The Penn State game was tied at seven at halftime, but Ryan Shazier's 17-yard interception return for a touchdown keyed the 35-23 win in Happy Valley. Miller ran for 134 yards and two one-yard touchdowns, and passed for 143, about half of it on one play, a 72-yard scoring play to Stoneburner to match the longest pass play of the year. The defense held the Nittany Lions to 32 yards on the ground with a long of nine.

The Buckeyes had a 567-170 edge in total yards in the 52-22 win over Illinois, posting 24 points in the second quarter. Hyde ran for 137 yards and three touchdowns, and Miller passed for 226 yards and two scores.

In the second overtime game in four weeks, the Buckeyes beat Wisconsin 21-14 in Madison. Last year, the home team Buckeyes had scored with 20 seconds remaining in regulation, and, this year, the home team Badgers scored with eight seconds remaining in regulation. In both overtime games this year, Carlos Hyde scored the winning touchdown on a run of two yards or less, and in each game, he had a touchdown in regulation. The Buckeyes were outgained in total offense, 360-236, but Corey Brown scored the first touchdown on a 68-yard punt return. Ryan Shazier denied a Badger score with under three minutes remaining in regulation by forcing a fumble at the 2-yard line, the only turnover in the game, and Christian Bryant broke up the Badgers' fourth down pass in overtime for the win.

Drew Basil had half of his field goal total of the year by kicking four in the 26-21 win over Michigan, including a 52-yarder on the last play of the first half, his longest of the year, and two more in the second half, the only scoring in the second half for either team. Hyde ran for 146 yards, and Miller passed for 189. Michigan's 279 yards of total offense, including two scoring plays of 67 and 75 yards and with only 60 yards in the second half, represented the Buckeyes defense's second best performance of the year.

In the post-game TV interview, Meyer, who had said the week before that he considered his team good but not great, said that yes, this was a great team. This would be Coach Meyer's only season at OSU in which the defense gave up at least 10 points in each game.

FUN FACTS:

- Miller had a 72-yard scoring run and two 72-yard passing touchdowns.

- Bradley Roby scored touchdowns on a punt, interception, and fumble return.

- The team scored 104 points in the third quarter and 104 in the fourth.

- The team scored 224 points in the first half and 222 points in the second half and overtimes.

- The edge in rushing touchdowns was 37-14.

- Hyde's 16 rushing touchdowns were two more than the opponents' total.

- The edge in passing touchdowns was 17-15, even though the opponents had 179 more passes and 106 more completions.

- The edge in interception return yardage was 164-6.

- The two closest games came in front of the two smallest crowds of the year, at Michigan State and Indiana.

- Half of the 12 wins came by seven points or less.

2013 (12-2)

The spring game was at Paul Brown Stadium in Cincinnati. For Paul Hummel, our software expert who recorded stats and lived in the Cincinnati area and made the trip to Columbus for the home games no matter if it was a noon or 8 p.m. start, this was a short jaunt for him. Paul Brown Stadium marked the fifth different site where I had seen a spring game—adding to Ohio Stadium, Crew Stadium, the practice field south of the Woody Hayes Athletic Center, and a spring game in the Kings Island area in the 1980s.

The Buckeyes scored the first 23 points and the last ten in the opening 40-20 win over Buffalo. Jordan Hall ran for 159 yards and two touchdowns, and Miller passed for 178 yards and two scores. Chris Fields caught a touchdown pass from Miller and one from Guiton. The big play for the Bulls was a 45-yard interception return for a score by Khalil Mack, the longest interception return against the Buckeyes all year.

The Buckeyes led 35-0 at halftime and coasted to a 42-7 win over San Diego State. Miller was injured in the first series and was done for the day. Guiton passed for 152 yards and two touchdowns, both to Corey Brown, and ran for 83 yards and another score. The defense held the Aztecs to 64 yards on the ground.

Miller was out of action for the 52-34 win at California, but Guiton had a Miller-like game, running for 92 yards and passing for 276 and four touchdowns, three of them in the first quarter, including two to Devin Smith of 90—the longest pass play in OSU history—and 47 yards. Jordan Hall ran for 168 yards and three touchdowns, and Smith finished with 149 yards. The two teams combined for 1,111 yards, 608 by the Buckeyes. Future NFL quarterback Jared Goff passed for 371 yards and three touchdowns for the Golden Bears, to 12 receivers.

Five different Buckeyes scored in the first quarter as the Buckeyes scored 34 and cruised to a 76-0 win over Florida A&M. In all, eight Buckeyes had a touchdown, and ten caught a pass. The two leading ball carriers would make a bigger name for themselves next year—Ezekiel Elliott ran for 162 yards and two touchdowns, and Cardale Jones for 52 and another score. Jordan Hall carried four times and scored twice. Total offense was 603-80 in favor of the Buckeyes, and Florida A&M's longest play was 10 yards.

Miller returned for the 31-24 win over Wisconsin and passed for 198 yards and all four touchdowns, two to Corey Brown. The Badgers scored the last 10 points of the game and had another possession, but it was after Cameron Johnston's 55-yard punt pinned them at their 10-yard line with 1:29 remaining.

In a tight game at Northwestern, the Buckeyes trailed 20-13 at half-time and 23-13 in the third quarter before winning 40-30. Bradley Roby scored the first touchdown on a blocked punt return, and Joey Bosa's recovery of a fumble on the last play of the game accounted for the final score. In between, Hyde ran for 168 yards and all three offensive touch-downs, all of them in the span of 14 minutes starting in the third quarter. Miller passed for 203, and Corey Brown had six catches for 127 yards.

The home game against Iowa was tied at 24 at the end of three quar-ters before Hyde scored his second touchdown and Drew Basil added a 25-yard field goal for the final 34-24 score. Hyde ran for 149 yards, and Miller ran for 102 and passed for 222 and two touchdowns. If you like round numbers, note that the Buckeyes had 35 minutes of possession times, and the Hawkeyes had 25.

Nineteen years after losing at Penn State 63-14, the Buckeyes beat the Nittany Lions by the same score in Columbus. Hyde, Miller, and Guiton each ran for two touchdowns. Hyde ran for 147 yards, and Miller passed for 252 and three touchdowns to three different receivers, as the Buckeyes rolled up 686 yards on offense. Playing against his home state, the Buckeyes' other Corey Brown, nicknamed "Pitt," had his only interception of the year.

Seven Buckeyes scored touchdowns, starting with Doran Grant's 33-yard interception return on the second play of the game in the 56-0 win at Purdue, leading 42-0 at halftime. Total offense was 640 to 116 in favor of the Buckeyes. Hyde ran for 111 yards, Miller passed for 233 and four touchdowns, and Jeff Heuerman led eleven receivers with five catches for 116 yards and a score. Cardale Jones completed his only pass of the year for three yards. The defense had six sacks and held the Boilers to 27 yards on the ground.

Miller had a 70-yard run on the third play of the game, the team's longest of the year, and Bradley Roby had a 63-yard interception return, the team's longest of the year, in the first quarter of the 60-35 win at Illinois. Hyde ran for 246 yards and four touchdowns, and had a fifth on a reception, matching the five scores by Keith Byars against Illinois in 1984. Miller ran for 184; both he and Hyde had more yards on the ground than Illinois did as a team. The lead was only 12 with 8:49 remaining, but Hyde ripped off his fourth and fifth touchdowns on runs of 51 and 55. The two teams combined for 1,011 yards, and the 60 points resulted in a scoring total of 179 points in the last three games.

The Buckeyes led 42-0 and coasted to a 42-14 win over Indiana. For the second straight game, Miller (144) and Hyde (117) had over 100 yards on the ground, and each had two touchdowns. Miller passed for 160 and two more scores. The two teams combined for 913 yards.

Make it three straight games with over 100 rushing yards for Hyde (226) and Miller (153) in the Instant Classic 42-41 win at Michigan. Hyde made up for a fumble in the fourth quarter that allowed Michigan to tie the game at 35 by scoring the go-ahead touchdown with 2:20 remaining, his only score of the game. Miller ran for three touchdowns and passed for two more, and the two teams combined for 1,129 yards. The Wolverines scored with 32 seconds remaining and went for two and the lead. The Buckeyes had no official interceptions in the game, but Tyvis Powell picked off Devin Gardner's pass to seal the win. I was grateful for Michigan Coach Brady Hoke going for two, because the time that I had to leave to work a high school playoff game was fast approaching, and I would have had to miss the overtime if he had gone for the tie. It was the only one-point game ever played in Ann Arbor.

One of the most impressive plays of the year was Bradley Roby making up 30 yards to track down Jeremy Gallon at the end of an 84-yard pass play on Michigan's first possession.

In the Big Ten Championship Game, the Buckeyes trailed Michigan State 17-0 in the second quarter, came back to lead 24-17, and eventually lost, 34-24, Coach Meyer's first loss at Ohio State. Miller accounted for all three touchdowns, two on the ground and a scoring pass to Corey Brown. The key play of the game came with the Buckeyes down 27-24. On fourth and two on the MSU 39, Miller's run to the short side was stopped short of the first down marker with 5:41 remaining. In the fourth quarter, the Buckeyes had only 25 yards, all on the ground, and 12 plays. For the fourth straight game, Miller (142) and Hyde (118) topped 100 yards on the ground.

In the Orange Bowl, the Buckeyes led Clemson 35-34 in the fourth quarter but lost 40-35. C.J. Barnett intercepted Tiger quarterback Tajh Boyd with 1:27 remaining, but Miller was intercepted nine seconds later at the Clemson 39. Hyde ran for 113 and had a touchdown rushing and one receiving, and Miller passed for 234 yards and two scores. Corey Brown had eight receptions for 116 yards. The two teams combined for 1,003 yards.

FUN FACTS:

- How many teams have had a 24-game winning streak after a four-game losing streak?

- Hyde ran for 1,521 yards and Miller for 1,068, despite Hyde missing three games and Miller essentially missing three.

- Kenny Guiton, Ezekiel Elliott, and Dontre Wilson each averaged over eight yards per carry. The team averaged 6.8.

- Tight end Jeff Heuerman had the highest yards per catch with 17.9, almost three yards more than the next highest.

- The edge in rushing touchdowns was 45-9.

- Hyde (15) and Miller (12) had more rushing touchdowns than the opponents.

- The edge in passing touchdowns was 38-31, even though the opponents had 166 more passes and 92 more completions.

- The Buckeyes had 1,003 plays, and the opponents had 1,000.

- For the fourth straight year, the leader in kick scoring had the initials *DB*—Devin Barclay in 2010 and Drew Basil the last three years.

2014 (14-1)

With Miller injured before the season started, Coach Meyer turned to redshirt freshman J.T. Barrett. After the opening 34-17 win against Navy, played at M&T Bank Stadium in Baltimore, I said to myself, *Well, Barrett was a pleasant surprise.* He had 12 of 15 passing for 226 yards and two touchdowns in the second half, including an 80-yard play to Devin Smith. He also led the team with 50 yards on the ground. The Buckeyes trailed 7-6 at halftime and 14-13 in the third quarter, with their only touchdown a Darron Lee 61-yard fumble return. A few years before, I had worked games at New Albany High School, when Lee was a slender quarterback and kick returner. Ezekiel Elliott's 44 yards for the game gave no clue to what he would do this year. Navy ran on 63 plays, passed on only four, and had more first downs—22 to 19. The last time the Buckeyes had opened in the opponent's home state (1998 at West Virginia), the score was the same, 34-17. When the Buckeyes opened at Minnesota in 1974, 40 years previously, they also scored 34.

Barrett had a step back in the 35-21 loss to Virginia Tech, going nine for 29 with three interceptions, including a 63-yard pick-six with 46 seconds remaining. The Buckeyes trailed 21-7 at halftime, but they tied it at 21 in the fourth quarter. LeBron James and Orlando Pace were on the sideline taking in the action. It was the Buckeyes' first home-opening loss since losing in 1978 to Penn State. Coincidentally, both Penn State and Virginia Tech were independents in 1978. The Buckeyes had the four longest completions, the longest run, and a slim 327-320 edge in total yards. Despite losing for the third time in the last four games, Coach Meyer said in the post-game press conference that he had confidence in the team. He would be right.

Curtis Samuel had a breakout game with 100 yards and two touchdowns rushing, and Michael Thomas had two in as many catches as the Buckeyes rolled up 628 yards in the 66-0 rout of Kent State. Barrett passed for 312 yards to 11 receivers and threw six touchdown passes, tying a school record. The defense held Kent State to 126 yards, 47 on the ground. Elliott tied for the team high with four receptions, but, after three games, he had only 141 of his 1,878 rushing yards for the season.

The offense surpassed the previous week's output with 710 yards, and Elliott got untracked with 182 yards in the 50-28 win over Cincinnati. Each quarterback—Barrett and Gunner Keil for the Bearcats—had four touchdown passes, and they combined for 682 passing yards. Barrett connected with ten receivers, and Devin Smith had two scores. During the game, a fan ran onto the field, only to be tackled by assistant strength and conditioning coach Anthony Schlegel. In hindsight, the fan was fortunate that Schlegel was only the assistant coach.

The Buckeyes returned to the state of Maryland to welcome the Terrapins to the Big Ten and won, 52-24. Seven Buckeyes had one touchdown each, with Raekwon McMillan scoring the last one on a 19-yard interception return. Three other defenders also had an interception. Elliott ran for 139 yards, and Barrett passed for 267 and had touchdown passes to four different receivers, giving him 14 scoring strikes in the last three games.

The Buckeyes welcomed Rutgers to the Big Ten and Ohio Stadium with a 56-17 win. Barrett had over half of the team's 585 total yards with 107 and two touchdowns on the ground and 261 and three scores through the air, two of them to Nick Vannett. With the Buckeyes' Joey Bosa on defense and Gary Nova quarterbacking the Scarlet Knights, Jeff Logan told me during the week to look for the Bosa-Nova matchup.

The Buckeyes had a 17-0 halftime lead at Penn State, but they needed double overtime to win 31-24. Barrett scored both touchdowns in the overtimes. Elliott ran for 109 yards and the first touchdown, as the two teams combined for only 533 yards. The Nittany Lions scored on a 40-yard interception return on the Buckeyes' first possession of the second half and on a field goal with nine seconds remaining in regulation. Joey Bosa ended the game with a walk-off blind side sack, the team's fifth of the game. As in the 1995 and 2003 games in Happy Valley, the Buckeyes had huge breaks, kicking their field goal without the officials noticing that the play clock had expired and scoring a touchdown after Vonn Bell was credited with an interception, although he didn't catch it cleanly. Barrett had only 74 yards passing, his only game of the year under 167, but no one was complaining.

The Buckeyes had a balanced offense in the 55-14 win over Illinois, with Barrett passing for 167 yards and Cardale Jones for 82—two touchdowns each—and Elliott the leading rusher with 69 yards. Barrett had his two lowest passing games back-to-back with this one. Samuel ran for two touchdowns, and Devin Smith had two touchdown receptions.

The Buckeyes trailed 21-14 in the second quarter at Michigan State before Barrett hooked up on scoring strikes with Michael Thomas for 79 yards and Devin Smith for 44 yards about two minutes apart late in the quarter to ignite a 49-37 win. Elliott ran for 154 yards and two touchdowns, and Barrett passed for an even 300 and three scores. Smith finished with six catches for 129 yards. Barrett added two more touchdowns on the ground. This set a record for consecutive Big Ten regular season wins with 21. The two teams combined for 1,104 total yards, 658 passing.

The Buckeyes had their second 31-24 win in four weeks in frigid Minnesota. The Gophers scored twice to tie it at 14 in the second quarter and scored the last 10 in the fourth quarter, including a field goal with 1:19 remaining. Jeff Heuerman covered the onside kick to secure the win. Barrett ran for 189 yards, including the team's longest of the year and the longest ever by an Ohio State quarterback, 86 yards, and passed for 200 and three touchdowns. The 86-yard run meant that the two longest runs in team history on the road were at Minnesota, with Eddie George having an 87-yard run. The 189 yards set a single-game rushing record for an Ohio State quarterback. I recall Coach Meyer, who had spent six years coaching in the Sunshine State, saying after the game that anyone who thought that playing in Big Ten weather like this—15 degrees with a light snow—was easy should "have at it."

The Buckeyes trailed Indiana 20-14 midway through the third quarter, but Jalin Marshall had a 54-yard punt return—his first of four scores in less than 15 minutes—to ignite the 42-27 win. His three scoring receptions of the fourth quarter covered six, 15, and 54 yards. The four touchdowns represented half of his total for the year. Elliott ran for 107 yards, and Barrett passed for 302, with a fourth touchdown pass going to Heuerman.

The Buckeyes trailed Michigan 14-7 before Barrett scored on an improvised 25-yard run—Michigan had only a three man front on the play—that capped an 83-yard drive with seven seconds remaining before halftime in the 42-28 win. The Buckeyes were up 28-21 when on the first play of the fourth quarter, Barrett suffered a fractured ankle. Cardale Jones was unable to move the team on that drive, but he ran for 18 yards on a second-and-15 play on the next drive, which saw Elliott go 44 yards for a score on fourth and one. Darron Lee had a 33-yard fumble return to extend it to 42-21, giving him the first and last touchdowns of the regular season games. Elliott ran for 121 yards and another score. The Buckeyes became the first team in Big Ten history to go 8-0 in three straight seasons in conference play.

Thirty-five years earlier in Columbus, in 1979, the Buckeyes had beaten Wisconsin 59-0. They duplicated that score in the Big Ten Championship Game. Each game had a defensive score—a pass interception in 1979 and Joey Bosa's fumble recovery in this one. Elliott ran for 220 yards and two touchdowns, with a long of 81; Jones passed for 257 and three scores, averaging 21 yards per completion; and Devin Smith had 137 and all three receiving touchdowns on plays of 39, 44, and 42 yards. Samuel had two touchdowns on his four carries. The offense rolled up 558 yards, averaging 10 yards per play, and the defense picked off three passes, two by Doran Grant.

As in 1979, the Buckeyes followed the 59-0 win over Wisconsin by scoring 42 in the next game. In the 42-35 win over Alabama in the semifinal game, the Buckeyes trailed the Tide 21-6 but gained the momentum 12 seconds before halftime when Evan Spencer's only pass of the year went to Michael Thomas, who barely got his foot down in bounds in the end zone. They extended the lead to 34-21 when lineman Steve Miller returned an interception 41 yards for a score, the Buckeyes' longest return of the year. Four years earlier, an interception by lineman Solomon Thomas sealed the win against another SEC team, Arkansas, in the same stadium. With the ball on the OSU 15-yard line, it was time for (#15) Elliott's 85-yard run, his longest of the year, making the score 42-28, and Tyvis Powell intercepted in the end zone on the last play. All three interceptions by the Buckeye defense came in the last 18 minutes.

Elliott finished with 230 yards and two scores, and Jones passed for 243, as the Buckeyes totaled 537 yards, with a 348-139 edge in the first half. The last time that the Buckeyes faced Alabama in the Superdome, in the 1978 Sugar Bowl, the Crimson Tide also scored 35 points, in their 35-6 win.

Oregon scored first in the national championship game in Arlington, Texas, and trailed only 21-20 in the third quarter before Elliott scored his second, third, and fourth touchdowns of the game in the 42-20 win. The Buckeyes outscored the Ducks 21-10 in each half despite losing four to one in the turnover category. Elliott ran for 246 yards, and Jones passed for 242, as the offense rolled up 538 yards. The receiver with the most receptions for each team was Marshall—Jalin with five for the Buckeyes and Byron with eight for the Ducks. Eli Apple intercepted on the last play of the game, just as Tyvis Powell had against Alabama. The Buckeyes had almost 15 more minutes of possession. The last two times that these teams met, including the Rose Bowl of the 2009 season, the total advantage was 38 minutes.

It was Cardale Jones' second straight game in which his longest pass was 47 yards. In the last three games, Jones passed for 742 yards, and Elliott ran for 685.

FUN FACTS:
- Mantle and Maris were not the only M&M Boys. The Buckeyes' two interceptions for touchdowns were by Raekwon McMillan and Steve Miller, and for each it was his only pick of the year.

- Rod Smith and Marcus Baugh each had one reception, and it was for a touchdown.

- The two leaders in touchdowns scored were Elliott (#15) with 18 and Devin Smith (who had worn #15 as a freshman and sophomore) with 12.

- In '14, Devin Smith, who had only 14 receptions in 2011, averaged 28.2 yards per catch for 931 yards and 12 touchdowns.

- The Buckeyes had 41 rushing touchdowns and 42 passing touchdowns.

- The edge in rushing touchdowns was 41-24.

- The edge in passing touchdowns was 42-17, even though the opponents had 86 more passes and 16 more completions.

- Opponents punted exactly twice as often as the Buckeyes—96 to 48.

- Opponents averaged four yards per game in punt returns.

- The Buckeyes had a 451-58 edge in punt return yardage.

2015 (12-1)

During the season, Doral Chenoweth of the *Columbus Dispatch* recorded and uploaded a few minutes of video showing our official stats crew at work and including comments from Scott Rex, Mike Basford, and me.

In the opening 42-24 win on Labor Day at Virginia Tech, the answer to the question of who would be the starting quarterback came only moments before the game started: Jones took the field instead of Barrett. It was reminiscent of 1978—Rod Gerald or Art Schlichter? Similar to 1978, a former quarterback—Gerald in 1978 and Braxton Miller in 2015—switched to receiver. The Buckeyes trailed 17-14 at halftime, but two huge scoring plays by Miller in the third quarter turned the game around. He had his longest run of the year—53 yards (only Elliott would have a longer one in this game, 80 yards)—and his 54-yard reception was the team's longest of the year.

Five of the six touchdowns were at least 24 yards long. Elliott finished with 122 yards, and Barrett's only pass in relief was a 26-yard scoring strike to Michael Thomas. The total offense was 572 yards. This was the fifth time in the last six games, going back to the previous year, that the Buckeyes scored 42 points.

Five days later, Elliott ran for 101 yards and three touchdowns in the 38-0 home opening win over Hawaii. Vonn Bell scored on a 14-yard fumble recovery and added an interception, and the defense held Hawaii to 165 yards.

Even though Northern Illinois led 10-3 in the second quarter, the Buckeyes squeaked by with a 20-13 win. Jones started but threw two interceptions, so Barrett came in the second quarter and finished. Each team had one offensive touchdown, as Darron Lee had a 41-yard interception return for a score. Elliott ran for 108 yards, and for the second straight game, the defense held the opponents under 200 yards of offense.

Jones got the start in the 38-12 win over Western Michigan and passed for 288 yards and two touchdowns. For the third straight game, the defense had a touchdown when Adolphus Washington had a 20-yard interception return. Elliott ran for 124 yards and a score, and the offense totaled 511 yards. The Broncos had more than 14 more minutes of possession time.

For the second straight year, Indiana had a third quarter lead before the Buckeyes secured a 34-27 win. Elliott had scoring runs of 55, 65, and 75 yards in the second half and finished with 274 yards, 243 of those in the second half. Jones passed for 245 yards, and Jalin Marshall had six receptions for 110 yards, as the two teams combined for 919 yards.

The Maryland game was tied at 21 in the third quarter before the Buckeyes scored four straight times and won 49-28. Elliott ran for 106 yards and two touchdowns, Jones passed for 291 and two scores, and Michael Thomas had seven receptions for 107 yards. Barrett passed only twice, but he ran for three scores and had the team's longest run of 23 yards.

Penn State led 3-0 at the end of the first quarter before the Buckeyes scored three times in the second and cruised to a 38-10 win. Elliott ran for 153 yards, and Barrett ran for 102 and was involved in 15 plays, producing four touchdowns, two on the ground and two in the air. Saquon Barkley had 194 of the Nittany Lions' 195 rushing yards. Of the Lions' 315 total yards, 112 came on two plays.

The defense had a shutout until 13 seconds remained in the 49-7 win at Rutgers. Elliott ran for 142 yards and two touchdowns, and Barrett ran for 101 yards and two scores and passed for 223 yards and three scores to three different receivers. Michael Thomas had five catches for 103 yards, and the offense rolled up 528 yards.

After a bye week, and after a scoreless first quarter, Vonn Bell got the Buckeyes on the board with a 16-yard interception return in the 28-14 win over Minnesota. Elliott ran for 114 yards, and Cardale Jones's 38-yard scoring run with 1:53 remaining was five yards longer than the Gophers had on the ground for the entire game. Barrett was serving a one game suspension.

The Buckeyes scored a touchdown in each quarter in the 28-3 win at Illinois. Elliott ran for 181 yards and two touchdowns, and Barrett returned to run for a score and pass for another. It was the Buckeyes' fourth straight game without giving up a rushing touchdown.

In front of a new Ohio Stadium record crowd, Michigan State's Michael Geiger kicked a 41-yard field goal on the last play to pull the upset, 17-14. The Spartans had 22 more plays and more than 16 more minutes of possession, and the Buckeyes had only five first downs and 132 total yards—86 yards rushing and 46 yards passing. In all other games, their lows were 162 and 123. Elliott with 33 yards rushing was less than 100% health-wise for this game, the only time this season that he would not have at least 100 yards in a game. As in 1972, 1974, 1998, and 2013, the Spartans gave the Buckeyes their first loss, in November or December. In each of these five years, the Buckeyes beat Michigan.

The Buckeyes bounced back in a big way in the 42-13 win over Michigan in Jim Harbaugh's first year. The score was only 14-10 at half-time. Elliott and Barrett accounted for all six touchdowns—Elliott ran for 214 and two scores, and Barrett ran for 139 yards and three scores and passed for another. The defense held the Wolverines to 57 yards on the ground, with a long of eight.

It was the third time in the last five trips to Ann Arbor that a running back had over 200 yards—Chris Wells in 2007 and Carlos Hyde in 2013. It was the third straight year that the Buckeyes scored 42 on Michigan. Joey Bosa nearly had a pick-six interception late in the game. If he had scored, would Coach Meyer have gone for 50?

In his last game as a Buckeye, Elliott ran for 149 yards and four touchdowns in the 44-28 win over Notre Dame in the BattleFrog Fiesta Bowl in Glendale, Arizona. Barrett passed for 211 yards and had a scoring pass to Michael Thomas. Sean Nuernberger kicked three field goals in the fourth quarter. The two teams combined for 901 yards. Tyvis Powell had a knack for interceptions late in the game and in late-year games—picking off the two-point attempt against Michigan in 2013, on the last play against Alabama in 2014, and in the last six minutes in this game.

Like the bowl game against the Irish in the Phoenix area 10 years ago, Notre Dame's quarterback was from Ohio—Brady Quinn from Dublin in 2005 and DeShone Kizer from Toledo this year—and both would play for the Cleveland Browns.

FUN FACTS:
- Adolphus Washington and Darron Lee had interceptions for touchdowns. The Washington and Lee University football team went 10-1 in 2015.

- The opponents averaged 1:28 more possession time per game.

- The first quarter was the Buckeyes' lowest scoring quarter and also their best defensive quarter. The second quarter was the Buckeyes' best scoring quarter and also their worst defensive quarter.

- J.T. Barrett had 11 rushing touchdowns and 11 passing touchdowns.

- Opponents averaged 3.3 yards per game in punt returns.
- The edge in rushing touchdowns was 39-10.
- Elliott (23) and Barrett (11) each had more rushing touchdowns than the opponents.
- Elliott had more rushing yards (1,821) than the opponents (1,649).
- The edge in passing touchdowns was 19-14, even though the opponents had 86 more passes and three more completions.

2016 (11-2)

In the opening 77-10 win over Bowling Green, the first Buckeye touchdown of the year was a 47-yard pass from J.T. Barrett to K.J. Hill—Hill's longest of the year and his only touchdown of the year—and I said at the time, "Who is K.J. Hill?" Three years later, when he became the Buckeyes' all-time leader in receptions, my words were very tasty as I was eating them.

The first touchdown of the game was a 63-yard interception return of a Barrett pass by the Falcons, and the last touchdown of the game was a 75-yard interception return by the Buckeyes' Rodjay Burns. Barrett accounted for seven touchdowns, passing for six and 349 yards, and running for another. Joe Burrow added a seventh touchdown pass, freshman Mike Weber ran for 136 yards in his debut, and the offense rolled up 776 yards, an all-time team record. Curtis Samuel had nine receptions for 177 and two scores, and Dontre Wilson had two scoring receptions. Malik Hooker had two interceptions, one for 44 yards.

The first two touchdowns in the 48-3 win over Tulsa were on interception returns in the second quarter—Malik Hooker for 26 yards and Marshon Lattimore for 40. This meant that the last three Buckeye touchdowns were off interceptions, including the last one the previous week.

Lattimore would add a second interception. Barrett ran for two touchdowns, and the defense held Tulsa to 188 yards, 61 on the ground. This was the second straight game in which the Buckeyes played a team where a Buckeyes coach had coached—Urban Meyer at Bowling Green and John Cooper at Tulsa.

Noah Brown had four touchdown catches in the 45-24 win over Oklahoma in Norman, including one where he pinned the ball behind the back of the defensive back. Baker intercepted Baker—Jerome Baker intercepted Baker Mayfield—and returned it 68 yards for a score in the first quarter. The team ran for 291 yards, including 123 by Mike Weber. Lattimore had an interception for the second straight game.

Eight Buckeyes scored one touchdown each in the 58-0 win over Rutgers. Weber ran for 144 yards, and Barrett passed for 238 yards and four scores. Receivers Parris Campbell and Johnnie Dixon each had a 5-yard carry for a score. The total offense advantage was 669-116, with Rutgers passing for only 33 yards, and the Buckeyes had 17:36 more time of possession.

Barrett ran for 137 yards, 38 more than Indiana had as a team, in the 38-17 win in Columbus. Weber ran for two touchdowns, and Parris Campbell had the longest kickoff return of the year, a 91-yard non-scoring return.

Tyler Durbin kicked a 31-yard field goal with 3:57 remaining in regulation to force overtime in the Wisconsin game in Madison, and Noah Brown caught a 7-yard pass from Barrett in overtime for the 30-23 win. It was the second straight time that the two teams had needed overtime in Madison. The Badgers had a first-and-goal on the 4-yard line in overtime, but after three plays that netted no yards, Tyquan Lewis sacked the quarterback on fourth down. Barrett accounted for all three touchdowns—running for two scores and passing for 226 yards and the game-winner to Brown.

At Penn State, the Buckeyes had leads of 12-0 and 21-7 before losing 24-21 on a 60-yard blocked field goal return in the fourth quarter. I missed seeing the game because I was in Huntington, West Virginia, at the Marshall-Charlotte game. The Buckeyes had 137 more yards of total offense and 23 more plays, and recorded a safety, continuing a rash of defensive and special teams scores against the Nittany Lions:

- 1998: Jerry Rudzinski fumble recovery and Joe Cooper blocked punt return

- 1999: Gary Berry fumble recovery

- 2000: Mike Collins fumble recovery

- 2001: Derek Ross interception

- 2002: Chris Gamble interception

- 2004: Ted Ginn punt return and Tyler Everett interception

- 2006: Malcolm Jenkins and Antonio Smith interceptions

- 2007: Malcolm Jenkins interception

- 2010: Travis Howard interception

- 2012: Ryan Shazier interception

- 2016: team safety

The Northwestern game was tied at 17 in the third quarter before Curtis Samuel's 3-yard run put the Buckeyes ahead in the 24-20 win. Barrett passed for 223 yards, and Weber ran for two scores.

The next two games were back-to-back wins by an identical 62-3 score against Nebraska and at Maryland. Damon Webb gave the Buckeyes the only touchdown that they would need with a 36-yard interception return on the first possession of the Nebraska game, and Malik Hooker added a 48-yard interception return in the third quarter. Joe Burrow scored on a 12-yard run with 7:19 remaining in the game. Barrett passed for 290 yards with four touchdowns, two to Curtis Samuel, who had eight receptions for 137 yards. Total offense was 590-204 in favor of the Buckeyes.

Samuel had three touchdowns in the win at Maryland, two on the ground and one receiving, and Barrett passed for 253 yards and two scores, as the offense rolled up 581 yards and the defense held Maryland to 176. Barrett added two more touchdowns on the ground.

Michigan State Coach Mark Dantonio elected to go for a two point conversion with under five minutes remaining, but the Buckeyes intercepted and left East Lansing with a 17-16 win. The Spartans' eight-play drive for that touchdown consisted entirely of runs by LJ Scott, who ran for 160 yards and had 76 receiving for the day. Gareon Conley intercepted with 1:30 remaining to seal the win. Mike Weber ran for 111 yards and a score in his home state, and Barrett ran for 105. The last two games in this series were decided by four points. This was the second straight year that the winning team scored 17 points, and this was the second 17-16 win in East Lansing in the past five years.

Before the 30-27 double overtime win over Michigan, ESPN's Chris Fowler was prophetic when he said, "Let's hope the game lives up to the hype," at the start of the game. In the second quarter, Kirk Herbstreit asked, "Where has Curtis Samuel been?" Samuel would eventually make his presence known.

Malik Hooker's 16-yard interception return tied the game at seven in the second quarter. Weber had the other touchdown in regulation, scoring against both teams from his home state. Michigan had scored a touchdown with six seconds left in the first half, and OSU's Tyler Durbin, who had missed two field goals, nailed one from 23 yards with one second left in regulation to force the overtime. In both overtime games this year, Durbin kicked a field goal for the last points in regulation. The Buckeyes had 81 yards in the first half and 249 in the second half and overtimes. In the fourth quarter, the Wolverines had nine plays that netted a total of five yards.

Michigan's Jourdan Lewis returned the ensuing kickoff (An ESPN anchor once said, *Ensuing* is used only in the context of football kickoffs and signifies that something important happened), was hemmed in on the right sideline, cut to the left, made it all the way to the OSU 43-yard line, cutting to the middle of the field, and was tackled by Joshua Norwood and Tyler Durbin (!). If he had cut outside, he may have scored. Chris Fowler said, "heart in mouth time for the Buckeyes faithful." I flashbacked to Jonathan Wells cutting the wrong way in 1999, denying the Buckeyes a potential 24-10 lead. The Wolverines had 100 yards in kickoff returns, and the Buckeyes had zero.

In the second overtime, Barrett had the controversial run on fourth down to the 15-yard line, and Curtis Samuel leaped into the end zone on the next play for the win. The offense had 50 yards in the two overtimes, and Samuel officially had 41 of them. You could give him an assist on seven more, as Barrett faked to him on his run for the score in the first overtime, clearing out more space. Barrett ran for 125 yards and passed for 124 on the day.

Khalid Hill had an efficient game for the Wolverines, with four touches for 11 yards and both touchdowns in regulation on a run and a reception.

Comparing this game to the win over Miami for the 2002 national championship:

- Both were in double overtime, with the score 17-17 in regulation.

- Each game had a 17-7 score in the third quarter.

- Both had controversial plays in overtime—the Chris Gamble pass interference call in the end zone, and the J.T. Barrett run on fourth down.

- The Miami game had a field goal with no time left in

regulation, and the Michigan game had a field goal with one second left in regulation, both in the north end zone.

- In the Miami game, punter Andy Groom had an assist on the Roscoe Parrish punt return that led to the tying field goal at the end of regulation. In the Michigan game, kicker Tyler Durbin had an assist on the Jourdan Lewis kickoff return at the end of regulation.

- In regulation, the Buckeyes' two touchdowns were in the same end zone.

- In regulation, the opponent scored on a run and a pass, in the same end zone.

- The first overtime was played on the south end of the stadium, where both teams scored a touchdown, and the second overtime was played on the north end, where the Buckeyes had a touchdown and the opponent did not.

- In the overtimes of each game, the first Buckeye touchdown was on a run by the quarterback, and the second was on a run by a running back. The lone opponent touchdown was on a pass play.

- The Buckeyes converted on fourth down in overtime in each game.

- In the Miami game, the Buckeyes' touchdown drives were 17, 14, 25, and 25 yards long. In the Michigan game, the Buckeyes' touchdown drives were 0 (Malik Hooker interception return), 13, 25, and 25 yards long.

- The Miami game had a Buckeyes fake field goal that didn't work, and the Michigan game had a Buckeyes fake punt that didn't work.

- Mike Nugent and Tyler Durbin each missed a shorter field goal than one that he made.

Gareon Conley intercepted Deshaun Watson on Clemson's first possession, but it was all downhill from there in the 31-0 loss in the Fiesta Bowl in Glendale, Arizona. Samuel had the longest play for either team, a 64-yard run, and caught nine passes. Clemson scored 31 on the 31st, and the Buckeyes scored 0 with zero days left in the year.

The last two games of the regular season were decided by four points, and one point was the total difference at the end of regulation. The Buckeyes had their most points in the first game of the season and the least (obviously) in the last. The shutout by Clemson snapped a streak of 21 quarters in which the Buckeyes had scored in a postseason game, including the Big Ten Championship Game of 2014.

FUN FACTS:
- After two games, the Buckeyes had scored more points than in the entire 1966 season, 50 years ago.

- The Buckeyes had seven interceptions for touchdowns, and the opponents had seven total interceptions.

- The edge in rushing touchdowns was 33-8.

- Weber and Barrett had nine rushing touchdowns each, and Samuel had eight, compared to the opponents' total of eight.

- Samuel had the longest run of the year, 74 yards, and the longest reception of the year, 79 yards.

- Wide receivers Parris Campbell and Johnnie Dixon combined for five rushing attempts which resulted in two touchdowns.

- The Buckeyes scored in each quarter of the first six games plus the overtime of the sixth game.

- The opponents completed only 48.9% of their passes.

- The opponents averaged 4.2 yards per game in punt returns.

2017 (12-2)

Fun Fact: what Buckeye was last on the team in rushing and all-purpose yards but would win a Heisman Trophy? The answer is at the end of this year's section.

The opening 49-21 win over Indiana on a Thursday came while I was doing the stats for a televised high school game. The Hoosiers had leads of 14-6 in the second quarter and 21-20 in the third. J.K. Dobbins exploded for 181 yards in his debut, Barrett passed for 304 yards to 10 receivers and three touchdowns, and Parris Campbell had six receptions for 136 yards, as the offense racked up 596 yards. Antonio Williams ran for two scores in his seven carries. The defense gave up 17 yards rushing, with a long of nine, and 420 passing on 68 passes.

The Buckeyes lost to Oklahoma in Columbus, 31-16, in a game that was tied at 3 at halftime and was only a 17-13 Sooner lead after three quarters. The Buckeyes had only one touchdown, while Baker Mayfield passed for 386 yards and three scores.

This meant that the home team had lost every time in the four meetings with the Sooners, and it continued an odd trend in games against non-conference powers in which the home team lost in consecutive meetings (showing the Buckeyes first in each case):

- Penn State: won in Happy Valley in 1976, lost in Columbus in 1978

- Oklahoma: lost in Columbus in 1977, won in Norman in 1983

- UCLA: won in Los Angeles in 1979, lost in Columbus in 1980

- Stanford: won in Palo Alto in 1981, lost in Columbus in 1982

- Texas: lost in Columbus in 2005, won in Austin in 2006

- Virginia Tech: lost in Columbus in 2014, won in Blacksburg in 2015

- Oklahoma: won in Norman in 2016, lost in Columbus in 2017

Dobbins ran for 172 yards and two touchdowns, and Barrett passed for 270 yards and two scores in the 38-7 win over Army. The ground game for Army, of course, had 259 yards, with only 19 passing.

Seven different Buckeyes, all receivers, had one touchdown each in the 54-21 win over Nevada-Las Vegas. Barrett passed for 209 yards and five touchdowns, and Dwayne Haskins outpassed him in yards (228) and added two scoring strikes. Thirteen receivers had at least one reception. (By the way, the form that I use on the official stats has columns for only eight receivers.) The leading receivers were C.J. Saunders with six for 102 yards and Parris Campbell with three for 105. The total offense margin was 664-264, and the two defensive backs with interceptions were two Damons—Webb and Arnette.

Mike Weber scored three times, Johnnie Dixon twice, and Demario McCall twice in the 56-0 win over Rutgers. McCall ran for 103 yards, Barrett passed for 286 and three touchdowns, and Dixon had 115 receiving yards. Total offense was 628-209 in favor of the Buckeyes, as four Scarlet Knights passers combined for 92 yards. Damon Webb had an interception for the second straight game.

Nine different Buckeyes scored a touchdown each in the 62-14 win over Maryland. Barrett passed for 261 yards and three touchdowns, the offense had 584 yards, and Jerome Baker scored on a 20-yard fumble recovery. Maryland had 217 yards in kick returns, including one for 100, compared to 50 on the ground and 16 passing on three completions, with no first downs passing; 55 of their 66 total yards came on two rushes.

Barrett passed for 325 yards and five touchdowns and ran for two more, and Dobbins ran for 106 yards as the offense rolled up 633 yards in the 56-14 win at Nebraska. The Cornhuskers ran for only 44 yards, meaning that the Buckeye defense had given up a total of 94 yards on the ground in the last two games.

The 39-38 comeback win over Penn State was an Instant Classic, as Barrett hit Marcus Baugh with a 16-yard pass with 1:48 remaining. The Buckeyes trailed 38-27 with 5:42 to go. The Nittany Lions won the toss, and contrary to what most coaches do, elected to receive. It paid off, as Saquon Barkley returned the kickoff 97 yards for a touchdown. Going back to last year, the last two Penn State touchdowns came in the kicking game. With Penn State up 21-3, the scoring run for Penn State was 38-3 going back to last year. Penn State had allowed only 9.6 points per game on defense coming into the game.

Late in the game, Sam Hubbard couldn't tell if Barkley or quarterback Trace McSorley had the ball, so he tackled both, for a loss. The Buckeyes dominated on offense, 529-283. Barrett had 423 yards of total offense, and K.J. Hill had 12 receptions for 102 yards. With 36 coming on a second quarter score, Barkley netted 44 yards on the ground.

The wheels came off in the 55-24 loss at Iowa. It all started with a pick-six on Barrett's first pass of the game, though the score was 17-17 in the second quarter. Barrett passed for 208 yards and three touchdowns, two to Johnnie Dixon, but he was intercepted four times; in the other 13 games of the year, he had a total of five interceptions.

Weber had scoring runs of 47 and 82 yards and finished with 162 in the 48-3 win over Michigan State. Dobbins added 124 as the Buckeyes out-ran the Spartans, 335-64. For the second time this year, the Damons—Webb and Arnette—had interceptions. Interestingly, the Spartans had more than nine more minutes of possession time.

Total offense was 543-105 in the 52-14 win over Illinois, with the lead 38-0 at halftime. Weber ran for 108 yards and two touchdowns—his second straight with two—and Binjimen Victor had two scoring catches. Illinois had only five first downs.

While the Buckeyes were beating Michigan 31-20, I was calling an Ohio Wesleyan basketball game and would miss seeing most of the OSU game. I went to a fast-food place in Delaware which had a TV, only to find out that they had another game on and could not change the channel. So, I went to another place and was happy to see that true Buckeyes fans were in charge of their TV. During the basketball game, my broadcast partner informed me that in the third quarter J.T. Barrett went to the locker room with an injury.

The Buckeyes trailed 14-0 and 20-14 before scoring the last 17 points. The score was 20-14 after the Buckeyes blocked the PAT attempt, twenty years after blocking a Michigan PAT attempt in the same end zone, in a game with a final score of 20-14. Haskins was six-for-seven for 94 yards passing, and he added a big gain on a run. As in 2005 with #11 Anthony Gonzalez, this year's #11, Austin Mack, made a great catch to keep a drive alive. It was the 7-11 combination, Haskins to Mack. Like Gonzalez's catch and like Mike Lanese's catch in 1984, it was on the north side of the field. K.J. Hill had two key catches on crossing routes in the fourth quarter, something that would haunt the Wolverines in the game next year. Mike Weber (#25) had a 25-yard run to seal the game, carrying the ball with his inside arm, but no one was complaining. Dobbins ran for 101 yards.

Did J.T. Barrett's performance in the 27-21 win over Wisconsin in the Big Ten Championship Game on a surgically repaired knee remind you of Curt Schilling's performance on a surgically repaired ankle in the 2004 postseason against the Yankees? The Buckeyes had one more game to win, and the Red Sox had one more game to win to advance to the World Series. Barrett accounted for all three touchdowns, passing for 211 yards and two touchdowns, and running for another, and Dobbins ran for 174. Each team scored in each quarter.

All the scoring was in the first half as the Buckeyes beat Southern California 24-7 in the Cotton Bowl. Barrett ran for two scores, and Damon Webb had the team's only interception return of the year for a touchdown, a 23-yard return. The last time that the Buckeyes played in the Cotton Bowl game, in the 1986 season, they had two interceptions for a score. The defense had eight sacks and held the Trojans to 57 yards on the ground, with 44 coming on three plays. The Trojans had 26 more plays and a 413-277 edge in total offense. This broke a nine-game losing streak to USC teams, going back to the Rose Bowl following the 1974 season and including the two bowl losses to South Carolina.

Atypical Fact: The Buckeyes had one interception for a touchdown and none on kickoffs, while the opponents had three and two. Of course, the opponents had almost three times as many kickoff opportunities.

FUN FACTS:
- What Buckeye was last on the team in rushing and all-purpose yards but would win a Heisman Trophy? If you said Joe Burrow, you would be correct.
- Eleven receivers had a touchdown reception.
- The opponents averaged more than three more minutes of possession per game.
- The opponents averaged 3.9 yards per game in punt returns.

- The leading rusher, passer, and receiver were J.K. (Dobbins), J.T. (Barrett), and K.J. (Hill).

- The first two games of the year were against Indiana (school colors Cream and Crimson) and Oklahoma (school colors Crimson and Cream).

2018 (13-1)

During the year, I posted this question on Facebook: The Buckeyes have Tulane, Indiana, and Michigan on the schedule. What do Tulane, Indiana, and Michigan have in common? The answer is at the end of this year's section.

The Buckeyes had bookend wins over Pacific-12 teams, starting with a 77-31 stomping of Oregon State in a deluge and ending with a win over Washington in the Rose Bowl, Coach Meyer's last game. Ryan Day was the interim coach for the first three games, as Coach Meyer was suspended.

In the opener against Oregon State, despite the weather delay for 80 minutes during halftime—at which point the Buckeyes led 42-14—this would be the shortest game of the year, in three hours and six minutes. Weber ran for 186 yards and three touchdowns, and Haskins passed for 313 and five scores, with Terry McLaurin catching four for 121 and two touchdowns. Ten Buckeyes had a reception, and seven Buckeyes scored, including Nick Bosa recovering a fumble. The teams combined for over 1,100 yards, 721 by the Buckeyes. The Beavers had the two longest plays of the day, 78 and 80 yard scoring runs by Artavis Pierce, both in the third quarter. Pierce finished with 168 rushing yards and 41 receiving yards. For the second time in three years, the Buckeyes had scored 77 in the opener.

Haskins and Tate Martell combined to go 30-for-33 for 354 yards and five touchdowns—including Martell with a perfect 10-for-10 for 121 yards—in the 52-3 win over Rutgers. Martell led all rushers with 95 yards and scored the last touchdown on a 47-yard run, as the total offense advantage was 579-134. Ten Buckeyes had a reception again, and Johnnie Dixon had two of the scoring receptions.

The Buckeyes had two defensive scores—Davon Hamilton on a fumble recovery and Dre'Mont Jones on a 28-yard interception return—in the 40-28 win over Texas Christian in AT&T Stadium in Arlington, Texas. Jones's score was the team's only interception return for a touchdown on the year. This made it a total of three defensive scores in this stadium in the span of four games. Dobbins ran for 121 yards in his home state, and Haskins passed for 344 and two scores. The teams combined for 1,037 yards, with the Buckeyes having only 15 more than the Horned Frogs.

Total offense was 570-256 as the Buckeyes jumped out to a 42-6 halftime lead over Tulane and coasted to a 49-6 win. Haskins passed for five touchdowns and 304 yards to 14 receivers, and Parris Campbell had eight receptions for 147 yards and two scores.

The first Big Ten matchup was another Instant Classic at Penn State and a 27-26 win. I was in Lexington, Kentucky to see the Kentucky-South Carolina game, but I left it early and caught the deciding last eight minutes. The Nittany Lions had leads of 13-0 and 26-14, but the Buckeyes scored 13 points in less than five minutes of the fourth quarter on passes of 47 to Binjimen Victor—who was lined up on the right side, made a leaping catch on the left side, and cut to the middle of the field—and 24 to K.J. Hill, who pranced into the end zone. Similar to Joey Bosa's sack to end double overtime in 2014, Chase Young stopped the ball carrier on a fourth-and-five play with 1:16 to seal the win. Haskins passed for 270 yards and three touchdowns, and the Lions' quarterback Trace McSorley ran or passed for 461 of their 492 yards. This was the second straight win over Penn State by one point, and where the deficit was at least 11 in the fourth quarter. The last three games against the Nittany Lions were decided by a total of five points.

The offense rang up 609 yards and had more than 13 more minutes of possession time in the 49-26 win over Indiana. Haskins passed for 455 yards and six touchdowns, with Parris Campbell catching nine for 142 and two scores and Terry McLaurin adding two more receptions for touchdowns. The two quarterbacks combined for 777 yards and nine touchdowns in the air.

The defense blanked Minnesota in the second half for the 30-14 win, after a 17-14 lead at halftime. The offense ran for only 92 yards, but Haskins passed for 412 and three touchdowns, with K.J. Hill leading ten receivers with nine for 187 yards and two scores. Blake Haubeil kicked three field goals, including a season-long 47-yarder. The two teams combined for exactly 900 yards.

Haskins was 49 for 73 passing, both team records, for 470 yards, as the Black-and-Gold road game jinx bit the Buckeyes for the second straight year in the 49-20 loss at Purdue. The Boilers scored four touchdowns in the fourth quarter, the last on a 41-yard interception return. In last year's loss at Iowa, the first touchdown of the game was on a pick-six. The two quarterbacks combined for 848 passing yards, and the two teams combined for 1,085 total yards. K.J. Hill led 11 receivers with nine receptions—for the second straight game—for 105 yards. As in 1998, 20 years ago, the only loss of the year was to a team with six wins.

Nebraska led 21-16 at halftime, but the Buckeyes rallied for a 36-31 win. Dobbins ran for 163 yards and three touchdowns, and Haskins passed for 252 yards and two scores. The two teams combined for 931 total yards.

The Buckeyes were up only 7-3 at halftime and 9-6 at the end of the third quarter, before posting 17 points in the fourth quarter to beat Michigan State 26-6 in East Lansing. In the second half, Drue Chrisman's punts forced the Spartans to start inside their own 7-yard line on their first five possessions, with one resulting in a safety. Dre'Mont Jones scored his second touchdown of the year on a recovered fumble. Mike Weber ran for 104 yards in his home state, and Haskins passed for 227. The defense held the Spartans to 54 yards on the ground, with 47 on one play, and the offense had nearly 15 more minutes of possession time.

I was in Bowling Green, Kentucky to see the Western Kentucky vs. Texas-El Paso game, but I caught the end of the 52-51 win over Maryland in overtime, a game that took exactly four hours to play in front of only 38,177 fans. Haskins connected with Victor on a 3-yard pass with 40 seconds remaining in regulation to force the overtime. In overtime, the play of the year was an 11-yard pass on 4th-and-1 play to Rashod Berry to the Maryland 5-yard line, Berry's only catch of the game. Dobbins carried 37 times for 203 yards, and in his home state, Haskins passed for 405 yards and three touchdowns, adding three more on the ground, including the game-winner. He would have only one other rushing touchdown this season. The Buckeyes survived a two-point conversion attempt by the Terrapins that would have won it for them. The two teams combined for 1,223 yards, 688 by the Buckeyes. Dixon had six catches for 102 yards, and McLaurin had four for 118, among the 10 receivers. For the second time in three years, the Buckeyes had a one point win on the road the week before the Michigan game.

The halftime score of the Michigan game was only 24-19, thanks to a Blake Haubeil field goal on the final play, but the Buckeyes erupted for 38 points in the second half for the 62-39 win. This was Chris Olave's coming out party, with two touchdown catches and an assist, blocking a punt that Sevyn Banks returned for a score. His first score was on a crossing route that ended in the north end zone, the second was on a leaping catch in the south end zone.

In the fourth quarter, Parris Campbell scored on a 78-yard play that appeared to be a handoff from Haskins, but after several looks at the replay, it was clear that Haskins flipped the ball forward, crediting him with one of his six touchdown passes. Mike Weber ended his three year career with a touchdown in all three years against Michigan State and the Wolverines, the two teams from his home state. The offense rolled up 567 yards, with Haskins passing for 396 and Campbell with six catches for 192 and two scores.

It could have been worse—the Buckeyes' 150 yards in penalties were an all-time team record. Michigan had almost 11 more minutes of possession than the Buckeyes; in the previous game against Maryland, the Buckeyes had 18 more minutes of possession than the Terrapins. Both teams had 28 first downs.

The Buckeyes had given up 90 points in the last two games, but they won both by scoring 114.

The Buckeyes were up only 24-21 in the third quarter of the Big Ten Championship Game against Northwestern before pulling away, 45-24. Terry McLaurin, playing in his hometown of Indianapolis, caught two of Haskins' five touchdown passes, and Johnnie Dixon had seven receptions for 129 and another score. Haskins passed for 499 yards, an all-time team record, and the offense rolled up 607 yards and had almost 12 more minutes of possession time. Between the two teams, 22 players caught a pass.

In Coach Meyer's last game, the Buckeyes had a 28-3 lead over Washington entering the fourth quarter of the Rose Bowl and held on for a 28-23 win. This game matched the two winningest active coaches by percentage with a minimum of 10 years at FBS schools—Coach Meyer and the Huskies' Chris Petersen. Brendon White had a key defensive play, intercepting the two point attempt after Washington's last touchdown with 42 seconds remaining. Haskins had scoring passes to three different receivers, all in the first half, and finished with 251 yards. The Huskies had 22 more plays, 10 more minutes of possession time, and more total yards—444 to 364. The two teams combined for 92 passes, but the game was turnover-free. For the second straight year in the bowl win against a Pacific-12 team, the Buckeyes were outgained.

The score was identical to the Fiesta Bowl win 25 years ago in 1983. In Coach Meyer's last three bowl games, the team scored a total of seven points in the second half. This was exactly 50 years from the last time that the Buckeyes beat Michigan at home and won the Rose Bowl in the same season.

What do Tulane, Indiana, and Michigan have in common? They are all streets in Columbus and within a few miles of the campus.

FUN FACTS:

- After the first five quarters of the year, the Buckeyes had scored more points than in the entire 1959 season.
- The Buckeyes had 5,100 yards passing and 51 touchdown passes.
- The edge in passing touchdowns was 51-18.
- For the second straight year, 11 receivers had a touchdown reception.
- Mike Weber had the longest run of the year for the second straight year.
- Tate Martell was the third leading rusher behind Dobbins and Weber, despite playing in only six games.
- Opponents averaged 3.1 yards per game in punt returns.

2019 (13-1)

Quarterback Justin Fields, a transfer from Georgia, got the Ryan Day era off to a bang with a 51-yard scoring run—with a semi-block from an official and his longest of the season—on the first possession of the year in the opening 45-21 win over Florida Atlantic. The team scored 28 in the first quarter, and five different Buckeyes had touchdowns, with tight end Jeremy Ruckert catching two of Fields's four scoring passes. Total offense was 469-228; the defense held the Owls to 22 rushing yards.

Luke Fickell's Cincinnati Bearcats were supposed to provide a test, but the Buckeyes dominated 42-0. Fields again ran for the first score of the game and ran for another in the third quarter. Dobbins ran for 141 yards and two touchdowns, and Fields passed for 224 and two scores, as the offense rolled up 508 yards.

The Buckeyes traveled to Indiana, and so did I, except that I went to South Bend to check New Mexico off my list of teams to see. While the Irish were thrashing the Lobos 66-14, the Buckeyes had no problem with the Hoosiers, 51-10. Dobbins ran for 193 yards, Master Teague added 106, and Fields passed for 199 yards and three touchdowns. Damon Arnette had the team's only interception return for a score in the year, a 96-yard effort. The offense had 520 yards, and the defense held the Hoosiers to 42 yards on the ground, with 20 coming on one play.

The Buckeyes spotted the Miami RedHawks the first five points before running away with a 76-5 win, scoring 42 points in the second quarter. All three Buckeye quarterbacks had touchdown passes—Fields had four to go along with his 223 yards, Chris Chugunov had two, and Gunnar Hoak had one. The running game added 227 yards and four touchdowns, and 13 receivers had a catch, as the total offense was 601-130. Miami had three more minutes of possession, thanks in part to this in the official account: "Lightning was spotted in area with 2:40 to go in game. Game ended with 2:40 on the clock. Remaining 2:40 was given to Miami who had ball at end." Weather issues had no effect on the Buckeyes the last two years, scoring 77 on Oregon State in 2018 and 76 in this game.

The game at Nebraska was also supposed to provide a challenge, but the Buckeyes won 48-7. Dobbins ran for 177 yards, and Fields passed for 212 and three touchdowns. The offense racked up 580 yards, and the defense had three interceptions, with Jeff Okudah picking off two in the first quarter. Drue Chrisman had a light day with one punt—down from his two of last week—and the offense had almost 14 more minutes of possession time.

The Buckeyes led Michigan State 27-10 at halftime and won 34-10. Dobbins ran for 172 yards, and Fields passed for 206 yards and two scores, while the offense posted 529 yards. The defense held the Spartans to 67 yards on the ground.

Chris Olave and Dobbins each had two touchdowns in the first half of the 52-3 win at Northwestern on a Friday night. It was the identical score as in the 1984 game in Evanston which I flew to with the WOSU-TV crew. Fields passed for four touchdowns, Dobbins ran for 121 yards, and Master Teague had the longest Buckeye run of the year, a 73-yard scoring effort in the fourth quarter. Total offense was 480-199; the Wildcats had only 42 passing yards.

The Wisconsin game had only a 10-7 lead in the third quarter, but the Buckeyes scored four more times to win 38-7. Dobbins ran for 163 yards and two touchdowns, Olave had two more touchdown receptions, and the total offense advantage was 431-191. The defense held the Badgers to 83 yards on the ground.

The Buckeyes scored 21 in the first, second, and fourth quarters in the 73-14 win over Maryland. Master Teague led the ground game with 111 yards, Fields passed for 200 and three touchdowns, ten receivers had a catch, and total offense was 705 for the Buckeyes and 139 for the Terrapins, 396 fewer yards than they had last year in this contest. Olave scored for the third straight game.

Rutgers had almost three more minutes of possession, but the Buckeyes had 35 more points in the 56-21 win. Fields passed for 305 yards and four touchdowns, two of them to Binjimen Victor. Olave had four receptions for 139 yards, and the total offense edge was 594-231.

The Buckeyes appeared to be cruising when the lead was 21-0 over Penn State in the third quarter, but two fumbles—they lost three in the game—got the Nittany Lions to within 21-17. Fields's 28-yard pass to Olave in the right corner of the south end zone in the fourth quarter secured the 28-17 win. Dobbins ran for 157 yards and two touchdowns.

In the 56-27 win at Michigan, Dobbins ran for 211 and four touchdowns, and Fields passed for 302 yards and four scores to four different receivers—one of them to Garrett Wilson on his first play upon returning from a visit to the medical tent. Wilson had three receptions for 118 yards, and the total offense edge was 577-396. It was the second time in the last three road trips to Michigan that the Buckeyes won by 29 points. It was the fourth time in the last seven trips to Ann Arbor that a running back had over 200 yards—after Chris Wells in 2007, Carlos Hyde in 2013, and Ezekiel Elliott in 2015.

The 34-21 win over Wisconsin in the Big Ten championship game has to rank among the best OSU wins ever, taking into account the 21-7 halftime deficit and the importance of qualifying for the College Football Playoff. The Buckeyes came out firing in the second half, with Jeremy Ruckert's one-handed touchdown catch on the first possession. Dobbins ran for 172 yards, and Fields passed for 299 yards and three touchdowns, two to K.J. Hill. The defense gave up 294 yards in the first half and 138 in the second.

The Buckeyes had a 16-0 lead over Clemson in the College Football Playoff semifinal game, but two officiating calls that were upsetting to OSU fans were significant in the 29-23 loss. The first one was a targeting call against Shaun Wade on a third down play that kept the Tiger drive alive and resulted in their first touchdown. The second was an officials' review that overturned a fumble return for a touchdown by Jordan Fuller. Dobbins ran for 174 yards, and Fields passed for 320, but his last pass was intercepted on a miscommunication with 37 seconds remaining after the Buckeyes had reached the Clemson 23-yard line. To this point, the Buckeyes lost to Clemson in all four postseason games, and three of them had an interception on their last possession in a game decided by six points or less. The Buckeyes' 46 passes were eight more than in any previous game of the season. The Tigers had the longest rush play and the longest pass play against the Buckeyes all season. They were the only opponent to have two touchdown passes in a game. The Buckeyes had seven more first downs and 99 more total yards, but like the loss to another Tigers team, LSU for the 2007 national championship, it was no consolation.

FUN FACTS:

- The Buckeyes scored more points in the second quarter than the opponents scored in the entire season.

- In the regular season, the offense averaged 52.6 points per game on the road and 48 at home, despite having games of 76 and 73 at home.

- Gunnar Hoak had the longest pass of the year—61 yards to Jameson Williams against Miami.

- The Buckeyes averaged a touchdown for every 8.5 passes. Opponents averaged a touchdown for every 43.7 passes.

- If punter Drue Chrisman had not completed his pass against Wisconsin in the Big Ten Championship Game on a trick play, all passing yards on the year would have been by quarterbacks who had transferred—Fields, Chris Chugunov, and Hoak.

- The edge in passing touchdowns was 48-9.

- Chris Olave had 12 touchdown receptions, and K.J. Hill had 10, each with more than the opponents' total of nine.

- Twelve receivers had a touchdown reception.

- Jake Hausmann and Marcus Crowley combined for three receptions and two touchdowns.

- The edge in rushing touchdowns was 39-14.

- J.K. Dobbins ran for 21 touchdowns, seven more than the opponents had in total.

- Dobbins ran for 2,003 yards, and the opponents ran for 1,452.

- Tuf Borland and Damon Arnette had an interception return that was longer than the opponents' return yards in the entire year.

- Garrett Wilson had a 52-yard punt return, 16 more yards than the opponents had the entire year.

- Opponents averaged 2.6 yards per game in punt returns.

2020 (7-1)

In college football week #8 of the COVID-19 pandemic year, the Buckeyes finally played their first game, a 52-17 win over Nebraska. Fields was nearly perfect—20 of 21 for 276 yards and two touchdowns, running for a third. Olave and Wilson each had over 100 yards receiving, and the team had only three penalties for 14 yards. Sevyn Banks, wearing #7, returned a fumble 55 yards for a touchdown. Freshmen had the last two touchdowns, Jaxon Smith-Njigba with a foot-dragging catch and quarterback Jack Miller with a 2-yard run.

Pandemic control restrictions required a reduced statistics crew; therefore, I was sidelined for the season, and this was the first home game since the 1970 opener that I had missed.

In the 38-25 win at Penn State, the defense held the Lions to 44 yards rushing, with 23 coming on one play. Olave and Wilson became the first two Ohio State receivers to each have 100 or more receiving yards in consecutive games, combining for 18 receptions in this game. Fields passed for 318 yards and four touchdowns, and had 16 consecutive completions over two games, tying a school record previously set by J.T. Barrett. Master Teague ran for 110 yards. The Buckeyes had been the beneficiary of officiating calls in the 1995, 2003, and 2014 wins at Penn State, but this time the Lions profited from a quirk. With two seconds remaining in the first half, the Buckeyes took a knee on fourth down, but only one second came off the clock, allowing the Lions to kick a 50-yard field goal. Each team had two kickers attempt field goals.

Fields followed his 318 yard performance with 314 and five touchdown passes in the 49-27 win over Rutgers. Wilson had a touchdown catch and his third straight game with over 104 yards receiving, and Olave had two scoring catches. The Scarlet Knights may have set a modern record by scoring four touchdowns without a successful conversion.

The November 14 game against Maryland, the November 28 game against Illinois, and the December 12 game against Michigan all were cancelled. The Buckeyes' last two regular season games were against Indiana and Michigan State.

During the tight second half against Indiana, a 42-35 win, I tweeted, "This looks like OSU-Illinois 1980," when the Buckeyes won 49-42, also had a 35-7 lead, and saw the defense give up 621 passing yards. The defense gave up only 491 passing yards in this game, with minus one on the ground, and the offense ran for 307, with Master Teague gaining 169 and scoring two touchdowns, and passed for 300. Shaun Wade had a 36-yard interception return for a score. Chris Olave had 101 receiving yards, and Garrett Wilson had 169, his fourth straight game with at least 100.

In the 52-12 win over Michigan State, the ground game had 300 plus yards for the second straight game with 322. Trey Sermon ran for 112 with a 64-yard touchdown, and Justin Fields added 104 to go along with 199 yards passing and two touchdowns. Chris Olave had 10 receptions for 139 yards and a score. In 2018 in East Lansing, Drue Chrisman had six punts downed inside the 20-yard line, one of them setting up a safety, and this time, he had three, one of them setting up Haskell Garrett's interception in the end zone for a touchdown. Shaun Wade had an interception for the second straight game. C.J. Stroud became the third Buckeye quarterback with a rushing touchdown on a 48-yard run. With Ryan Day sidelined with COVID-19 issues, Larry Johnson filled in, making it the third straight year that a different coach had been in charge of at least one game.

In the Big Ten Championship Game, the Buckeyes trailed Northwestern 10-6 at halftime before using the run game for a 22-10 win. The 16-0 second half scoring meant that the Buckeyes had outscored the opponents 43-0 combined in the second half of the championship game the last two seasons. The Buckeyes scored 22 points despite the absence of 22 players. Trey Sermon exploded for a team record 331 yards rushing, with 271 and his two touchdowns in the second half. When the Buckeyes had to settle for three field goals with the score 16-10 in the fourth quarter, I flashed back to similar post-season games they had lost while scoring three field goals—the Rose Bowls of the 1979 and 1984 seasons and the Clemson loss last season. The 22 points scored and the 10 points given up were the lowest of the season.

This game and the 1973 Michigan game had several similarities:

- It was the last game of the season against a Big Ten opponent, played in a state adjacent to Ohio.

- The defense gave up 10 points, with all 10 in one half.

- A Buckeye running back had an explosive game—Archie Griffin had 163 yards in 1973.

- The Buckeye quarterback had an injured thumb and his most uneventful game of the year.

- Each team advanced to its next game thanks to a greatly disputed vote.

- Each team's next game was a 21-point win against the team that they had lost to in the postseason the year before. In 1973, it was against SC (Southern California), and in 2020, it was against a team (Clemson) from the state with the initials SC.

In the 49-28 College Football Playoff semifinal win over Clemson in New Orleans, despite a hard hit in the first half, Fields was 22 for 28 for 385 yards and six passing touchdowns. Olave had six receptions for 132 yards and two scores, and tight ends Jeremy Ruckert and Luke Farrell combined for three touchdown catches. Trey Sermon ran for 193 yards, giving him 524 in the last two games. Four Buckeye receivers had a longer reception than Clemson's longest of 29 yards. The defense held the Tigers to 44 net yards rushing, an average of two yards per carry. Like the 2014 semifinal win over Alabama in New Orleans, the combined score was 77 points. In Fields's two games against Clemson, he was 52 for 74 for 705 yards and seven touchdowns.

Dabo Swinney had ranked the Buckeyes #11 in the final Coaches Poll. The Eleven Warriors played Alabama on January 11 for the national championship, losing 52-24. Eighteen years after beating Miami in the title game, the Buckeyes played in Miami. Sermon suffered an injury on the first play of the game and was done for the game. Fields (33) and Teague (29) had the longest runs of the game.

Jake Seibert and Drue Chrisman, both graduates of Cincinnati LaSalle High School, handled all of the kickoff, PAT, field goal, and punting duties.

In the national championship game of the 2014 season, the Buckeyes had used the Smith (Devin) and Jones (Cardale) battery, and in this game, the Crimson Tide relied on DeVonta Smith (215 yards receiving and three touchdowns, all in the first half) and Mac Jones (464 yards passing and five touchdowns).

Not-So-Fun Fact: The two postseason losses by 28 points came 100 years apart, in 1920 (28-0 loss to California in the Rose Bowl) and 2020.

FUN FACTS:

- The last time that the Buckeyes played eight games, in 1941, they also had one loss, with a 6-1-1 record.

- Trey Sermon's record breaking performance against Northwestern meant that the top six individual rushing games against Big Ten teams all came against a team from a state that starts with the letter *I*—Eddie George (314 in 1995 against Illinois), Ezekiel Elliott (274 in

2015 against Indiana), Keith Byars (274 in 1984 against Illinois), Carlos Hyde (246 in 2013 against Illinois), and Archie Griffin (246 in 1973 against Iowa).

- In the Northwestern and Clemson games, the two transfers, Fields and Sermon, combined for 95% of the total offense.

- For the second straight year, all passing yards in the regular season were by transfers.

- Trevor Lawrence's only two losses came against a quarterback who transferred from Ohio State (Joe Burrow) and one who transferred to Ohio State.

- In the season that ended in '21, the Buckeyes had 2,100 passing yards, all by Justin Fields.

- The edge in points off turnovers was 48-7.

- The longest run and pass plays were 65 yards each. For the opponents, they were 66 and 68.

- C.J. Stroud and Jack Miller combined for three carries for two touchdowns,

- Before the win over Clemson, the Buckeyes had lost all six postseason games against teams whose mascot is the Tigers: Clemson 0-4, LSU 0-1, and Auburn: 0-1.

- The opponents had 91 more passes and 41 more completions, but the Buckeyes had a 22-6 edge in passing touchdowns.

- Drue Chrisman's punting averages by year were 44.2, 43.2, 44.3, and 45.0.

- The last four games were away from Ohio Stadium, and the 2021 opener is scheduled at Minnesota.

CHAPTER 8

Nerd Alert!

FOR OCD PEOPLE LIKE ME, ENJOY!

To answer Jeff Logan's trivia question, the only two father and son combinations to play for the legendary Woody Hayes at Ohio State are Dick and Jeff Logan and Howard and Craig Cassady.

The Terrible 1's: The Buckeyes have often struggled in years ending with a 1 since the 1950s:

- 1951: 4-3-2, the second worst record of the decade

- 1971: 6-4, the worst record of the decade

- 2001: 7-5, the worst record of the decade

- 2011: 6-7, the worst record of the decade

Threes and Sixes: In 1973 and 1976, and in 1983 and 1986, and in 1993 and 1996, the Buckeyes won the bowl game:

- Each decade had a different coach for those wins.

- In the other years of those decades, the combined bowl record was 4-16.

- Since then—2003, 2006, 2013, 2016—the record is 1-3.

- The combined record against Michigan in those six years was 0-5-1.

Three's a charm: In five of six consecutive decades—the 1940s, the 1950s, the 1960s, the 1980s, and the 1990s—the Buckeyes won three Big Ten championships:

Postseason games other than the Big Ten Championship Games:

- The most common difference in the score is three and seven, with eight occurrences of each. The eight seven-point games came between 1991 and 2014.

- Three of the four seven point losses came to SEC teams.

- The two one-point games were losses to Southern California in the Rose Bowl.

- Three of the five three-point wins were in the Rose Bowl.

- The two six-point games were losses.

- The two 12-point games were losses.

- The only nine-point and 11-point wins are in the Rose Bowl, and each had a combined 43 points.

- The two 21-point games were wins.

The Seven-Year Itch: From 1954 through 1975, the combined record for every seventh year (1954, 1961, 1968, and 1975) was 37-0-1 in the regular season and 39-1-1 overall. Following that in seven-year cycles, the 1982 team had a seven-game winning streak, the 1989 team had a six-game streak, the 1996 team had a 10-game streak, the 2003 team had two five-game streaks, the 2010 team had two six-game streaks, and the 2017 team had a six- and a five- game streak.

The Terrible Nines: From 1919 through 2019, OSU was 2-9 in the last game of the season of a year that ended in a 9. The two wins came in the Rose Bowl of the 1949 and 2009 seasons.

Double Digit Dilemma:

- In the 1920s, the 1960s, the 1980s, the 1990s, and the 2010s, the Buckeyes had their worst record of the decade in 1922, 1966, 1988, 1999, and 2011.

- The Buckeyes lost to Michigan in 1911, 1922, 1933, 1966, 1977, 1988, 1999, 2000, and 2011. In 1900, it was a 0-0 tie.

The Buckeyes' worst records since 2002 were in 2004 and 2011, the only two seasons where they lost in overtime.

In their first 17 bowl games, the Buckeyes had no scores on defense or special teams. In 13 of the next 32 postseason games (excluding the Big Ten Championship), they had a score on defense or special teams.

- 1983: kickoff return for a touchdown
- 1985: interception for a touchdown
- 1986: two interceptions for a touchdown
- 1990: safety
- 1991: blocked punt for a touchdown
- 1993: blocked punt for a touchdown
- 1997: safety
- 1998: blocked punt for a touchdown
- 2003: blocked punt for a touchdown

- 2006: kickoff return for a touchdown
- 2013: safety
- 2014: interception for a touchdown
- 2017: interception for a touchdown

Note: this has occurred in each of the last four games in a year ending in 3.

In all four seasons of the Bowl Championship Series and the College Football Playoff eras when the Buckeyes played in national championship games, they faced a coach who either was born in Ohio or served on the Ohio State staff—Coker (2002), Meyer (2006), Miles (2007), and Saban (2020).

The last five Ohio State non-interim presidents—William Kirwan (1998), Karen Holbrook (2002), E. Gordon Gee (2007), Michael Drake (2014), and Kristina Johnson (2020)—all took office in a year where the Buckeyes either won or tied for the Big Ten Championship. In four of those years, the Buckeyes played in the national championship game, winning two. In that span, the university also appointed an interim president in 2002, 2007, and 2013, and the football teams were Big Ten champs in 2007 and won its division in 2013.

The 1968, 2002, and 2014 national championship teams each had wins by a score of 31-24. In 1968, it was against Illinois; in 2002, it was against Miami; and in 2014, it was against Penn State and Minnesota.

- All four games were not in Ohio Stadium.
- The Miami and Penn State games were in double overtime, and in each of those games, OSU trailed 24-17 after the first overtime.
- Miami kicked a field goal as time expired in regulation, and Penn State kicked a field goal with nine seconds left in regulation.

- Each season had a key defensive play involving a participant with the initials *TP*—Ted Provost in 1968, Terry Porter in 2002, and Tyvis Powell in 2014.

More on the 1968, 2002, and 2014 national championship teams:

- The names of coaches Woody Hayes, Jim Tressel, and Urban Meyer all contain 10 letters. Even replacing "Wayne" for "Woody" retains the pattern.

- The starting quarterbacks—Kern, Maciejowski, Krenzel, Barrett, and Jones—had a combined two starts before the season started, both by Krenzel in 2001. Those two games for Krenzel were the entire Michigan game and the bowl game, where he had a combined six rushes and passes.

- Each team had a player from New York City. The 1968 and 2014 teams had a running back from Brooklyn—John Brockington and Curtis Samuel—and the 2002 team had Will Smith, born in Queens.

- Each team had played the opponent of the national championship game within the previous five years:
    - The 1968 team played USC in the 1963 and 1964 seasons.
    - The 2002 team played Miami in the 1999 season.
    - The 2014 team played Oregon in the 2009 season.

In both the 1968 and 2002 national championship seasons:

- The calendar was identical both years, so that both teams played on each Saturday from September 28 through the Michigan game on November 23.

- Each team had a player on defense named Tim Anderson.

- Jim Otis played on the 1968 team, and his son Jim Otis played on the 2002 team.

- The starting quarterback's last name started with *K*. The letters in *Kern* appear in *Krenzel*.

- Each team played a team from Texas in the opener— SMU in 1968 and Texas Tech in 2002.

- Each team had an October game in Columbus in which they scored 13 points and had an interception for a touchdown against a team that started with the letter *P*—13-0 over Purdue in 1968 with Ted Provost's interception and 13-7 over Penn State in 2002 with Chris Gamble's.

  - In each case, the team was one they had lost to the year before.

  - Each play started with the ball on the far hash mark, each interception was returned down the right sideline and was scored in the south end zone, and each was on the opponent's first possession of the third quarter.

  - In each case, the opposing quarterback's last name ended with the letter *S*—Phipps and Mills.

- In each game, the Buckeyes had another interception by a lineman—Jim Stillwagon in 1968 and Will Smith in 2002—and it was his only interception of the year.

- Both Provost and Gamble had four interceptions that year, and the interception for the score was the only one with any return yards.

- Each team played a regular season game against a team from the conference now known as the Pacific-12—Oregon and Washington State, respectively.

- Each team had a 27-16 and 31-24 win away from Columbus, a 45-21 win at home, and wins at home in which they scored 13, 25, and 50 points.

- Each team beat Illinois by seven points in Champaign and scored the last touchdown to break a tie.

- In each case, in the Michigan game the year before, the Buckeyes had all three touchdowns on runs in the first half, had a 21-0 lead, and kicked a field goal in the fourth quarter.

- The game for the national championship—the Rose Bowl and the BCS Championship:

  - saw the Buckeyes outgained on offense but record five turnovers on defense.

  - saw the defense give up two touchdowns and a field goal in regulation.

  - matched the #1 and #2 ranked teams.

  - In the Rose Bowl of the 1968 season, all three Buckeye touchdowns were in the south end zone. In the Miami game of the 2002 season, both Buckeye touchdowns in regulation and the third one were in the south end zone.

Kern's teams were 27-2, and Krenzel's were 25-2 in his two full years:

- Each had a 2-1 record against Michigan, with a loss at Michigan.
- The Buckeyes never lost at home in Kern's three years or in Krenzel's two full years.
- The two losses for Kern's teams were by a combined 22 points, and the two losses for Krenzel's teams in his two full years were by a combined 21 points.

In both the 1968 and 2014 national championship seasons:

- Each team had one shutout in the regular season.
- Each team played Oregon.
- Each team ended the season with a win over a team from the conference now known as the Pacific-12—USC and Oregon, respectively.
- The opposing quarterbacks in the championship game had alliterative names—Steve Sogge and Marcus Mariota.

In both the 2002 and 2014 national championship seasons:

- The main quarterback wore #16 and had seven letters in his last name.
- Each team had one player from Michigan—Craig Krenzel and Damon Webb.

- Each team had defensive players named *Grant*—Cie in 2002, and Curtis and Doran in 2014.

- Each team played Kent State and Cincinnati.

- Each team played a Tech school—Texas Tech and Virginia Tech, respectively.

In both undefeated seasons of 1968 and 2012:

- In the previous season, the team won six games.

- Each team played teams from the current Pacific-12 Conference—Oregon and USC in 1968, and California in 2012.

- Each team's main quarterback was a sophomore.

- Each team's leading running back was a junior—Jim Otis with 985 yards and 17 touchdowns, and Carlos Hyde with 970 yards and 16 touchdowns.

In both undefeated seasons of 2002 and 2012:

- In 2002, the Buckeyes doubled their seven wins from the previous year to go 14-0. In 2012, the Buckeyes doubled their six wins from the previous year to go 12-0.

- Half of each team's wins came by seven points or less.

- The combined record of the previous year was 13-12.

- The combined score of the previous year's Michigan game was OSU 60, Michigan 60.

- The Buckeyes lost two games the next year.

- Each team beat Michigan by five points.

- Against Penn State each year:

  - On October 26, 2002, Chris Gamble returned an interception for a touchdown in the south end zone in the first two minutes of the third quarter.

  - On October 27, 2012, Ryan Shazier returned an interception for a touchdown in the south end zone in the first two minutes of the third quarter.

- Each team trailed Purdue with under two minutes remaining in regulation.

- Each team played a team from the MAC—Kent State and Miami.

- Each team played a team from the current Pacific-12 Conference—Washington State and California.

- Each team played a team from California—San Jose State and California.

- Each team played Miami—the 2002 team played the Hurricanes, and the 2012 team played the RedHawks.

- Each team played a team from Florida—Miami and Central Florida.

- Each team gave up 14 points to Wisconsin in Madison.

- The next to last regular season game in each season was a seven point win in overtime on the road—Illinois and Wisconsin.

Heading into the 1968 national championship season, the Buckeyes were on a four-game winning streak. However, heading into the other seven national championship seasons, they had not finished the previous season with a win, or were at best 1-1 in their last two games:

- 1942: tied Michigan in 1941
- 1954: lost to Michigan in 1953
- 1957: shut out by Iowa and Michigan in 1956
- 1961: beat Michigan but lost to Iowa the week before, in 1960
- 1970: lost to Michigan in 1969
- 2002: lost to South Carolina in 2001
- 2014: lost to Michigan State and Clemson in 2013

Since 1968, the Buckeyes played in the game for the national championship—or entered the bowl game with a perfect record—and faced a Heisman Trophy winner:

- 1968: O.J. Simpson
- 1970: Jim Plunkett
- 1979: Charles White (and future winner Marcus Allen)
- 2006: future winner Tim Tebow
- 2014: Marcus Mariota (and future winner Derrick Henry in the semifinal game)
- 2020: DeVonta Smith

Craig Krenzel:

- Two of his three rushing touchdowns in 2002 came in the national championship game. His other rushing touchdown also came in an away game in the dramatic (yes, they were all dramatic) win against Cincinnati. In the two games against Miami and Cincinnati, his combined passing numbers were only 21 for 50, and he had the team's longest run in each game.

- He was the MVP of both the 2002 (Miami) and 2003 (Kansas State) bowl games despite completing less than half of his passes in each game.

The Buckeyes tied for first place in the Big Ten three times between 1981 and 1995, but they lost out on the Rose Bowl bid because another team decided to double (or better) their win total from the previous year. The Buckeyes did not have Iowa on the schedule in 1981 or Northwestern on the schedule in 1995, for a chance to settle the conference outright:

- 1981: Iowa improved from 4-7 in 1980 to 8-4.

- 1993: Wisconsin improved from 5-6 in 1992 to 10-1-1.

- 1995: Northwestern improved from 3-7-1 in 1994 to 10-2.

In the 1970s, the Buckeyes lost seven bowl games. In five of the seven games, the opposing coach (below) went on to coach in the NFL. The next occurrence of this was in 2006, with Urban Meyer of Florida being named head coach of the Jacksonville Jaguars in 2021. The other two coaches who beat OSU in a 1970s bowl game were Bear Bryant of Alabama and Danny Ford, who played at Alabama. The Buckeyes also lost bowl games to Gene Stallings of Alabama in the 1994 season and to Lou Holtz in the 2000 and 2001 seasons, and they previously had been an NFL coach.

- 1970: John Ralston of Stanford coached the Broncos.

- 1972 and 1974: John McKay of USC coached the

Buccaneers.

- 1975: Dick Vermeil of UCLA coached the Eagles, Rams, and Chiefs.

- 1979: John Robinson coached the Rams.

In the 1970s, Woody's teams had one touchdown pass in bowl games (1977 season). When Coach Bruce came on board, his teams had a touchdown pass in five of his first six bowl games.

Both OSU and Clemson won national championships in the 2010s, and both had a 6-7 season in the 2010s. Alabama won multiple national championships starting in 2009 and had been 6-7 in 2006.

After losing to USC in the Rose Bowl of the 1974 season and to Missouri in 1976, when the opponents were successful on a two point conversion, the Buckeyes survived the last six such situations in which the opponent's two point conversion attempt in the fourth quarter if successful would have won the game, or given them the lead, or tied the game:

- 1992: Louisville

- 1994: Northwestern

- 2009: Navy

- 2013: Michigan

- 2016: Michigan State

- 2018: Maryland

The 1990 Michigan game was decided on a field goal on the last play of the game. The Buckeyes had no other games in the 1990s where a field goal attempt on the last play of regulation or in overtime affected the outcome, but eight have occurred since 2000:

- 2000: Dan Stultz's field goal to beat Illinois

- 2001: South Carolina's field goal to win the bowl game

- 2002: Illinois' field goal to extend the game into overtime

- 2002: Miami's field goal to extend the game into overtime

- 2003: Penn State's miss gave the Buckeyes the win

- 2004: Mike Nugent's field goal to beat Marshall

- 2009: Devin Barclay's field goal to beat Iowa in overtime

- 2015: Michigan State's field goal to win

The G Men—players whose last names start with *G*, the 7th letter of the alphabet, and who wore number 7. All but Gordon played on a team that lost one game or less:

- Cornelius Greene

- Sonny Gordon

- Joey Galloway

- Joe Germaine

- Chris Gamble

- Ted Ginn, Jr.

Note: A first name *G*, quarterback Greg Castignola, wore #7 on the 1979 team that lost one game.

The top three performances for rushing touchdowns in a year came in 20-year intervals—Pete Johnson in 1975, Eddie George in 1995, and Ezekiel Elliott in 2015.

CHAPTER 9

Ohio State vs. Michigan

WITH THE EXCEPTION of Bo Schembechler, between 1958 and 2014, six out of seven Michigan coaches lost their last game to Ohio State.

The Buckeyes scored 100 points against Michigan in the three years of the Rich Rodriguez era and 103 points in the first three years of the Jim Harbaugh era.

The Buckeyes scored a combined 118 points in the 2018 and 2019 games, compared to a total of 111 in the ten games of the 1970s.

The only two games with a score of 9-3 came in 1950 (the Snow Bowl) and in 1980, exactly 30 years apart, with the Wolverines winning both in Columbus. In both years, Michigan finished first and the Buckeyes tied for second in the conference.

Hail to the Chief.

- The only three games with a combined score of 46 points came in 1989, 2001, and 2005—the same years where a George Bush started a new term as president. Two of those games had a score in the last 1:20. Thank you, teams!

- The last three times that the Buckeyes started a winning streak of at least four games in the rivalry were in 1960, 2004, and 2012, each of them a presidential election year. The Buckeyes started a 3-0-1 streak in 1972, another presidential election year. The last time that the Wolverines started a four game winning streak was in 1988, another presidential election year.

The only two games with a combined score of 83 points occurred six years apart in 2013 and 2019. If Brady Hoke had not gone for two points in 2013, this would have been a different story.

The most common combined score is 21 points, with six such games, but the last occurrence was in 1947.

The only two games decided by 13 points were the two 13-0 games in 1930 and 1933.

The only two games decided by 17 points were in the consecutive games in Ann Arbor in 1955 and 1957.

The only two games decided by 20 points were in the consecutive years of 1952 and 1953.

The only two games decided by 22 points were the two 22-0 games won by Michigan in 1907 and 1976.

The only two games decided by 29 points occurred four years apart in 2015 and 2019.

The only two games decided by 40 points were the two 40-0 games won by Michigan in 1905 and 1940.

The most common difference in the score is three and ten points (nine times each). Ten of these 18 occurred in the 20 games between 1971 and 1990, and 12 of them occurred in the 27 games between 1964 and 1990.

Prime Time: In the Buckeyes' last six wins in Ann Arbor (2007, 2009, 2013, 2015, 2017, and 2019), the difference was a prime number five times—11, 11, 29, 11, and 29—and one point in the other (2013).

Using 1961 as Year Zero, the Buckeyes have beaten or tied Michigan using the Fibonacci Sequence (0, 1, 1, 2, 3, 5, 8, 13, 21, 34, etc.): 1961, 1962, 1963, 1965, 1968, 1973 (tie), 1981, 1994, and 2015. Place your bets now on the 2049 game!

OSU's defensive or special teams' touchdowns:

- 1971: Tom Campana punt return
- 1979: Todd Bell return of a blocked punt
- 1994: safety
- 2001: safety
- 2009: Cameron Heyward fumble recovery
- 2010: Jordan Hall kickoff return
- 2014: Darron Lee fumble return
- 2016: Malik Hooker interception return
- 2018: Sevyn Banks return of a blocked punt

The last two games in the series to end in a tie—1973 and 1992—saw the home team rally from 10 points down.

Starting in 1941, OSU and Michigan alternated favorable results every ten years in years that end in *1*.

- OSU had a tie in 1941 and won in 1961, 1981, and 2001.
- Michigan won in 1951, 1971, 1991, and 2011.

Starting in the 1910s, in years ending in *1* and *2*, the two teams have had the better record or a split in alternating decades:

- 1921 and 1922: OSU 1-1

- 1941 and 1942: OSU 1-0-1

- 1961 and 1962: OSU 2-0

- 1981 and 1982: OSU 2-0

- 2001 and 2002: OSU 2-0

- Combined: OSU 8-1-1

- 1911 and 1912 Michigan 2-0

- 1931 and 1932 Michigan 1-1

- 1951 and 1952 Michigan 1-1

- 1971 and 1972 Michigan 1-1

- 1991 and 1992 Michigan 1-0-1

- 2011 and 2012 Michigan 1-1

- Combined: Michigan 7-4-1

The Not-Terrible-2s: Beginning in 1942, OSU has been 7-0-1 against Michigan in a year ending in 2, with the tie coming in 1992.

Four Sure: The next best streak is in years that end in 4. The Buckeyes have won each of the five games since 1974. Of course, I was at the 1964 game. Before 1964, the Buckeyes won in 1934, 1944, and 1954.

The 6's

- In the four years ending in 6 from 1986 through 2016, the margin of victory was two, four, three, and three points, with each team winning two games. The 2016 game was tied in at the end of regulation.

- The Buckeyes have won the last two games in years ending with 6 (2006 and 2016), outscoring Michigan only by a combined three points in regulation. Starting in 1946, Michigan won the six previous games in years ending with 6, outscoring OSU by a combined 113 points.

Crazy 8s: In each of these decades, OSU scored its most points against Michigan in the year ending with 8:

- 1900s: 6 in 1908 (tied with 1904 and 1909)
- 1920s: 19 in 1928
- 1960s: 50 in 1968 (tied with 1961)
- 1980s: 31 in 1988 (all 31 in the second half)
- 1990s: 31 in 1998
- 2000s: 42 in 2008 (tied with 2006)
- 2010s: 62 in 2018

The Terrible 9's: from 1939 through 1999, OSU was 1-5-1 against Michigan in the seven years that ended in a 9. The tie came in 1949, and the win came in 1979.

Starting in 1952, the Buckeyes had a passing touchdown every nine years against Michigan—followed by 1961, 1970, 1979, 1988, 1997, 2006, and 2015. The 1970 and 1979 games were two of the three games in the 1970s with a touchdown pass against Michigan, with 1975 being the other.

Lucky number 13: starting in 1929, the Buckeyes have beaten Michigan every 13 years—1929, 1942, 1955, 1968, 1981, 1994, and 2007, with the ill-fated 2020 season next in line. Note: Michigan was not on the schedule in 1916, Chic Harley's freshman year, when the Buckeyes were 7-0, outscoring the opponents 258-29.

Other than the 13-year interval, the Buckeyes have beaten or tied Michigan every:

- year since 2012
- two years since 2002*
- three years since 1998
- four years since 1994
- five years since 2002
- six years since 1992
- seven years since 1987
- eight years since 1994
- nine years since 1992
- 10 years since 1942
- 11 years since 1987*
- 12 years since 1958
- 14 years since 1970
- 15 years since 1942
- 16 years since 1982
- 17 years since 1941
- 18 years since 1974
- 19 years since 1941
- 20 years since 1921
- 21 years since 1900
- 22 years since 1935
- 23 years since 1929

- 24 years since 1910
- 25 years since 1929
- 26 years since 1929
- 27 years since 1928
- 28 years since 1942
- 29 years since 1900
- 30 years since 1919
- 31 years since 1936
- 32 years since 1910
- 33 years since 1921*
- 34 years since 1900
- 35 years since 1900
- 36 years since 1900
- 37 years since 1920
- 38 years since 1929
- 39 years since 1928
- 40 years since 1921
- 41 years since 1900
- 42 years since 1900
- 43 years since 1919
- 44 years since 1910
- 45 years since 1920
- 46 years since 1921
- 47 years since 1910

- 48 years since 1910

- 49 years since 1900

- 50 years since 1910

* No game in 2020 to extend the streak

Howard Jones (1910), Sam Willaman (1929), and Paul Brown (1941) were good luck charms, each with multiple streaks beginning in his first year.

From 1973 through 1981, OSU was 1-3 in Columbus and 3-1-1 in Ann Arbor.

In the six games between 1972 and 1977, the team with more total offense won only one game (1976).

From 1971 through 1980, Ohio State scored seven offensive touchdowns total against Michigan. In the 2018 and 2019 games, they scored seven and eight, respectively.

In the five games from 1976 through 1980, OSU scored one offensive touchdown, and that was on a pass that was tipped by Michigan defensive back Mike Jolly in 1979. In those five games, the Buckeyes had no PATs.

In the four consecutive games in Columbus—1974, 1976, 1978, and 1980—the Buckeyes had no touchdowns. In the next three games in Columbus—1982, 1984, and 1986—the Buckeyes had three touchdowns in each game.

Both Stanley Edwards and Braylen Edwards, father and son, played for the Wolverines in a 14-9 loss to the Buckeyes—Stanley in 1981 and Braylen in 2002.

In 1973, freshman Pete Johnson scored against Michigan. It would be 14 years before another freshman would score a touchdown against Michigan—Carlos Snow in 1987. It would take 15 years after Snow's before another freshman would score a touchdown against Michigan, but then a flurry followed, especially in Columbus in the even years:

- 2002: Maurice Clarett
- 2003: Santonio Holmes
- 2004: Anthony Gonzalez and Ted Ginn, Jr.
- 2006: Chris Wells
- 2008: Dan Herron
- 2011: Braxton Miller
- 2014: Darron Lee and J.T. Barrett
- 2016: Mike Weber
- 2017: J. K. Dobbins
- 2018: Chris Olave and Sevyn Banks
- 2019: Garrett Wilson

Five Buckeye quarterbacks forced into action when the starter had to leave the game:

- 1987: Greg Frey completed his only pass for 19 yards to keep the drive alive for the winning field goal.
- 2003: Scott McMullen, 8 of 13 passes for 108 yards
- 2014: Cardale Jones, an 18-yard run for a first down, and 2 of 3 passes for seven yards
- 2017: Dwayne Haskins, 6 of 7 passes for 94 yards, and three carries for 24 yards
- 2019: Chris Chugunov completed a pass for 11 yards and a first down.

Beat the Clock: In four straight games in Columbus, the Buckeyes had a late score to end a half:

- 2012: Drew Basil had a 52-yard field goal as time expired in the first half.

- 2014: J.T. Barrett had a 25-yard run with seven seconds remaining in the first half.

- 2016: Tyler Durbin had a 23-yard field with one second remaining in regulation.

- 2018: Blake Haubeil had a 19-yard field goal as time expired in the first half.

From 2011 through 2014, the two teams each had 79 points in the first half, with one point being the biggest margin in any game:

- 2011: OSU 24-23 lead

- 2012: Michigan 21-20 lead

- 2013: tied at 21

- 2014: tied at 14

Even the next four years, 2015 through 2018, saw the biggest half-time margin of only five points, with the Buckeyes having a combined advantage of 59-53.

1968: In the game in Columbus, with a grass field, the north end zone had *MICH* painted onto it. Would Urban Meyer have had the *M* replaced with an *X*? He also would have been distraught by the maize and gold painted grass in that end zone.

CHAPTER 10

The Coaches

JOHN COOPER'S 111 WINS + Jim Tressel's 94 wins = Woody's 205 wins. They rank second and third in OSU victories.

John Cooper and Jim Tressel both doubled their win totals in their second years.

Woody's house number of 1711: 17 + 11 = Woody's 28 years at OSU.

The names of Paul Eugene Brown and Urban Frank Meyer, the first and most recent coaches to win a national championship, each contain 15 letters.

Paul Brown and Jim Tressel won a national championship in his second year, Urban Meyer in his third year, and Woody in his fourth.

Jim Tressel had 10 bowl games.

- In four of the games, the opposing coach, like Tressel, had his first FBS head coaching position in 2001: Larry Coker (2002 season), Les Miles (2004 and 2007 seasons), and Urban Meyer (2006 season).

- In two of the games, the opposing coach was in his first season as a FBS head coach: Charlie Weis (2005 season) and Chip Kelly (2009 season).

Jim Tressel and Woody Hayes:

- Tressel's first year (2001) was exactly 50 years after Woody's.

- Each faced a Pennsylvania team on the road in the seventh game in his first year—Pitt in 1951 and Penn State in 2001.

- Each had a non-conference game embedded in the schedule in his first year—Pitt in the seventh game of 1951 and San Diego State in the sixth game of 2001.

- Each was left-handed.

- Each was the son of an educator.

- Each had been a head coach at colleges in Ohio—Woody at Denison and Miami, Tressel at Youngstown State. Also, Tressel was an assistant coach at Miami.

- Each had a worse record in his first year than his predecessor. Woody was 4-3-2, compared to Wes Fesler's 6-3, and Tressel was 7-5, following Cooper's 8-4.

- Each won a national championship within four years.

- Each wore a tie at games. Note: Minnesota's Coach P.J. Fleck was a graduate assistant at OSU under Jim Tressel and says that he wears a tie to emulate him.

Jim Tressel and Earle Bruce:

- Each had his first OSU game on September 8.

- Each won two more bowl games than he lost—Bruce was 5-3 and Tressel was 6-4.

- Each lost his first bowl game and won his last two.

- Each was on the same staff as Urban Meyer. Tressel and Meyer were on Bruce's OSU staff in the 1980s, and Meyer was on Bruce's Colorado State staff.

- Each beat Michigan on the road in his first season, and each beat Michigan in his last season.

Urban Meyer and Jim Harbaugh:

- Born less than seven months apart in the same Toledo hospital

- Bowling Green State University: Meyer was the head coach, and Harbaugh's father Jack played for and was an assistant coach for the Falcons.

John Cooper and Lloyd Carr:

- Each was born in Tennessee.

- Each lost his last game in the rivalry.

Francis Schmidt and John Cooper:

- Each came from a college in the southwest—Schmidt from Texas Christian and Cooper from Arizona State.

- Each was followed by a coach who won a national championship in his second year.

- Each coached against Notre Dame twice.

- Cooper had been the head coach at Tulsa; Schmidt had been the head coach at Henry Kendall College, which later became the University of Tulsa.

- Schmidt was born in Kansas, and Cooper was an assistant for the Kansas Jayhawks.

Francis Schmidt and Urban Meyer:

- Each was the head coach for seven years.
- Each ran an up-tempo offense.
- Each won his first four games against Michigan. The similarity ends there, as Schmidt lost his last three and Meyer won all seven.
- Each had been the head coach at a current Southeastern Conference college—Schmidt at Arkansas and Meyer at Florida.

Jim Tressel and Urban Meyer:

- Each had multiple national championships in his previous job.
- Each served under Earle Bruce at OSU.
- Each had his first head coaching job in the Football Bowl Subdivision in 2001 with an Ohio team.
- Tressel beat Michigan 26-20 in his first year, and Meyer beat Michigan 26-21 in his first year.
- Tressel's only loss in his last year was a Big 10 loss on October 16, and Meyer's only loss in his last year was a Big Ten loss on October 20. Each team played five more games against a Big 10 team.

Earle Bruce and Urban Meyer each won five postseason games. Hayes, Bruce, Tressel, and Meyer: The calendar in each coach's first year was the same; therefore, nearly all games for each one occurred on the same dates.

The last six coaches who coached at least two years—Wes Fesler (loss), Hayes (loss), Bruce (win), Cooper (loss), Tressel (win), and Meyer (win)—had the same result against Michigan in his first and last year.

Schmidt, Hayes, Bruce, and Cooper each lost four games in his last year.

Schmidt, Bruce, Tressel, and Meyer were all age 48 at the time of their first OSU game.

Woody Hayes and Luke Fickell were age 38 at the time of their first OSU game.

Paul Brown and Wes Fesler, two of the four coaches in the 1940s, were born less than three months apart.

Woody Hayes and Bear Bryant were born less than seven months apart in 1913. Bear Bryant was born in a county (Cleveland County, Arkansas) with an Ohio-like name.

The first game for Tressel, Fickell, and Meyer was against a team from the Mid-American Conference:

- 2001: Akron
- 2011: Akron
- 2012: Miami

Woody Hayes and Paul Brown:

- Valentine's Day: In his book, *Paul Brown*, Andre O'Toole writes that on Valentine's Day of 1941, the Stark County Ohio State Alumni Club held a dinner in Brown's honor before Paul began his OSU coaching duties. Woody was born on Valentine's Day in 1913.

- Woody coached at OSU for 28 years. Brown coached

at the college and pro levels in Ohio for a combined 28 years.

- Both coached a high school in Northeast Ohio—Brown at Massillon and Woody at New Philadelphia.

Earle Bruce and Ryan Day:

- Their first years were 40 years apart—1979 and 2019.
- Each had an undefeated regular season record in his first year.
- Bruce succeeded Woody Hayes, who won 76% of his OSU games, and Day succeeded Urban Meyer, who won 90% of his games. With Jim Tressel in second place with 83%, Meyer and Hayes are two of the top three winningest OSU coaches among those who coached at least four years.
- Each succeeded a coach with multiple national championships.
- Each had been an assistant coach at OSU.
- Bruce was a head coach in the state of Florida—Tampa. Day first worked for Meyer as a graduate assistant in the state of Florida—the Florida Gators in 2005.
- Neither was born in Ohio. From 1947 to the present, they are two of the three coaches—John Cooper being the other—not born in Ohio.
- In his first loss, which occurred in the postseason, his team kicked three field goals.
- In Bruce's first loss, USC had the winning score with

1:32 remaining. In Day's first loss, Clemson had the winning score with 1:49 remaining.

Sam Willaman and Earle Bruce:

- In 1929, former Iowa State coach Willaman became the Ohio State coach.

- Fifty years later in 1979, former Iowa State coach Bruce became the Ohio State coach.

- They replaced the two coaches with the longest OSU tenures—John Wilce and Woody Hayes.

- Each won his first game against Michigan in Ann Arbor and lost the next year at home, failing to score a touchdown in the Columbus game.

- Each was an OSU alumnus.

- Willaman's first year as an OSU player was 1911, and Earle Bruce's first year as an OSU varsity player was to have been 1951, 40 years later.

ACKNOWLEDGMENTS

I OBTAINED MOST OF MY FACTS AND FIGURES from the OSU Athletics website: https://ohiostatebuckeyes.com/football-archive.

Any mistakes in this book are solely my own.

Thanks to the following who gave me opportunities and support throughout the years:

- From Time Warner: John Gordon and Jeff Logan

- From WOSU-TV: John Prosek, the late Ed Clay, Jack Kramer, Paul Warfield, Cornelius Greene, Jeff Logan, and Jim Henderson

- From the OSU official stats crew: Mike Basford, Kyle Kuhlman, Scott Rex, Andy Powell, Dave Saffle, Tom McDonald, Kendra Willard, Paul Hummel, Stan Anderson, Tom Stevenson, the late Bob Starr, and the late D.C. Koehl

PHOTO MEMORIES

The Rose Bowl of the 1970 season, a 27-17 loss to Stanford. The Buckeyes had a 17-13 lead heading into the fourth quarter.

Halftime of the Rose Bowl of the 1972 season. The 7-7 score would evolve into a 42-17 loss to USC.

The Tournament of Roses parade for the Rose Bowl of the 1973 season. The irony was that the Buckeyes rarely passed—or had to, in Archie Griffin's sophomore year—but would pass well in this 42-21 win.

Tom Klaban (#6), Archie Griffin (#45), and Jeff Logan (#34) warm up before the 1975 game at Purdue. If you really needed the jersey numbers to identify them, you are not a Buckeye fan. Archie would set the record for the all-time rushing yards in this game.

Talk about the royal treatment in the city where the King lived! The Liberty Bowl welcomed me when I worked the stats for the 1981 Liberty Bowl telecast.

Two Hall of Famers—Harry Kalas and Joe Theismann—and me before the 1981 Liberty Bowl telecast.

Behind the scenes at the 1981 Liberty Bowl telecast.

Along with Jack Kramer and Paul Warfield before taking off from Don Scott Field to tape a road game broadcast for WOSU-TV in the 1980s. I was the statistician for the WOSU-TV broadcasts from 1981 through 1990.

Mark and me with Jeff Logan before Jeff's radio show at the national championship game against LSU in New Orleans. Jeff had me on the show, where I incorrectly identified the Buckeye with the most rushing yards in a bowl game. So much for being a Buckeye trivia expert!

The 2002 team is my all-time favorite team, and the 31-24 double overtime win over Miami is my all-time favorite game. Seats on the 45 yard line were not bad, either.

Made in the USA
Las Vegas, NV
02 June 2023

72849868R00184